Anthropological Studies

in Theravada Buddhism

Manning Nash, Gananath Obeyesekere, Michael M. Ames,

Jasper Ingersoll, David E. Pfanner, June C. Nash,

Michael Moerman, May Ebihara, Nur Yalman

Cultural Report Series No. 13

Southeast Asia Studies

Yale University

Yale University Southeast Asia Studies

Karl J. Pelzer
Director

Harry J. Benda
Associate Director

Adrienne Suddard
Editor

Library of Congress Catalog Card No. 66-19029

ⓒ Copyright 1966 by Yale University Southeast Asia Studies

distributor

The Cellar Book Shop, 18090 Wyoming, Detroit, Michigan 48221

Printed in U.S.A.

PUBLISHER'S NOTE

As Professor Manning Nash points out in his introduction, the purpose of the Conference on Theravada Buddhism, held at the University of Chicago in 1963, and of the resultant papers published here was to bring to the study of this great religious system the methodological resources of social and cultural anthropology. A pioneer effort in comparative analysis of Theravada Buddhist practices, this volume offers both rich empirical description and stimulating theoretical speculation and should interest a wide audience -- from students of the area and of Buddhism to the growing number of anthropologists and others concerned with comparative Asian studies. We wish to thank Professor Nash and his colleagues for turning their papers over to us for publication and for their generous cooperation in the preparation of the book for press. Special thanks are also due Miss Ward Whittington of the Peabody Museum at Yale, who drew the maps and charts, and Mrs. Ruth S. Memmott, who made the final typescript.

H. J. B.

ACKNOWLEDGMENTS

The authors are deeply indebted to the Committee of South Asian Studies of the University of Chicago for making the Conference on Theravada Buddhism, held under their auspices in May 1962, so pleasant a meeting for the exchange of views and data. To Professor Milton B. Singer, Executive Secretary of the Committee, we owe special thanks. Dr. Nur O. Yalman was instrumental in organizing the conference and seminal in his participation, infusing the whole proceedings with his spirit and help. Of several visitors during the conference whose comments and advice contributed to making these papers better were Dr. and Mrs. Winston King of Grinell College, Dr. Alex Weyman of the University of Wisconsin, and Dr. Aung Thein of Rangoon University. I also wish to thank those of the faculty of the University of Chicago who visited or participated in the conference.

M. N.

CONTENTS

CONTENTS (continued)

INTRODUCTION

These nine papers by anthropologists are the products of recent fieldwork among the peoples of Southeast Asia and were written at the request of Dr. Nur Yalman and myself, who convened a conference on Theravada Buddhism at the University of Chicago. These two features of the papers -- their origin in recent anthropological fieldwork and their adaptation to an assigned topic in the wide field of Buddhism in Southeast Asia -- explain both the title and the contents of the volume.

As studies by anthropologists, they carry some of the distinguishing features of modern theory and research in social and cultural anthropology; as studies on Buddhism they confront an established tradition of historical and textual scholarship; and as studies of the relations of religion and society they explore and venture into a large region of philosophical uncertainty. Three major canons of contemporary field research are exemplified here. First, the basis is the writer's own observations, made during a protracted residence among the people reported on. The immediacy, the richness of detail, the careful attention to informant and observer bias in these reports all stem from the anthropological dedication to firsthand fact and observation. The second, growing out of the first, is that the reports are on bounded, named, and real societies or social systems. The papers deal with aspects of Buddhism in a village in Burma, or a region in Ceylon, or a segment of the Cambodian peasantry, or a quasi-tribal people in northern Thailand. Where in older anthropological writings description and analysis of the bounded, located social system observed and reported by the fieldworker himself had usually sufficed, these papers exemplify the shift from the study of tribal to peasant peoples. All the authors show an awareness of the fact that their unit of study forms but part of a large social and cultural system. One of the repeated themes in this volume is the attempt to take systematic account of the "part-whole" problem which arises in the study of civilizations and their peasantries. The various formulations put forth in the papers demonstrate, however, that a general, accepted conceptual treatment of the relations of parts of social and cultural systems to their larger spatial and cultural, historical and dynamic contexts is still to be fashioned. Even then, these papers move the problem by suggesting fresh approaches. Third, the volume manifests the anthropologists' emphasis on comparison. In fact, without a drive to compare, this volume would never have been conceived. The comparative method, in one form or another, is the anthropological equivalent of, or substitute for, experimentation in the physical and biological sciences. It is through comparison that the essential can be distinguished from the peripheral, and only through comparison can a systematic idea of "what goes with what" in the realm of social and cultural phenomena be approached. The comparative stance of anthropology, then, is the major mode of formulating and of testing hypotheses.

The phenomenon examined and discussed in this volume is Theravada Buddhism. The first questions about it are the simple, elementary ones that are usually the most vexing and difficult to answer. The authors, in their attempt to lay the basis for a systematic comparison of Buddhist practices in the Theravada countries, addressed themselves to the common features of this system of belief and behavior in Ceylon and mainland Southeast Asia. The major task was to determine the factors of unity and variety in this religious system, and then to account for them in terms of the varying social, cultural, and historical contexts in which Theravada Buddhism was found. The comparisons, in some cases explicit, in others implicit, are made in the framework of a controlled comparison. The controls are set by the restriction to countries or peoples whose dominant religious orientation is tied to the Pali canon of the Theravadin and who, over time, have had some cultural and social interconnections. This restriction to Theravada countries (although Laos is not reported on here) presents for analysis a common body of belief and behavior, with historical continuity, and a range of small variations which possibly could be accounted for with the data at hand.

The internal variety of what from some other scholarly perspective might seem more monolithic is an interesting and significant result of this careful attention to a limited segment of the Buddhist world and experience. Significant differences among the various Theravada Buddhist communities exist with regard to the nature and content of the pantheon, the ritual and ceremonial cycles, the roles of religious specialists, and the interconnections between religion and society. Just to point up some of the more striking differences revealed in the papers: monks are present at marriage ceremonies in Cambodia, while in all other Theravada communities the Buddhist cleric is symbolically antithetical to marriage and procreation; the structured nature of the more or less unordered animistic nat system of Upper Burma is clearly differentiated from the animistic spirits and beings elsewhere, like the phii of Thailand; the parish head duties of the Thai monk may be contrasted with the role of the Sangha in all the other communities reported on; finally, we find very different sets of relations between Sangha and polity in the different Theravada countries.

The reported data on contemporary Theravada Buddhism raise some important theoretical and historical problems. Of these, the most interesting are, first, the line of demarcation between what has been called "Theravada" and what goes by the name of "Mahayana." These two systems of religion are certainly more distinct at the literary and philosophical level than they are at the behavioral and community level. Second, the reports in this volume render problematical any generally valid stipulations concerning the minimal structure and content of Theravada Buddhism as a system of action and thought for both laity and monkhood. In the third place, the interaction of pre-Buddhist and non-Buddhist elements with the traditional Buddhism of the region also poses pressing questions for further research and exploration. And, fourth, the relations between "text and context" -- the relations between the ongoing behavior of the ordinary Buddhist (both monk and laity) and the voluminous canonical (in the Tipitaka) and semicanonical literature of Theravada Buddhism -- opens the door to cooperation between field anthropologists (sometimes accused of "seeing everything and reading nothing") and historians of Buddhism and textual scholars of Sanskrit and Pali (sometimes maligned by anthropologists as "reading everything and understanding nothing").

Ideally the understanding of Theravada Buddhism should rest on factual history of the rise, spread, and development of Buddhism throughout Southeast Asia; this would be supplemented by a history of the social and cultural forces that influenced the movement of Buddhism in the area; to these comprehensive historical accounts would be added a description and functional analysis at the community, regional, and national levels of contemporary beliefs and practices; and such a magnificent edifice would then be capped by a study of how the various forms of Buddhism are adapting and modifying in the face of the movements toward modernity and nation building in all the newly independent Buddhist nations of Southeast Asia. Anyone familiar with the status of textual studies, of the historiography of Southeast Asia, and of the amount and reliability of anthropological fieldwork analysis in the region knows how far contemporary scholarship is from the full and intellectually satisfying explanation my ideal posits.

In the first place the reliable history of the rise and diffusion of Buddhism has not yet been written. Such heroic efforts as those of Eliot, Mus, and Conze, or more specialized studies like those of Dutt, Finot, and Berval, have cleared away much historical debris and provided a solid basis for further work.* Southeast Asian historiography itself is undergoing a rebirth, and with modern historians writing from the point of view of the development of the region and peoples, rather than from the point of view of a mythological or static East being changed and awakened by a dynamic West, we may expect the kind of social history that social scientists find valuable. Certainly the history now known points to some of the sources of unity and variety in Theravada Buddhism as it is described in this volume. Sinhalese Buddhism is often styled "original" or "primitive" and is supposed to be closest to the earliest Pali canon. The renowned Buddhaghosa codified the canon around the middle of the fifth century A.D. But it is clear that this monk was dealing with a tradition already containing elements of Hinduism, Mahayanist teaching, and possibly even Tantric elements (for the Tantrist Amogha went to Ceylon in 741 A.D. and found some parallels and perhaps introduced some Tantric elements then). The nature of Theravada Buddhism in Ceylon is similar to that practiced throughout mainland Southeast Asia: it is everywhere mixed with elements of Brahmanic Hinduism, with Mahayanist doctrine, and with indigenous elements, but at the same time it is Theravada Buddhism which is dominant, continuous, and national in scope. The differences among the communities described in this volume stem in part, obviously, from the differential impact and retention of the Hindu and Mahayanist traditions on the Theravada communities and in part from the differing indigenous bases which Buddhism encountered.

In Burma, the Pali canon seems present about the sixth century A.D., but Theravada only became the dominant religion in the middle of the eleventh century under Anawrahta. His victory over the so-called Ari monks shows that he too contended with Mahayanist influences (recorded in the architecture of Pagan), some possible Tantric elements, as well as with Brahmanism probably diffused from Bengal and Orissa. Thailand, too has the same mix-

---

*Sir Charles Eliot, Hinduism and Buddhism (3 vols. London, Routledge and Kegan Paul, 1921); Paul Mus, Barabudur: Esquisse d'une histoire du Bouddhisme (Hanoi, 1936); Edward Conze, Buddism: Its Essence and Development (New York, Harper, 1958); Nalinaksha Dutt, Early History of the Spread of Buddhism and the Buddhist Schools (London, Luzac, 1925); L. Finot, "Outlines of the History of Buddhism in Indo-China, " Indian Historical Quarterly, 2 (1926), 672-89; and René de Berval, "Expansion du Bouddhisme en Asie," France-Asie, 153-157 (1959, "Présence du Bouddhisme"), 685-96.

ture of traditions. When Siam was a province of Cambodia, it is likely that Brahmanism was strong, and Eliot reports the linga cult at Wat Pho in Bangkok; and, of course, the court ceremonies of Siam required the presence of Brahman astrologers and sooth-sayers (as did those of Burma and Cambodia). In short, the his-torical record shows the interaction of several religious traditions, with the final dominance of Theravada Buddhism in mainland South-east Asia and in Ceylon. A fuller history would tell us just how and why Theravada Buddhism has had this remarkable tenacity in Southeast Asia (though the remnant Chams, once Buddhist, are now mainly Muslim and without traces of their former religion); it would make clearer for us how Buddhism could become the re-ligion of whole populations while Hinduism, Mahayana Buddhism, and some of the Chinese traditions never penetrated deeply beyond the king and his court. The field data of anthropologists may prove a welcome stimulus to new historiological efforts to answer these questions.

In turning to the content of the papers in this volume, I shall be extremely brief, for a discerning reader can find for himself the information and point of view of each of the authors, and I do not want artificially to place the writers in more accord than they in fact are. What most strikingly unites the contributors is their attention to Buddhism and to anthropology, at one and the same time. They all treat their data as having relevance not only in the descriptive sense of interpreting various forms of religious life in Southeast Asia, but also as bearing on the systematic analysis of religion in general, and on the theory of religion and society. Ames, for example, treats the content of the Sinhalese pantheon as a problem in understanding the structure of any hierarchy of sacred elements. Obeyesekere handles the same Sinhalese pantheon, but his concern is to analyze the relations between the village, the pro-vince, and the nation in terms of their ordering and definition of the deities of Buddhism. Ingersoll's paper is an essay in the appli-cation of role analysis, as that perspective is now practiced in anthropology and sociology, to the status and activities of monks in Thailand. And Pfanner provides a similar analysis for a village in Lower Burma. The close parallelism of these two studies brings into sharp relief the latitude in role expectations for monks in neighboring Theravada countries. M. Nash's paper uses material from Upper Burma in an attempt to provide a generalized scheme for accounting for any ritual and ceremonial cycle. J. Nash's paper suggests a system and order among the nats of Upper Burma and shows with great detail just how this system is articulated within the dominant Theravada beliefs and practices. Moerman for the Lue-Thai and Ebihara for Cambodian peasants show some of the empirical connections between Buddhism and its social context and provide some incipient generalizations on the meaning of these observed connections.

Together, these papers constitute a first attempt to provide an empirical basis for the serious comparative study of Theravada Buddhism as a living religious system. Indeed, most of the information in them is new and expands our grasp of what it means to be a Theravada Buddhist in the varying communities where that system is dominant. They are, in addition, good anthropology in that they raise and treat with some of the most interesting of current debates in theory and in method. And, finally, we may hope that our symposium will encourage fruitful interaction between those whose habitat has been the library and those who prefer the peasant hut. On the growing body of data and theory from field and book, a deeply enriched understanding of Buddhism, of Southeast Asia, and of man in society can emerge.

MANNING NASH

ANTHROPOLOGICAL STUDIES IN THERAVADA BUDDHISM

THE BUDDHIST PANTHEON IN CEYLON AND ITS EXTENSIONS[1]

Gananath Obeyesekere

University of Ceylon

Anthropologists studying peasant societies in Southeast Asia have
generally chosen the "village" as their object of study, though
sometimes it is difficult to know where one village ends and another begins or whether the particular village one chooses to study
is actually a village or merely a named hamlet or neighborhood.
The vagueness associated with the term is less of a disadvantage
than at first appears, however, for like the similarly vague but
indispensable "society," the term "village" has its utility. Probably its widest use is to designate the "society" selected by the
anthropologist for study, typically a social group living in a physically demarcated area within whose confines are articulated the
major social relations of the individuals constituting the group.
Very often the village is "named," is characterized by economic
interdependence among its members, and has a local village deity,
a common ritual idiom, and a common set of cultural norms that
distinguish it from other villages and regions (Opler 1956; Singh
1956). The fact that in the village the major social relations, in
both a qualitative and a quantitative sense, are contained within
certain limits, whether artificially demarcated by the anthropologist or naturally demarcated by the culture, and that the village
has a commonality of shared norms (a "moral community"), provides empirical justification for the methodological assumption
anthropologists often make in describing a social system, namely,
that the system in respect to its empirical dimensions is a closed
one.

Yet it is all too easy to make the mistake of translating a
set of methodological assumptions into empirical "facts." Consider, for example, two common assumptions often made by anthropologists studying religion in peasant societies. Some anthropologists make the empirical assumption that the religion of the village
is a microcosm of the religion of the nation, province, or culture
area, while others assume that the village religion has empirical
reference only in respect to the community studied--and nothing
outside it. Both assumptions result from a confusion of empirical
and conceptual frames of reference, i.e. "as if" type methodological assumptions, so necessary for certain theoretical purposes,
come to be treated as true empirical assumptions. But it is obvious that the village, in an empirical sense, is not a closed group,
for individuals engage in several important, especially qualitatively
important, social relationships with persons outside their village,
with other villages, and with the organizational apparatus of the

state. Redfield's contribution to the study of peasant cultures and
societies was that his theoretical interests required a clear recognition of these empirical facts and of the need to give these facts
conceptual formulation. He attempted to conceptualize the "openness" of peasant culture and society, though some of the terms he
employed to formulate this "openness," e.g. "half-society" and
"half-culture," involved an unfortunate reification of such useful
concepts as "culture" and "society" (Redfield 1956: 68).

The present paper is a further attempt to demonstrate the
"openness" of the village and the relationship between the Sinhalese
village and the nation as a whole in terms of a single institutional
variable, religion--or, more specifically, the religious pantheon.
The problems posed here are as follows: (a) To what extent does
the Sinhalese village possess a unique and discrete religious system and how far could the village be seen as a single moral community? (b) To what extent is the village, in respect to its religion, a part of a larger religious and moral community? (c) What
are the mechanisms by which the religion of the village is articulated with that of other villages and with the larger moral community of Sinhalese Buddhists?

Since I have been influenced by the work of Redfield, some
Redfieldian concepts will appear in this paper, notably, "Great
Tradition" and "Little Tradition." The term "Great Tradition"
will be used with reference to doctrinal Theravada (Hinayana)
Buddhism of the Pali Canon, and in this sense the Great Tradition
is typical not only of Ceylon but also of Cambodia, Thailand, and
Burma. The Great Tradition is ideally the tradition of world-re-
nouncing monks. In contrast with this is Sinhalese Buddhism,
which is the religion of the Sinhalese masses. Sinhalese Buddhism,
though based on the Great Tradition, is not its equivalent and can be
conveniently thought of as a "Little Tradition." The Little Traditions of Southeast Asian "Theravada" societies differ from one to
another: their Great Traditions are the same. Sinhalese Buddhism
as I approach it will not be viewed as a composite structure consisting of several strata or systems within systems but as a unitary
tradition amenable to systemic differentiation. Sinhalese Buddhism
is locally institutionalized in each village: the village religion, too,
could be seen, for methodological purposes, as a unitary structure.

The Traditional Sociopolitical Background of
Rambadeniya Village

The data presented in this paper comes from intensive field
work done in a geographically isolated jungle village, Rambadeniya,
in the Laggala pattu (district) in the northeast corner of the central

province of Ceylon. In the interpretation that follows, I have also drawn upon my field experience in other parts of Buddhist Ceylon, especially in placing the religion of Rambadeniya in the larger institutional framework of Sinhalese Buddhism. The cultural and geographic isolation of Rambadeniya has helped me to frame my questions in terms of traditional Sinhalese religious behavior, rather than in the context of modern changes, without resort to "pseudohistory," though what I have to say would also be relevant for Sinhalese Buddhism in its modern context.

Situated in the heart of the jungle, Rambadeniya is inaccessible by car. It requires a five-mile walk through hilly terrain from the nearest jeep track or motor road to reach it. There is no post office; few newspapers trickle in; and during my stay in 1959 and 1960 there was only one radio, which belonged to the village headman, a salaried government official recruited from the local aristocracy. Rambadeniya is a well-defined village, i.e. it has its own paddy fields, jungle, and waste, and its territorial limits (sīma) are clearly demarcated. There are three castes: two subcastes of the dominant goigama (farmer) caste, which formed a numerical majority, and a few households of the dura caste, a servant caste of the goigama, whose service duties were attendance at goigama rites of passage and performance of the "flute" in exorcistic and temple ceremonies. Of the two goigama subcastes, the named subcaste of pattiya was considered inferior to the other goigama subcastes -- though the theoretical rule of subcaste endogamy was ignored in a few instances. Kinship is bilateral, among all the castes; the residence rule is virilocal, the women being largely recruited from other villages in the Laggala pattu. Women, however, had a very inferior status in the society -- in spite of the fact that their jural status was superior to that of women in unilineally organized societies, for theoretically they had equal inheritance rights with men and divorce was by mutual consent. Yet this was a male-dominated society with sharp status cleavages between the sexes and marked intersex antagonisms. Women, though jural equals of men, were their ritual inferiors, an inferiority defined and legitimated by the mechanisms of kili or ritual pollution. Kili was associated with the menstrual flow, childbirth, puberty, and death, i.e. with the major sources of pollution, tendering those directly or indirectly associated with them "untouchable." Women are directly associated with the sources of untouchability and pollution, men only indirectly through contact or proximity. Men are directly polluting only at death -- when they have moved out of the social structure for good; women are polluting between two phases in their life cycle, puberty at one end and menopause at the other -- when they occupy certain definite points in the social structure. Children, both girls and boys, are considered ritually neutral, but jurally they are viewed as minors. Without going into further details one could sum up by saying that important status distinctions exist in this society between men and women, between castes, and between children and adults.

Laggala traditionally was part of the feudally organized Kandyan kingdom and, unlike the western seaboard which was under European domination for several centuries, came under European control with its annexation by the British in 1815. Since the ideology of feudalism is crucial to the comprehension of the Sinhalese ritual idiom, I shall briefly describe how the traditional Kandyan kingdom was organized.[2] The king was theoretically an absolute monarch, considered a living god or Bōdhisatva. Highly elaborate ceremonials of prostration and obeisance symbolized the vast social distance between ruler and ruled; his personal attendants often had to wear "mouth masks" when approaching him. The rituals and ceremonials performed by his personal attendants, e.g. fanning, anointing, and bathing the king, were called the tēvāva. The king was assisted in his administrative duties by several (about four) ministers or adikāramvaru. The king and his ministers formed an informal council which controlled the central administrative, judicial, and legislative apparatus of the state.

For purposes of administration, the Kandyan kingdom was divided into twenty-one divisions, the major ones called disāvani, each under the control of a governor or disāva, and the smaller ones called rata, under the control of a ratē mahatmaya. Each "governor" had certain legally defined executive and judicial functions. The provinces were subdivided into smaller ones or koralēs in charge of a korāle responsible to the disāva; the koralēs were further subdivided into pattu (districts), which consisted of several contiguous villages. Each village in the pattu, had its own ancestral paddy fields (pravēni), the highest property right an individual could legally have, which "conferred heritable title in perpetuity" (Pieris 1956: 44). But even the ownership of such land was contingent on the performance of certain services -- personal service or payment in money or kind -- known as rājakariya. These could be considered villages of "free peasants."

Rambadeniya was part of the disāvani of Matale, but unlike most villages in the area, it was not a village of free peasants but rather one of tied serfs. In Sinhalese feudalism there were, in addition to "free villages," other villages directly attached to the king (gabadāgam), a chief (nindagam), or temples (vihāragam). These villages were private estates of the owner and directly under his administrative control. Peasants in these villages were almost tied serfs who could be evicted by the proprietor of the estate. Their rights over the land were contingent on the performance of various services to the lord and a yearly customary visit (dākum)

with pingo loads of gifts. Up until about ten years ago, Rambadeniya folk continued to perform these services and pay the yearly
"däkum" to the disāva who "owned" the village at his valauva
(manor) in Kandy. Since then, these services have been commuted
for a small, almost token money payment.

The Structure of the Rambadeniya Pantheon[3]

For purposes of clarity I have presented here a simplified
picture of the Rambadeniya pantheon, constructed almost entirely
from the rituals performed in the village and the mythology associated with these rituals (see Figure 1). The pantheon is presented
as a pyramidal structure, depicted for purposes of easy reference
in five levels. In level one, at the apex of the pantheon, is the
Buddha, who occupies a presidential position vis-à-vis the other
deities: he is worshiped in practically every ritual performed in
Rambadeniya. He is not viewed as a deity in the conventional sense
of a being who intercedes on behalf of humans and brings fertility,
prosperity, weal, or woe to humans who propitiate him. The prayers addressed to him are commemorative rather than propitiatory
or petitionary. He does not possess a human status either, for by
virtue of having achieved enlightenment and release (mōksha,
nirvāna) he has transcended his humanity. His outstanding characteristics are his compassion, benevolence, and nonpunitiveness:
he is goodness incarnate. So far the attitude of the peasant is close
to the scriptural, but there is a point where doctrinal Buddhism
and Sinhalese Buddhism seem to part company. Logically, from
the point of view of the doctrines, the Buddha does not exist. He
can have no active role in the affairs of the world, for this would
contradict the fact that he has achieved nirvāna. In the Buddhism
of Rambadeniya the Buddha is generally seen as in some sense
"living." Prayers (albeit commemorative) are addressed to
images and other symbols of the Buddha presence; and dietary
offerings are given to him. Though direct propitiation never occurs, the prayers addressed to the Buddha recognize some notion
of his "presence." A popular prayer, for example, runs as follows: "Pardon me, Venerable world sage, Blessed one, the 'sins'
I have committed with body, word, thought, or by carelessness."
On the psychological level the problem is relatively easy to understand, for it is doubtful that worship and oblations, however ration-
alized as commemorative, could be directed to any phenomenally
nonexistent being. Moreover the Sinhalese like other humans worship deities (gods and demons) of a conventional sort. These
beings are perceived as living. Thus one could expect the attitudes
toward the conventional gods to be generalized to the Buddha, who
belongs to the same stimulus-set.

Cognitively then the Buddha is viewed as nonliving; psycholo-

Figure 1. SIMPLIFIED DIAGRAM OF THE RAMBADENIYA
PANTHEON

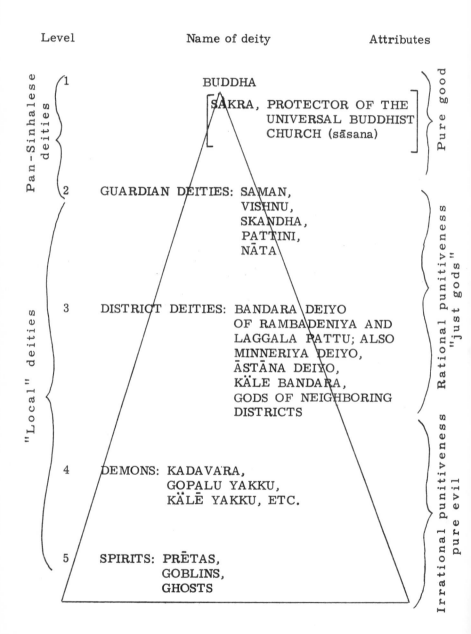

Level   Name of deity   Attributes

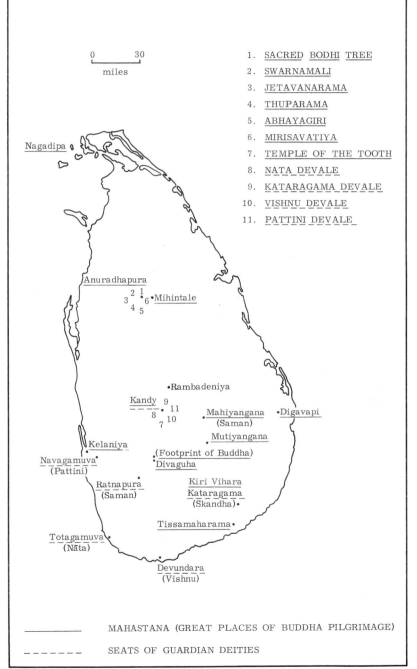

Figure 2. MAIN CENTERS OF PILGRIMAGE IN CEYLON

0 ___ 30
miles

1. SACRED BODHI TREE
2. SWARNAMALI
3. JETAVANARAMA
4. THUPARAMA
5. ABHAYAGIRI
6. MIRISAVATIYA
7. TEMPLE OF THE TOOTH
8. NATA DEVALE
9. KATARAGAMA DEVALE
10. VISHNU DEVALE
11. PATTINI DEVALE

Nagadipa

Anuradhapura
3 2 1
     6 •Mihintale
   4 5

•Rambadeniya

Kandy 9
       • 11
    8
    7 10

Mahiyangana   •Digavapi
(Saman)

Mutiyangana
•

Kelaniya

Navagamuva•
(Pattini)

(Footprint of Buddha)
•Divaguha

Ratnapura•
(Saman)

Kiri Vihara
Kataragama
(Skandha)•

Tissamaharama•

Totagamuva•
(Nāta)

Devundara
(Vishnu)

_____ MAHASTANA (GREAT PLACES OF BUDDHA PILGRIMAGE)

_ _ _ _ _ _ SEATS OF GUARDIAN DEITIES

gically he is perceived as living. How is it possible to reconcile these seemingly irreconcilable positions? This is done through the symbolism of the Buddha relics with its underlying notions of sympathetic (contagious) magic. Though the Buddha is not living, his presence is manifested in the dhātu, or relics. Such a point of view is completely consonant with other aspects of Sinhalese religion, as for example where ingredients used in magic, altars, and images become activated (jīvan) through the dishti (essence) of the deity, who in ritual is invited to cast his eye (bälma) on these objects. Through this process the deity is present in the object: not his phenomenal presence as a separate being but his essence which, as a part of his being, can sympathetically represent the whole and thus act on behalf of the whole. A similar, though not identical, attitude prevails in respect of dhātu. The Sinhalese say that the Buddha is present in his relics (Buduhāmuduruvō dhātuvala jīvamānava innava). Hence relics are addressed as dhātun vahanse, i.e. "Venerable Relic." Practically every Buddhist temple has a relic casket and a relic chamber (dāgoba) where Buddha and arhat relics are enshrined. The word "dhātu" is used in other contexts too and generally means "elemental substance" or "basic constituents of larger bodies or entities." As Leach points out, orgasm and conception are viewed by Sinhalese as the conjunction of male and female dhātu (1961: 35). Thus dhātu seems to have the connotation of "life force" or "vital principle." When the Buddha personality is viewed as incarnated in his dhātu, the notion is that of an immanent presence only: no assistance could therefore be sought from the Buddha personality incarnated in his relics.

The Sinhalese Buddhist concept of an immanent Buddha personality or presence is probably rooted in an important ambiguity in the Buddhist doctrine itself regarding the state of nirvāna. A question that comes up often in Buddhist theology and debate is one which was asked by a disciple from the Buddha himself, namely the state of an arhat (one who has achieved nirvāna) after death, whether he is alive or dead, or both, or neither. This is one of the "unanswered questions" of the Buddha for such questions were dismissed as not "conducive to the holy life" and therefore "profitless." It is quite unlikely that such a view would ever have found popular acceptance or that popularly nirvāna was ever defined as an extinction of personality, or "a blowing out" as the texts state. In some sense the nirvāna-achieved personality "lives": thus the dhātu is the visible representation of the immortal nirvāna state. It is no accident that arhat and Buddha relics are believed by Sinhalese Buddhists to possess irdhi (the capacity to float in air) and are depicted in paintings and mythology as floating, for irdhi is the defining attribute of the arhat in Sinhalese Buddhism. The conception of Buddha and arhat relics, and other sacred symbols of Buddha worship, is probably based on popular notions of the

immortality of the nirvāna state. There is an interesting Sinhalese
myth which states that in the flood that heralds the destruction of
this age all the Buddha dhātu found in various parts of the world
will assemble together through irdhi and the Buddha himself will
be refashioned out of these substances. He will then utter a last
sermon. This is strikingly similar to the notion that male dhātu
and female dhātu unite in orgasm to form a new being.

Slightly below the Buddha is Sakra, the protector of the universal Buddhist church (sāsana). Though constantly referred to
in myths, he is never directly propitiated or worshiped in Rambadeniya for he has delegated his authority to Saman, the protector
and guardian of the Buddha sāsana in Ceylon. Saman then occupies
level two of the pantheon along with the four (sometimes five) other
deities of equal status: Vishnu, Skandha (Kataragama), Nāta, and
Pattini. These four gods are also viewed as defenders of the faith,
but their special task is to protect the secular kingdom; they are
collectively addressed as hatara deiyo.⁴ I shall for convenience refer to all deities in level two as guardian deities. These deities
are differently conceived from that of the Buddha -- they are gods
in a conventional sense, granting favors. They are both punitive
and benevolent but their punitiveness is a "rational punitiveness, "
i. e. they are just gods punishing humans only for transgressions
or sins. Level three consists of Bandara Deiyo, the presiding
deity for Laggala pattu. Almost on the same level are deities of
equal status who preside over other districts near and around
Laggala. These district deities have more or less the same attributes as the guardian deities. From the point of view of the worshipers these gods are seen as provident father figures in relation
to whom the petitioner is a "newborn baby" or "a child" (lē bilinda,
ladaruva). Level four of the pantheon consists of demons and other
inferior deities and level five of ghosts and prētas, the malevolent
spirits of dead ancestors. Supernatural beings on levels four and
five are viewed as completely evil and "irrationally punitive, " i. e.
causing harm without just cause or principle.

The pantheon thus represents a morality structure with pure
goodness and benevolence represented at the apex of the pantheon
and pure evil at the base. The morality represented is that of
karma and the status of the deities of the pantheon are products of
karma (karma pala, karma vipāka). The Buddha represents the
highest goal of Buddhist aspiration: nirvāna and enlightenment.
The gods are several steps below this ideal -- as beings who have
done good and have achieved their position in the pantheon by virtue
of this but who still have a long way to go before they can achieve
salvation. They are viewed as Bōdhisatvas or future Buddhas and
are addressed in rituals as "Lord who will be future Buddha. " Of
the several guardian deities, the god Nāta is viewed as the very

next Buddha, Maitreya. This incidentally is the typical Sinhalese
Buddhist conception of Bōdhisatva; he is a just god granting favors
to his devotees rather than a self-sacrificing savior who has postponed his own salvation to save the world, which is the orthodox
Mahayana position. The demons and prētas, the spirits of sinful
ancestors, are all inferior and sinful beings who have been born in
their degraded status because of their bad karma. Myths associated with them clearly exemplify this fact. Moreover, these inferior beings, owing to their "irrational punitiveness," continue to
accumulate bad karma. They are thus caught in a vicious circle:
by nature they must perforce do evil but by continuing to do evil
they increase their load of "sin," thus denying themselves the
chance of improving their present degraded status. Though salvation is not completely denied to them, they come close to a Buddhist
analogue of eternal damnation.

    The morality of karma governing the pantheon is symbolically
communicated in the ceremonies of obeisance and worship adopted
toward the deities. The Buddha as head of the pantheon is worshiped with the hands on the head or forehead. In rituals performed
for the Buddha in Rambadeniya vegetarian foods and fruit juices are
placed on his altar daily. He is, furthermore, honored with incense and flowers. The gods are worshiped with the hands held
somewhat lower or with the fists clenched and placed against the
chest. Since gods are considered noble beings (and potential
Buddhas) they too are offered vegetarian foods, auspicious flowers,
and incense. They are fanned (tēvāva) and anointed (nanumura)
as kings are. This respectful obeisance is not given the demons at
all. They are offered neither auspicious flowers nor soft incense
but typically invoked with certain flowers considered inauspicious
and with resin, an inferior "incense." The food given to them is
typically puluta (burnt meat, fish, or egg) and riri (blood). Of
the lowest class of supernaturals, the only kind propitiated are
prētas, who are also never worshiped but are given inferior foods
like puluṭa, marihuana, arrack, spittle, and sometimes fecal matter. The kind of offering given to the deity could be considered,
once again, as symbolizing his status in the pantheon. The Buddha
and the gods are never offered "meat." The vegetarian sacrifice
symbolizes their high status, while the low position of the demons
and lesser supernaturals is symbolized by the blood and burnt meat
sacrifice. In a Hindu social situation, one might be tempted to
relate the foods offered to deities to the dietary prescriptions of
the various castes. Drawing a parallel in Ceylon, one might say
that the Buddha and the gods reflect a clean caste status and the
demons and prētas an impure caste status. But there has been no
tradition of prescribed foods in Ceylon relating to the caste hierarchy. Indeed, there has not been historically even a tradition of
vegetarianism equally applicable to all strata of society: meat and

fish eating cuts across caste lines. The only food traditionally
held in abhorrence was beef, hence the killing of cattle was the
caste duty of the numerically small Rodiya caste, the only caste
in Ceylon approximating, even vaguely, the status of the Indian untouchable. The Ceylonese maintain that these foods have nothing
to do with caste status but have to be seen in relation to the Sinhalese Buddhist pantheon as a "morality structure." The foods symbolize the principle of ahimsā, or nonviolence, with its logical consequence in a vegetarian dietary. In Ceylon, though meat eating
is common, all castes recognize that such an act is a violation of
the ethic of ahimsā. Everyone subscribes to an ideal of vegetarianism. The actual practice and fulfillment of the ideal did not depend
on one's caste affiliations but on one's Buddhist affiliations. Those
who were better Buddhists tended to be vegetarians, irrespective
of their caste status, in order to better equip themselves for salvation. Thus the offerings given to the Buddha and the gods indicate the high status accorded to them by a community subscribing
to an ideal of ahimsā. The demons and prētas are given impure
foods for they are sinful beings, like their meat-eating counter-
parts who have violated one of the fundamental precepts of their
religion. Traditional Hindu concepts of purity and impurity are
retranslated, however imperfectly, into the idiom of Sinhalese religion. This is further apparent in the myths underlying and justi-
fying the oblations and obeisance where blood, feces, and violence
are given karmic and ethical meaning.

The moral basis of the pantheon is further evident in the relations between man and deity. It is true that the deities, even the
most sinful, are more powerful than man and that man may even
depend on them. But, as Durkheim said, if man needs the deities,
it is also true that the deities need man (Durkheim 1915: 215 ff.).
This dependence of the supernatural being on man is most manifest
in the lower levels of the pantheon. The demons and prētas have
just about no opportunity to improve their lot by their own volition.
Their best chance is through the generosity of the worshiper, specifically through the Sinhalese Buddhist mechanism of merit transfer, pin amumōdan kirīma. But not all demons are fortunate in
this regard, for the human being is not motivated to transfer merit
to demons who capriciously injure him. Their only other chance
of acquiring merit is by leaving the body of the person possessed
by them or by refraining from causing illness and death. Ghosts
and prētas are more fortunate in this respect, for the Sinhalese
Buddhist may out of sympathy for a dead ancester perform "good
works" and transfer some of the merit to the prēta, thereby en-
hancing the salvation chances of that tormented spirit. But even
other mean spirits are not completely left out for a stereotyped
Sinhalese wish attached to acts of piety gives some hope for all
living things, demons and mean spirits included: "May all living

things be released from disease, suffering, and death."

It is in relation to the gods, however, that merit transfer becomes significant, linking the deity and the worshiper in a morality
of mutual self-interest. Man needs the providence of the gods, who
protect him and banish the demons of disease, but man in return
transfers some of his accumulated merit to the gods and thus assists the latter in their spiritual progress toward nirvāna and enlightenment. A universal Pali prayer uttered by all Sinhalese Buddhists gives concrete expression to this:

> Let the gods and nagas of great power who dwell on heaven
> and earth partake of this merit and long protect the Sāsana.

> Let the gods and nagas of great power who dwell on heaven
> and earth partake of this merit and long protect me.

The god is protector of man and of the faith: his reward is the
merit transferred to him by the devotee.

It has been customary to think of Buddhism in Southeast
Asian societies as consisting of discrete strata, one on top of the
other, e.g. a Buddhist stratum, a Brahmanic stratum, and a
animistic stratum. The pantheon described here is neither a
Theravada Buddhist nor a specifically animist one but a Sinhalese
Buddhist pantheon held together by the morality of karma. The
Buddha, gods, demons, and an array of lesser supernatural beings
constitute a single pantheon which displays a wholly consistent
structure. Moreover, the gods in the Sinhalese pantheon are not
necessarily those found mentioned in the Theravada Pali texts but
deities, both "local" and "foreign," who have been incorporated
into the pantheon by various mechanisms. For example, the Gods
of the Four Quarters, the various Brahmas and Nagas, so often
mentioned in the Pali texts, are given only nominal reference in
Sinhalese rituals, whereas gods like Vishnu and Skandha, who are
worshiped by the same names in Hindu India, play a far more
significant role. Yet they too are by no means "Hindu," for they
have been given statuses and attributes consonant with their roles
in a Buddhist pantheon.

One of the mechanisms by which the supernatural beings are
related to one another and to the Buddha at the top of the hierarchy
is through the distribution of power and authority or varan. Varan
is a term which is, once again, derived from the idiom of Sinhalese
feudalism. The king, who is the source of all political power, de-
legates his authority (or gives varan) to lesser political personnel
of the feudal state. In Sinhalese Buddhism likewise, the Buddha is
the ultimate repository of the power and authority possessed by

deities and demons: these latter have their powers delegated to
them by the Buddha. In other words, these beings have a varan
or what might be called a warrant from the Buddha to accept sacrifices from humans and bring relief to their woes, as kings give
varan to their chiefs to rule over an area. The idea of delegated
authority and power is surely an attempt made by Sinhalese Buddhism to meet a Great Tradition assertion, namely that the demons,
by virtue of the supremacy of the law of universal causation (karma),
have no real power. Sinhalese Buddhism, which like any other institutionalized religion could not afford to dispense with supernatural beings possessed with power (or capacity to do good or bad),
meets the doctrinal challenge by stating that these beings are in-
trinsically powerless and only wield powers derived directly or indirectly from the Buddha. Authority thus branches outward from
the apex of the pantheon and converges once again at the top.

One of the questions arising from this concept of varan
relates again to the personality of the Buddha. How could any
supernatural being obtain varan if the Buddha no longer exists?
This difficulty is overcome by positing two types of varan, direct
and indirect. Direct varan is that obtained directly from the Buddha
when he was alive by certain supernatural beings, e.g. Sakra and
Kataragama. Later on, after the Buddha was no more, these
beings in turn gave varan to others, thus redistributing power and
authority initially obtained from the Buddha. But all varan, direct
or indirect, ultimately devolves from the Buddha.

In Rambadeniya there are several myths linking their most
important deities with the Buddha and the guardian deities through
varan. For example, their local god Bandara Deiyo obtained varan
from Skandha to rule over the Laggala pattu. They also have their
own version of a pan-Sinhalese myth which describes the varan
given to demons by the Buddha. This myth states that in ancient
times demons ravaged the earth, killed humans, stole their belong-
ings, and carried these away to their abode in Sakvala gala. The
Buddha, seeing all this, flew through the air and created huge
flames that made Sakvala gala unbearably hot. The demons were
alarmed and fell prostrate before the Buddha, who then ordered
them to listen to his words. (Because they did so without batting
their eyelids, demons to this day don't shut their eyes.) "Here-
after," the Buddha intoned, "you shall not destroy humans and
take their goods. Instead you have my varan to accept sacrifices
and offerings from human beings." Varan was probably an important mechanism whereby "non-Buddhist" deities were incorporated
into the Sinhalese pantheon without disrupting the pantheon as a
unitary structure.

Analogous to varan is a kind of feudal overlordship that

exists between greater and lesser supernatural beings. In Rambadeniya the lesser gods of level three are viewed as ministers or
attendants of the guardian deities, making up their retinue
(pirivara); the demons of level four are viewed as servants of the
lesser gods and constitute their following (pirisa). This concept
of feudal overlordship, or a jajmani relationship between different
levels of deities, was also probably an important mechanism whereby parochial deities were incorporated into the Sinhalese pantheon.
Thus a whole idiom derived from Sinhalese feudalism links the
deities of the pantheon, creating one interconnected structure.

The Manipulation of the Pantheon and Delimitation
of the Moral Community

In the rituals performed by the village the total or "ideal"
pantheon as depicted earlier is not activated. Hence a distinction
has to be drawn between the "active" pantheon and the "ideal"
pantheon. The active pantheon consists of the deities directly propitiated by the people. In village rituals, level two of the pantheon
is largely "inactive"; the guardian deities are never directly propitiated in the village rituals. This is in harmony with the feudal
concepts underlying Rambadeniya ritual idiom. The district deity,
Bandara Deiyo, rules over the village on a varan from the greater
deity, Skandha; thus it is Bandara Deiyo that has to be propitiated
in the local rituals. This acknowledgment of the suzerainty of the
guardian deities is more than a formal affair; it is very real from
the point of view of the villagers. Periodically the kapurāla from
the great Skandha devāle at Kandy visits every single household in
Rambadeniya (as well as other villages in the area) to invoke the
blessings of the deity on the family. This is analogous to the yearly visits of the monarch through his domain and serves to reestab-
lish the suzerainty of Skandha over the local deities.

The pantheon is manipulated by the villagers of Rambadeniya through their ritual system. Since it would be impossible to
describe here the total ritual system of the Sinhalese, suffice it to
say that the system can be dichotomized in terms of the religious
goals or orientations of the masses. The rituals performed for
the Buddha have largely to do with the other-worldly orientations
of the masses, rituals for demons and gods with their this-worldly
goals. The allocation of specialist religious roles also reflects
this dichotomy. Living within the temple or monastery, the Buddhist monk is concerned for man's salvation. The kapurāla (also
known as yakdessa or kattāndiya), who is associated with a devāle
(temple of the gods), acts as intermediary between man and the
gods in the obtainment of material goods and rewards.

As to the ritual cycle in Rambadeniya, the nearest Buddhist temple (vihāra) was five miles away in the neighboring village of Ettamgoda, but the villagers performed daily rituals before an image of the Buddha placed on a cement altar under a large bōdhi tree near the village preaching hall (banagē). Rituals for the gods were performed by the villagers collectively after harvest. Demons were propitiated during sickness, the theory being that the rationally punitive god would banish his servant, the demon, who had possessed the patient. But these different rituals are by no means airtight. In rituals to the Buddha the gods are "remembered," and rituals to gods and demons commence with a "homage" to the Buddha, the Dhamma, and the Sangha.

Many points may become clearer in the following description of the ritual performed for Bandara Deiyo during the biannual rites of intensification after the harvests, for this ritual more than any other defines Rambadeniya village as a single moral community. The Bandara Deiyo ritual, called adukku, is essentially a ceremony of first fruits and each villager brings a fistful of rice from the "new harvest" (alut sāl) together with coconuts and jaggery for use in preparing the gods' feast (deiyanne dāne). In eating of the gods' feast at the conclusion of the ritual, men become commensals of the gods. The ritual also serves for some villagers as an occasion for making "vows" to Bandara Deiyo. The relative sizes of the altars constructed, in a sacred area near the river bank, symbolize to some extent the relation between the various supernaturals. A large elaborate altar is constructed for Bandara Deiyo and other gods of level three in the pantheon whereas two smaller ones are set up for deities of levels four and five. Obeisances and offerings follow the hierarchical pattern described earlier. For present purposes what are important are the social functions of the ritual, which validate and ritually legitimate the status structure of the village and define the limits of the moral community. Let me illustrate.

There is, first of all, a rule excluding women from participation in the adukku, a rule which validates the social inferiority of women and defines their inferior status in the social structure while fostering male solidarity and unity, for all males irrespective of caste can participate in this ceremony. Secondly, the adukku validates the status distinctions between the two major castes in the village, goigama and dura. All castes in the village assist in the performance of adukku; there is no caste division of labor in the allocation of tasks performed in the ritual (except that a kapurāla of the goigama caste should officiate at the ritual); in the feast that follows, all castes eat their food off banana leaves; and there are no special seating arrangements or no spatial separation of the castes, as in India. However, meals for the deities are cooked in two pots. One of these pots, the raja hāliya (royal

pot), is officially dedicated to Bandara Deiyo and placed on his
altar. The food in the royal pot can be eaten only by members of
the goigama caste whereas food from the other pot can be eaten by
both dura and goigama. The goigama kapurāla shouts aloud for
everyone to hear that no low caste member (hīnakulaätto) should
eat of the raja häliya. Furthermore, when a dura caste member
wishes to make a vow to Bandara Deiyo, he is introduced by the
kapurāla in the following manner, "Lord, listen to the plea of your
feudal tenant (or infant) so and so of inferior caste." Thirdly, the
adukku ritual legitimates the jural inferiority of children for sub-
adults, too, are forbidden to eat of the raja häliya. Fourthly, the
ritual is punctuated with invocations to the several deities of the
pantheon, the content of which may be summed up as follows: "Protect all beings within this sīma ("limit," here "limits," of this
village); banish disease, dangers, winds; protect the fields; banish
the leopard that steals our cattle; forgive us our evil thoughts and
evil deeds; and fulfill our secret wishes and thoughts. Extend your
protective benevolence within the sīma of this village for the sīma
(time limit) of one year -- and (by this good) may you achieve
future Buddhahood." These invocations end with a cryptic statement, "Buddharaksha Buddhasima; Devarakshadevasima," which
translated means, "May the protective benevolence of the Buddha
and the gods be effective for the sīma of the village." Thus the
ritual of the adukku validates the social structure of the village,
defines its limits, and demarcates the village as a moral community over which the gods have protective jurisdiction and authority.

Extensions of the Pantheon and Expansion of the
Moral Community

There is, then, a sense in which Rambadeniya is a single
moral community; the rituals performed for "local deities," i.e.
levels three and below of the pantheon, define the limits of the
moral community and validate the status structure of the village.
My thesis is that the major substantive differences in the religion
of each village occur at these levels. Thus the "local deities,"
the myths associated with them, their attributes, and the number
and modes of propitiation may vary from one village or region to
another. In each village they are closely involved in the social
structure of the group. There are no major substantive differences
on levels one and two of the pantheon in all Sinhalese villages for
two reasons: all villages share a common repertoire of meanings,
prayers, and rituals associated with the Buddha (a common "salvation idiom") and all acknowledge the suzerainty of the major
guardian deities over their local deities. In other words, the village religion is extended at levels one and two of the pantheon.

Crucial to this extension is the concept of sīma. From

the meaning "parish" in the Pali literature, sīma has acquired the more general meaning of "limit" in these political contexts:

(a) Relating to territory, as a "boundary" or "border" of a kingdom, province, or village.

(b) Relating to authority and control, as the "limit" of a political domain, e.g. the king has sīma over the kingdom, the disāva over a province, the headman over a village.

(c) Relating to time, as a "time limit" (kāla sīmāva) on the exercise of political authority, e.g. the kāla sīmāva for the king is the king's lifetime, for a disāva only a year (barring his reappointment by the king).

All these meanings of sīma, so important in the political idiom, are transferred intact to the religious context, so the deities in the pantheon all have their sīma in terms of territory, authority, and time. We could generalize and say that the limits of authority and power of deities increase in an ascending order from the base of the pantheon until one reaches the apex of the pyramid, i.e. in Sakra, whose sīma of authority is the universal Buddhist church, and the Buddha, who is beyond all sīma. As far as the major gods of Rambadeniya are concerned, Bandara Deiyo has sīma in the village and other villages of his district, and in the yearly rites of intensification the kapurāla asks him to protect the sīma of the village for one year. The other deities on the same level of the pantheon have their sīma in neighboring villages and districts. These several districts merge into a larger district or "province," forming the larger sīma which is presided over by one of the guardian deities with his seat and major sanctum in a special "sacred area" in the province. In the case of Rambadeniya the guardian deity who had this special authority was Saman, with a seat at Mahiyangana thirty-five miles away and another major sanctum in Ratnapura in the Sabaragamuva province of Ceylon. Similarly, Skandha has his sanctum in Kataragama, Pattini in Navagamuva, Nāta in Totagamuva, and Vishnu in Devundara. In Sinhalese theory, the guardian deities had general jurisdiction over the island but might also have a special area (sīma) over which they had more direct control. This has its analogy in Sinhalese feudalism where a king has political and administrative control over the whole island but in addition may have special areas where his authority and power are directly exercised. The village pantheon, then, is articulated with the seat of the guardian deity, Saman, through a set of cultural concepts derived from the idiom of feudalism. If in the village rituals levels three, four,

and five of the pantheon were strongly active, in the rituals performed at the seat of Saman these levels are largely "inactive";
on the other hand, level two of the pantheon, which was inactive
at the village level, is activated in the provincial rituals. There
is a reduction of power at the province: the various local deities
relinquish the powers at the seat of the guardian deity. Powers
delegated to and diffused among the numerous "local deities" of
the villages in the area are all recouped in the provincial seat.

The actual organization of the sacred precincts at Mahiyangana emphasize levels one and two of the pantheon. There is
the Buddha Vihāra, the dāgoba containing the collar bone relic of
the Buddha, the bōdhi tree, and the pansala of the monks. Then
there is the main devāle in which the god Saman is housed. Several
decades ago there were separate devāles for three other guardian
deities -- Pattini, Kataragama (Skandha), and Vishnu. These
deities are now propitiated in the main devāle sacred to Saman.
There are no devāles for the regional deities for, as we pointed
out, they have relinquished their powers at the center. But their
names are mentioned in the invocations (yātika) recited by the
kapurāla at the main devāle. If the rituals of the village bring
prosperity to its members, the rituals performed here bring prosperity to the whole area, e.g. there is the planting of the kapa,
to bring wealth and prosperity to the whole province, and the water-
cutting ritual, to ensure an adequate supply of rain. A very important ritual performed during the period of festivities is the
procession (perahära), a highly elaborate and colorful ceremony
in which the insignia of the deity Saman, his sister Maha Devi, a
servitor deity Kalu Devata, and the Buddha relics are paraded
through the sacred precincts before the gaze of the assembled
crowd. This type of ritual is probably what Milton Singer calls a
"cultural performance" (Singer 1958: 351). In the final night
(mahaperahära) the Buddha, the supreme head of the pantheon,
and Saman, the defender of the faith, parade the streets to acknowledge the homage of the assembled populace, thus reaffirming
their suzerain positions in the pantheon.

In the preceding analysis I have described the articulation
of the village pantheon with the seat of the guardian deity through
a set of concepts derived from the idiom of Sinhalese feudalism.
I suggest in addition that the extension of the pantheon has a direct
sociological counterpart in the expansion of the moral community
of the village through the institution of the "pilgrimage." Traditionally it was obligatory, if not compulsory, for the villagers of
Rambadeniya and other villages to visit Mahiyangana and participate in the yearly festival there. The custom is still strong and
at festival time the villages in the area are practically deserted.
During the pilgrimage, one has to be specially guarded in one's

thoughts, actions, and words lest the god Saman be offended. Each pilgrim party (nadē) winds along the jungle tracks singing religious songs -- generally in praise of the Buddha. Proceeding through the jungle, the pilgrims stop at various sacred spots and hang branches or leafy twigs on certain trees sacred to minor deities. This action signifies the recognition of the power of those beings through whose sīma the party has to pass. Near Mahiyangana there is a literal expansion of the moral community as pilgrim parties from different villages begin to merge in one large mass. On arrival at Mahiyangana the villagers purify themselves by bathing in the river. Next they go worship Saman and the other guardian deities at the devāle, and finally they proceed to worship the Buddha. A shift in allegiance has occurred: the villages have "renounced" the authority of Bandara Deiyo for the superior authority of Saman and the other guardian deities. All the several villages have renounced their parochial local deities and are now united in common worship under the benevolent, but austere, overlordship of Saman. If the rituals of the village define the limits of the moral community and validate the status differences in the social structure, the rituals at Mahiyangana are open to all, irrespective of caste and sex or other status factors. The once separate and discrete moral communities of the several villages now lose their identity in the larger moral community of Sinhalese Buddhists.

Evidence for the interpretation advanced here comes from one of the most spectacular rituals performed at Mahiyangana, the vädi perahära or "Procession of the Veddhas." The Veddhas, the aboriginal inhabitants of Ceylon, have always lived on the periphery of Sinhalese civilization, traditionally owing tenuous feudal obligations to the Sinhalese king and acknowledging his formal supremacy. Veddha religion was radically different from Sinhalese religion, notably in the absence of rituals to the Buddha (level one), though the Buddha was formally accepted as supreme and treated as some superior deity. More importantly connected with their religion were Skandha and Saman, within whose domain most of the Veddha communities are still found. The ritual of the vädi perahära clearly validates the position of the Veddhas vis-à-vis the moral community of Sinhalese Buddhists, and Veddha religion vis-à-vis Sinhalese Buddhism.

Veddhas (seventy-one in the ritual I witnessed) carrying poles representing spears line up near the devāle of Saman, led by a "chief" carrying a bow and arrow. After circumambulating the devāle three times in a graceful dance, the Veddhas suddenly increase the tempo of their dance, at a signal from the chief, and start hooting, yelling, and brandishing their "spears," frightening the assembled Sinhalese spectators. They stage several battles

in front of the devāle, during which they "assault" the devāle by
striking their spears on the devāle steps. They then run toward
the vihāra and try to enter the premises of the dāgoba, where the
Buddha relics are enshrined. Here the path is blocked by two
"watchers" (murakārayo) who shout, "You can't approach this
place. Go back to the royal altar (rajavidiya, the altar of the
guardian deity)." These mock battles are repeated several times
and end with the Veddhas placing their "spears" gently against the
dāgoba and worshiping it. They then run toward the monks' residence (pansala), stage a battle, but, as at the dāgoba, end by
worshiping the monks gathered there. Then, from the monks'
residence back to the devāle where they again "battle," beating
their spears against the stone steps of the devāle until the spears
break into small pieces and finally falling prostrate on the ground
to worship the gods housed in the devāle. After this they run
toward the nearby river ("the ferry crossing of the gods") and
bathe and purify themselves. Returning to the devāle calm and
self-possessed, they are now permitted to enter the inner sanctum
while the kapurāla chants an incantation for Saman, Skandha, and
the other major deities and blesses the Veddhas by lustrating each
person with "sandal water." The ritual ends with the Veddhas all
shouting "haro-harā" (from the Indian "hari-hara"), which in Ceylon
is the paean of praise for the god Skandha, the great guardian deity
of the Island and formal overlord of the Veddha pantheon.

The difference in the social functions of the rituals performed by Sinhalese and Veddha are impressive. In the case of
the Sinhalese there are no rituals that separate one group from
another: all the assembled groups form one moral community participating in common worship. In the case of the Veddhas, the rituals define their status in relation to the dominant religion in that
they are "prevented" from entering the vihāra and dāgoba. Though
they formally acknowledge the supremacy of the Buddha, they are
clearly outside the Sinhalese Buddhist moral community. Yet they
are not total strangers, for both Sinhalese and Veddha are united
in worship of the guardian deities, Saman and Skandha, protectors
of the secular and supernatural order of both Veddha and Sinhalese.

Village, Province, and State

It is at the provincial seat of the guardian deity that the
village, however isolated it may be, merges with the larger community of Sinhalese Buddhists. We have seen that levels three,
four, and five of the pantheon, so important in the village and substantively different in each village or region, are blurred, and
level two of the guardian deities, substantively the same in all
villages, "activated." Level two of the pantheon is even more
vividly institutionalized in the festivals still performed today at

the capital of the old kingdom at Kandy. The central spot in the sacred area at Kandy is the Dalada Maligawa, the temple of the tooth, containing the Buddhist holy of holies, the tooth relic in which is incarnated preeminently the nirvāna presence of the Buddha. The tooth is closely associated with Sinhalese kingship and with the legitimation of the king's political authority. Near the temple of the tooth are devāles for the four guardian deities (hatara deiyo) of the secular realm -- Nāta, Pattini, Skandha, Vishnu. (The devāles here are considered only slightly less powerful than the devāle of each deity at his main seat.) For our purposes the most important rituals are performed here during the month of August (äsala) and constitute a glorified elaboration of the rituals performed at the provincial seat, e.g. the water-cutting ceremony to create rain for the whole nation. Here, in these state ceremonies, the four guardians of the realm parade the streets in the perahära. During the first week of the festivities, each devāle performs its own parade, carrying the insignia of the deity in a procession three times around the devāle. Later on, in the last two weeks, the several processions merge and together with the procession of the temple of the tooth parade the major streets of Kandy, giving the assembled crowds a vivid and concrete representation of the upper two levels of the pantheon.

After Mahiyangana, the next major pilgrimage center for Rambadeniya villagers was Kandy during äsala. Practically all adult men and most adult women have been there several times. Rambadeniya was probably singularly well placed in this respect for many villagers had to visit the capital every year anyway to pay däkum to the proprietor of their village (nindagama), Mr. X. Disava, in his valauva there. This meant an opportunity to participate in the festivities of the temple of the tooth as well. But it would be true to say, I think, that these state ceremonies were themselves, and are still, a big attraction for Sinhalese villagers. Here too, and even more than at Mahiyangana, the village is articulated with the larger moral community. The pilgrimage to Kandy is less obligatory than to Mahiyangana and not all the villagers can consistently make it. However, if the villagers cannot make it to the rituals of the "center," the "center" is brought to the village in a very direct and realistic fashion. As mentioned earlier, once every year several kapurālas from the four devāles at Kandy visit the villagers in the Kandyan area, carrying with them the insignia of the deity. In effect, the hatara deiyo visit the villages, blessing each household. But the manner of blessing is interesting: the kapurāla asks the householders to face the direction of the Maligawa and worship the deity while he chants a blessing. This round of visits by the kapurālas is well established in Sinhalese custom, so that even if direct participation in the state rituals is not possible, every villager can at least vicariously participate.

The "Salvation Idiom" and the Moral Unity of a Civilization

We suggested earlier that the ritual system of the village could be dichotomized in terms of the religious goals or orientations of the people -- the Buddha being associated with their 'otherworldly' orientations and the gods and lesser supernaturals with their materialistic "this-worldly" orientations. If there is diversity in belief and worship in Sinhalese villages in respect to the latter, there is uniformity in respect to the former. The prayers and rituals associated with the Buddha (level one of the pantheon) are pāli gāthas, prescribed by the Great Tradition and uniform all over the Island. There are, in addition to these gāthas, a common set of concepts pertaining to man's destiny and salvation that Rambadeniya folk share with other Sinhalese villages. All derive from the Great Tradition of Theravada Buddhism, and the mediating agency for these ideas is the Buddhist monastery. These rituals, prayers, and meanings common to all Sinhalese villages are what I call a "salvation idiom" which, though not the exact equivalent of the salvation ethic of the Great Tradition, uses the same terms. This remains true despite the specific meanings attached to the terms in Sinhalese Buddhism to accommodate the religious needs of the masses. Thus Rambadeniya folk share with other villagers such terms as: pin (merit, good deeds), pau (sin, bad deeds), karma (law of universal causation), mōksha, nirvāna (release), dukkha (suffering), dāna (charity), maitreye (compassion), sila (virtue), karunā (kindliness), apāya (hell), devlova (heaven), and samsāra (life). There may be significant variations from region to region in the meanings given to these terms but, in so far as these concepts are derived from Theravada Buddhism, the monasteries serve to prevent any radical departure from a common "core meaning."

The salvation idiom unites the villages in a common world view, most matters of general concern being readily interpreted through these basic Buddhist concepts. Though "local deities" and "local beliefs" may differ from village to village, none can be called non-Buddhist, for all have been incorporated into a Buddhistic framework. As I have pointed out earlier, the differences among "local deities" (levels three, four, and five of the pantheon) are more apparent than real for the explanations of their powers, status, fortune, and attributes are uniform everywhere and invariably couched in terms of the "salvation idiom." Hence in a very fundamental sense Sinhalese Buddhists are a single moral community, for they have a common salvation idiom from which their world view is largely constituted. Far from being an abstraction, this "belonging" receives concrete sociological expression through, once again, the mechanism of the "obligatory pilgrimage."

There are several sacred places (mahastāna, literally
"great places") associated with the Buddha to which the people
can make a pilgrimage to earn pin (merit) toward their salvation.
These places of Buddha worship are the analogue of the sacred
places associated with the guardian deities and may occasionally
coincide with them. For example, the seat of Saman at Mahiyangana is also a great place of Buddha worship since it contains the
collarbone relic. Of several lists of such great places, the most
popular enumerates sixteen (see Figure 2) and is included in a
Pali prayer entitled "The Worship of Sixteen Great Places":

> Mahiyangana, Nagadipa,
> Kelaniya, Buddha's footprint at Adam's peak,
> Divaguha, Digavapi,
> The chetiya (dāgoba) at Mutiyangana,
> Tissamaharama Vihāra, the sacred bōdhi tree,
> Miriswati dāgoba, Swarnamali,
> Thuparama chetiya, Abhayagiri
> Jetevani Vihārana, Mihintale,
> Kiri Vihara at Kataragama,
> I worship those sixteen places with my hands on
> my forehead.

It is interesting to note that the tradition of worshiping at these
sixteen great places goes back at least to the eighteenth century
(Culavamsa 1930: 284, 216).

Since these sacred places are scattered throughout the
Island, the "ideal pilgrimage" takes the individual through practically the length and breadth of the country. Though it is doubtful
whether in the past many individuals had the time or opportunity to
do the grand round, it is more feasible than a trip to Mecca by a
contemporary Moslem citizen of Ceylon. In any case, some of
these places would be within the reach of most villages. In these
sacred places, Buddhists from all parts of the country meet together in a commonality of worship. This is always an important
social function of the "obligatory pilgrimage": it is a mechanism
which transfers the individual or group from the limited moral
community of the village to the larger moral community of the
civilization. Its role in building up a sense of universal religious
brotherhood transcending national barriers (comparable with that
found at Catholic places of pilgrimage or the Moslem's Mecca) and
in fostering a sense of national consciousness in feudal type societies is obvious. One is reminded of the lines in Chaucer's
Canterbury Tales:

> And specially from every shires ende
> Of Engelond to Caunterbury they wende,
> The hooly blisful martir for to seke,
> That hem hath holpen whan that they were seeke.

The Religious Pantheon and the Political Order

   An attempt was made in this paper to demonstrate the connection between the village religion and the larger religious tradition of the Sinhalese Buddhists in terms of the pantheon and its extensions. Obviously there exist other connections not emphasized
in this paper. We stated that the pantheon was institutionalized on
three major levels -- the village, the province, and the state --
and that this institutionalization was based on feudal notions pertaining to authority and the devolution of power. Indeed, one could
say that at several points the religious system is directly linked
with the feudal order. We stated earlier that the village rituals
validate the social structure of the group while, in the province
and the state, people from all parts of the Island participate in
common worship irrespective of status affiliations. The latter
statement is true only from the point of view of the worshipers
assembled at these sacred places and not of those responsible for
the organization, conduct, and performance of the rituals. Consider the perahära. Here the top levels of the pantheon were presented to the audience, but the "internal structure" of the perahära
also revealed a social order. The organization of the human personnel marching in the procession reflected in epitome the feudal,
social, and political structure of the province. The procession
was traditionally led by the disäva of the province, various state
officials, the kapurälas, and the chief Buddhist monks. The castes
were represented in their roles as drummers, dancers, washermen, flutists, smiths, and potters. Even the Veddhas, all of whose
service duties (rājakāriya) relate to performance in the perahära,
have their place in the "internal structure" of the procession. At
Kandy, this was doubly conspicuous, for the king and his ministers
(adikāramvaru) took part while an important officer of the king,
the diyavadana nilame, officiated at the water-cutting ceremony
(which is done by the kapurāla at the village level). This perahära
presents to the assembled crowd the powerful upper hierarchies
of not only the pantheon but also the political order, including the
major castes of the kingdom, in the "cultural performance" of
their social roles (Obeyesekere 1958). At the provincial level and
at the "center," the village becomes part of the larger political
and religious order of the state.

   In conclusion we may ask the question as to how far the
description presented above accords with the facts of contemporary
Ceylon in the throes of social change? A good deal, I think. The
neat articulation of the feudal and religious systems are no longer
important. But in so far as Ceylon still consists of villages, with
local traditions, the extensions of the pantheon and the obligatory
pilgrimage have similar significance.

Many of the villages still have their local deities and local beliefs while the upper two levels of the pantheon are common to all. The position and attributes of the Buddha have not changed at all. Better roads and better communications have made the pilgrimage so easy that the grand round is now within the reach of most villagers. With the decay of caste and feudalism and the democratization of the state, there is, I think, a tendency toward the universalization of the pantheon, e.g. village and regional deities are losing their authority and the guardian deities have taken over their powers. Even among the guardian deities some have become more popular than others so that Nāta, Vishnu, and Pattini -- traditionally very powerful deities -- are being propitiated less and less. One of the more impressive changes in modern times is the remarkable ascendancy of Skandha, whose seat at Kataragama is now the major pilgrimage center for Sinhalese people at level two of the pantheon. It is my belief that this deity will soon become, next to the Buddha, the predominant deity in the pantheon and may eventually displace the other guardian deities altogether. But though there have been changes in the structure of the pantheon, this has not necessarily meant a psychological shift or change. Deities of levels two and three of the pantheon have similar psychological attributes -- most of them (the male ones) being rationally punitive, providential deities or father figures, in relation to whom the worshiper is an infant (ladaruva). Hence there could be a reorganization of the formal structure of the pantheon without a necessary psychological reorganization in the individual's relationship to a deity. The psychological equivalence of deities makes a formal restructuring of the pantheon a not too difficult task.

NOTES

1.   The present article is based on field work done in Ceylon at various periods from 1958 to 1961. I wish to thank the Asia Foundation in Ceylon for generous financial assistance, which made this work possible. K.A.D. Perera, a student in the Department of Sociology, University of Ceylon, helped me in my field work, especially during the "pilgrimage" to Mahiyangana. Soon after the final version of this paper had been written, Mr. Perera died unexpectedly while still a young man. I dedicate this work to his memory.

2.   The following discussion of Kandyan feudalism is entirely based on the work of Ralph Pieris (1956).

3.   Much of the discussion of the pantheon is based on an earlier article by the author entitled "The Great Tradition and The Little in the Perspective of Sinhalese Buddhism."

4.   The hatara varan deiyo have in Sinhalese Buddhism probably
      usurped the place of the hatara varan deiyo of the Pali texts
      who are the guardians of the four quarters. The term hatara
      varan deiyo (or simply hatara deiyo) is used most often in the
      Kandyan area and the low country of Ceylon. In the low coun-
      try, Vibisana, whose sanctum is Kelaniya, is considered an
      equal of the hatara deiyo and also a guardian deity. It is also
      probable that Aiyanar mentioned by Leach (1961) has a simi-
      lar role in the dry zone of Ceylon. I have omitted reference
      to these deities as it would unnecessarily complicate the pic-
      ture presented here.

REFERENCES CITED

Durkheim, Emile

      1915   The Elementary Forms of the Religious Life, trans.
                J. W. Swain, London, George Allen and Unwin.

Leach, E. R.

      1961   Pul Eliya: A Village in Ceylon, Cambridge,
                Cambridge University Press.

Obeyesekere, G.

      1958   "Structure of a Sinhalese Ritual, " Ceylon Journal of
                Historical and Social Studies, 1 (No. 2).

      1963   "The Great Tradition and The Little in the Perspec-
                tive of Sinhalese Buddhism" Journal of Asian Studies,
                22, 139-53.

Opler, Morris E.

      1956   "The Extensions of an Indian Village, " Journal of
                Asian Studies, 16 (No. 1).

Pieris, Ralph

      1956   Sinhalese Social Organization, Peradeniya, Univer-
                sity of Ceylon Press Board.

Redfield, Robert

      1956   Peasant Society and Culture, Chicago, University of
                Chicago Press.

Singh, Rudra Datt

      1956   "The Unity of an Indian Village, " Journal of Asian
                Studies, 16 (No. 1).

Singer, Milton

      1958   "The Great Tradition in a Metropolitan Center:
                Madras," Journal of American Folklore, 71 (No. 281).

RITUAL PRESTATIONS AND THE STRUCTURE OF THE
SINHALESE PANTHEON[1]

Michael M. Ames

University of British Columbia

When anthropologists turn to the study of religion they seem to emphasize either psychological or cultural aspects. Religion is viewed as the source of a series of projective, cathartic, and adjustive mechanisms on the one hand or as a system of quasi-linguistic symbols, value orientations, and world views on the other. In either case the social structure of the religious community usually receives only passing notice. To most anthropologists, in fact, the term "social structure" is more likely to bring to mind a kinship system than anything else and most of the abstract models of social structure that have so far been created are, not surprisingly, models of kinship systems. When the anthropologist leaves kinship to study religion he often as not leaves behind as well his notions about structure.

Consider for example the recent works by the structuralists Lévi-Strauss (1955, 1958, etc.) and Leach (1958, 1961, 1962). Once they turned to the analysis of religious phenomena they discussed the logical arrangement of mythical symbols and the implications of this order for kinship and psyche. Leach almost begins to talk like a Freudian! And Lévi-Strauss, although he writes about the "structural" study of myth, actually refers to linguistic rather than to sociological notions of structure; these are not the same kinds of structure at all. Neither Leach nor Lévi-Strauss has yet to say much about the social structure of religion itself, although both are social structure specialists, and probably neither would disagree that interpersonal relations within the context of religion are just as structured as those within kinship. There are religious roles just as there are kinship roles, religious institutions as well as kinship institutions. Anthropologists treat the family, polity, and economy as analytically independent social systems, so why not give the religious system, or ecclesiastical organization (someone has suggested the term "religity"), comparable status?

Without intending to depreciate the value of the mythical studies, for certainly they are ingenious, I would like to make some attempt at redressing the balance by returning the concept of structure to religion and that of context to myth. The same analytical concept of social structure used in kinship studies can be applied to the study of religion. I present below one example of such an application. In doing so I want to reassert the old-fashioned functionalist dogma that myth and ritual are intimately

related; I will go even further and argue that certain aspects of
myth correlate precisely with certain aspects of ritual. My specific thesis is that the "structure" of the Sinhalese pantheon ("certain
aspects of myth") is a direct reflection of the arrangement of ritual prestations ("certain aspects of ritual"). This is a Durkheimian proposition: gods need man as much as man needs the gods,
for "without offerings and sacrifices they would die" (1915: 38). It
is precisely the offerings and sacrifices -- what I will call transactions or prestations -- that have created the gods in the first
place.

Let me be clear about what I mean. I have no desire to argue
the absurd by saying all aspects of myth or all religious beliefs
correlate exactly with all aspects of the social structure of religion.
It is only in certain very specific ways that religious beliefs provide the notorious "mirror image" of social phenomena. Those
specific aspects are what I want to explore here.

The structural aspect that concerns me is the patterning of
ritual offerings (transactions or prestations). I will also show how
my structural analysis -- and this is using "structure" in the traditional sense to mean social interaction -- leads naturally to a
discussion of sacred and profane value orientations, beliefs about
the spirit world, and even, should one desire, personal religious
experiences. I believe this should be the primary approach of
those who call themselves "structuralists." It is only when one
knows what the religious or ecclesiastical structure is -- the
"functional context" -- that one can sensibly talk about the meaning of religious symbols and psychic experiences. Myths can of
course be studied independent of their structural contexts, and
they can be related to secular institutions such as kinship; but as a
structuralist my first concern is in seeing how in fact they are related to their structural framework within the religious system.

The following discussion of Sinhalese rituals and religious
beliefs is based on two further assumptions: (1) all Sinhalese rituals are built around, or concerned with, a series of prestations
or transactions and (2) these transactions can be treated as structural units or "unit acts." Following Oliver (1958), I view transactions, or the "circulation of goods," as one dimension of social
interaction or social structure. The discussion will therefore
proceed in this manner. First I will distinguish several categories
of ritual transactions in terms of two criteria: (1) the specific
transaction involved and (2) beliefs about the purpose of this transaction. Next I will show how in practice these transactional units
are combined in various ways to form different types of rituals or
"ritual sequences." Finally I will illustrate how certain beliefs
about spirits reflect this sequential arrangement of ritual acts.

This is the "mirror image" phenomenon. It is part of my argument that only through such a social structural analysis of ritual can one discover what is the symbolic structure of the pantheon. Previous efforts to discuss the spirit world of the Sinhalese (Leach 1962; Yalman 1962), although insightful, are incomplete simply because they bypass the structure of spirit worship to concentrate on the logical arrangement, or "binary oppositions," among certain spirit symbols.

These "symbolicist" studies are based on several question- able assumptions. They assume that thought categories can best be described in terms of quasi-linguistic binary oppositions and that certain of these oppositions are particularly important -- es- pecially those between life and death, purity and impurity, sex and nonsex. But why these oppositions and not others? Why not sacred and profane? How does one decide which categories to select and which to ignore? What are the underlying psychological assump- tions involved in the selecting? The symbolicist approach seems to me to be primarily an intuitive process that depends more on insight or even genius than on empirical methods. In this re- spect it suffers from the same fault as the American school of cul- ture and personality. Another characteristic of the symbolicists is that they are primarily concerned with exploring the relations between religious symbols and kinship systems. Ecclesiastical structure, as I suggested above, tends to be ignored.

My intent is less to criticize these studies than to show how mine is different. We differ more in methods than in results. But this is crucial. How does one go about determining the various categories of spirits in a pantheon? My quest is much more re- stricted than theirs. I offer in this paper a heuristic, and empiri- cal, device for tackling this limited problem; if it is successful, we can then go on to talk about kinship. The device is subjected to a detailed application. Do not boggle at these details at the expense of general principles. The underlying proposition is simply that if people believe in different kinds of spirits then they will treat, or interact with, those spirits in different ways. The specific content of the interaction may vary for each society or religious commun- ity.

This is what I call a structuralist approach to spirit beliefs. Binary symbols are elusive; spirits cannot be seen; but ritual transactions can be counted and examined in the field. The fact that the results of my exploration, although more detailed, corres- pond more or less generally to those of Leach and Yalman only suggests to me that their intuitions have been empirically con- firmed. Their results are commendable despite their methods.

Two further explanatory notes are necessary to avoid possible misunderstandings. Part of my concern is with people's beliefs about the purpose of transactions. These are manifest beliefs, opinions, or suppositions; they are not subconscious or covert attitudes, values, norms, or psychological motives. I do not ask why people transact, for that presupposes a knowledge about individual psyches that I do not possess. The questions to be asked are: what objects or goods are transacted and what are the manifest intents or stated purposes for these transactions? As will be pointed out later, these simple distinctions have far-reaching implications. Finally, although I talk about "the Sinhalese," I am actually referring only to those Sinhalese Buddhists I observed in the Matara district of southern Ceylon during 1959 and 1960. Most of my research was done in Matara town itself and in a village ten miles from that town. How relevant the statements in this paper are for Sinhalese beliefs and rites elsewhere in Ceylon I leave for others to decide. Details will obviously differ. I believe, however, that the general principles to be propounded here will hold for all Sinhalese Buddhists.

II

I begin with the second criterion referred to above, the manifest intent or stated purpose of ritual transactions. All Sinhalese rituals may be divided, on this basis, into two main categories: transactions that are reciprocal and those that are not. These two categories may in turn be subdivided according to the first criterion: the kind of object or scarce good that is transacted. This will give a series of subcategories or "unit acts" of transactions. Within the category of reciprocal transactions, for example, there are three kinds of units differentiated from each other according to the degree of purity of the objects transacted. Within the nonreciprocal category there are at least six identifiable units, although they are not differentiated in any systematic way such as by degrees of purity or pollution. They are nevertheless distinguished from each other by the Sinhalese, as are the three unit acts within the reciprocal category.

Perhaps the distinction between reciprocal and nonreciprocal ritual transactions can be made clearer by introducing here several concrete examples of unit acts together with alternate acts belonging to the same general category.

An example of a unit act within the nonreciprocal category is an offering to the Buddha, sometimes called <u>Buddha pūjāva</u>[2] but more accurately termed <u>vändima-pidima</u>, that is, giving homage or reverence (<u>vändima</u>, or <u>vandanā</u>) and giving material goods

such as flowers and food (pidīma). To perform this act, both
monks and laity, individually or jointly, go before a Buddha statue,
pay homage, and then present offerings of flowers, vegetable curries, and beverages. The stated purpose is twofold. On the one
hand it is to show reverence for a great man and his sacred teachings. On the other hand, through presenting material objects, it
is practice in renunciation. In both cases the purpose is not to
influence the recipient but to improve one's own virtues, to become
self-perfected in mind and deed (satpurusa) as the first step toward
salvation (nirvānaya). Ego gives and alter receives. Alter's reaction, whatever it may be, is not necessary to validate ego's original act of giving. All alter has to do is accept the prestation.
That is why I call this type of transaction nonreciprocal.[3] The reward for making these offerings is in the form of merit that is
earned by the giver's own action. Buddha does not "bestow" merit.
The Buddha statue, alter, is merely a passive field of merit (pinak
keta) on which a person sows good actions in order to purify himself of mental defilements (kleśa) such as greed, anger, and spiritual ignorance. Buddha no longer exists and therefore can neither
be influenced by the offering nor reward the donor.

Consider another example: the laity give alms to monks.
Here an exchange may certainly occur in that monks "give" sermons to the laity. But the transaction is still nonreciprocal. Each
transaction, alms-giving or sermon-giving, may occur independent
of the other -- even in isolation. The official reason why a layman
gives alms to monks is "to earn merit through my own good actions."
The reward he receives is the merit he earns himself. The fact
that a monk, in response to receiving alms, may preach a sermon
to the layman, is irrelevant. Sermon-giving is a complete, separate, and independent merit act.

This is the point I am trying to make. A subtle form of exchange may occur: a layman prefers to give alms to a particular
monk who has performed special services for him. But I am not
interested in these subtleties. The layman's official or manifest
intent (adahasa) is to earn merit, not to repay a friendly monk.
It is only according to this official or ideal intent that a transaction
is said to be nonreciprocal or reciprocal.[4]

In addition to vāndīma-pidīma there are at least five other
unit acts manifestly intended to be nonreciprocal (see Table 1).
In each case the reward for the transaction comes not from the
recipient's reaction but from the donor's own action. They are
called "unit" transactions because each may vary independently
of the others.

Table 1. Nonreciprocal (Expressive) Transactional Units

1. Venerating Buddha (vändīma-pidīma)
2. Alms-giving (dan-dīma)
3. Preaching sermons (bana kīma)
4. Transferring merit (pin dīma)
5. Giving respect (garu kirīma)
6. Giving assistance (vatāvat kirīma)

People "give" respect to parents and elders; villagers "give" assistance to the needy or the stranger; the laity "give" alms to monks, which earns merit for themselves; monks present "gifts" of sermons or spiritual knowledge to the laity, a meritorious ploy for the monks; both monks and laity present "gifts" of alms to the Buddha statue. These nonreciprocal transactions taken together form an integrated network: laity give to each other, monks give to each other, laity give to monks, monks give to laity, and every-one gives to Buddha. It is a network of prestations that serves to bind all together in the same "Buddhist moral community" (Buñdāgama) or "Buddhist church" (Budhasāsanaya). What sets these transactions off from all others is the manifest intent to earn merit (pina) through one's own virtuous deeds. The recipi-ent's reactions, although perhaps an important factor in motivating further actions on the part of ego, are not necessary to validate ego's original action. It is in this sense, then, that these trans-actions are nonreciprocal.

All other Sinhalese ritual acts fall under the second category, that of reciprocal transactions. Here the manifest intent is quite the reverse of the first category. The purpose is specifically to fulfill or terminate a contract or "bargain" with alter. An example of this second type is dēva pūjāva, offering to the gods (deviyās).

To perform this act, an individual -- monk or layman -- pre-sents a tray of food, flowers, and incense to a deviyā and recites hymns and ballads in honor of the spirit. To this extent it is simi-lar to vändīma-pidīma to Buddha. A frequently occurring alterna-tive is for an individual to hire a medium or advocate -- a kapurāla or "priest" -- to present the offerings and perform the recitations for him.

The manifest intent is the direct opposite of the purpose of performing nonreciprocal prestations; here the purpose is always to influence the recipient on one's own behalf or to repay him for something he did in the past. Pūjāva is offered to the deviyā in return for his assistance and protection, for a specific and concrete reciprocity. The·purpose is not purification of mental defilements, as in nonreciprocal prestations, so much as it is purification from external defilements -- pollution (kili) caused by goblin attack, sickness, vengeance of an enemy. Broadly speaking therefore, we may characterize a reciprocal prestation by saying its purpose is self-protection (āraksāva) rather than self-perfection (satpuruṣa). It is a propitiatory (hence "magic") rite because the official intent is to enlist reciprocity. It is a "give and take" relationship (ganu-denu kirīma) between man and spirit: ego and alter barter for goods and services. If the deviyā renders a service then man gives him a pujāvā as "payment" (usually at the next annual festival held at the spirit's temple). No service, no payment. Nonreciprocal rites, in contrast, are meritorious because the intent is to improve one's own self. This distinction between nonreciprocal (expressive) and reciprocal (instrumental) is similar to Firth's division between sacramental and nonsacramental rites (1963: 223-24).

Dēva pūjāva is one of several reciprocal transactional units, all of which can be graded, as it was suggested earlier (see also Ames 1964a: 33-35), according to levels of purity (see Table 2). The less the purity of the offerings, the lower the status of the spirit who receives them, and the more harmful he may be. But more of this later. Reciprocal prestations to spirits do not serve to create moral bonds between individuals in the way Buddhist pres-tations do. No merit-making is involved. In contrast to Buddhist prestations, however, those involving spirits frequently involve as well ritual specialists (priests, magicians) who act as mediators between the "patient" (āturayā) and the spirit. This is a therapeu-tic relation rather than a moral one (Ames 1964b).

Table 2. Reciprocal (Instrumental) Transactional Units

1. Pure offerings (pūjāvas) are given to deviyās. Pūjāva includes flowers, incense, fruit, vegetables, cereals, but never meat (see note) or oily foods.

2. Pure and polluted offerings (baliya or balibili) are given to planetary deities (graha deviyās). Bali is similar to pūjāva, i.e. flowers, incense, and foods, but it also includes fried foods, oil cakes, and meat or bili (a living "sacrifice" usually in the form of a cockbird, although it may also mean human sacri-fice).

3. Polluted offerings (dola) are given to goblins (yakās). Dola is composed almost entirely of pol-luting objects -- roasted and fried meats, opium, arrack, toddy, ganja, cigarettes, animal and human bones, and a live cockbird (bili).

Note: There is one exception to the rule that a pure offering never
         includes meat. Kataragama Deviyā took as mistress a
         princess, Valli Ammā, of a tribe of hunters, the Veddahs.
         To commemorate this union, priests at Kataragama Deviyā's
         jungle shrine (in Kataragama town) present venison to him
         as part of the daily offering. Venison is said to be the food
         of the hunting tribe from which the god's mistress came.

     To summarize briefly, there is one main category of nonre-
ciprocal prestations, as illustrated by giving homage to Buddha
(vändīma-pidīma) or alms-giving (dan-dīma). This is giving with
the intent of earning merit; it is therefore a meritorious, Buddhist,
or "sacred" kind of transaction. On the other hand, we have two
main categories of reciprocal prestations: pūjāva to gods and dola
to goblins. (Balibili to graha deviyās is actually a combination of
these two.) These are prestations intended to propitiate or influence alter (the spirit), to make or fulfill a specific bargain. They
are therefore propitiatory, magical, or "profane" kinds of transactions. Here I call all these transactions "religious" -- whether
Buddhist or magical -- for the sake of convenience (Ames 1964a).

     For the individual, the function of nonreciprocal prestations
is to earn merit; for society, their function is integrative -- they
bind people together into one community concerned with moral or
sacred things. For the individual, the function of reciprocal prestations is manipulative -- to augment his personal fortunes, to remove misfortune (external pollution), or to win vengeance (sorcery). It is a therapeutic function in the broadest sense, for the
concern is with gratification and deprivation on the personality
level. For society, the function of reciprocal prestations is po-
tentially disruptive: insofar as spirit propitiation is successful it
leads to inequalities, or, via sorcery, to hostilities.

     There are secular transactions that roughly correspond to
this structuring of religious acts. In a restricted sense one is a
mirror image of the other. One informant phrased the corres-
pondence this way. Buddhist giving (dan dīma) is like presenting
"gifts" (täggas) to kinsmen and friends, i.e. to one's "equals."
Pūjāva to deviyās is like paying a "bribe" (allasa) to someone who
is superior -- a landlord, headman, government official -- in
order to enlist his assistance or protection, to ward off his displeasure. Dola to yakās is like paying a "fine" (dadaya) or tip
(santōsaya) to an inferior person (see Table 3).

Table 3. Secular Transactional Units

+ Bribes (allasa) to superiors (landlords, etc.)

± Gifts (täggas) to equals (kinsmen, etc.)

- Fines (dadaya) or tips (santōsaya) to inferiors
  (beggars, etc.)

Täggas are given "out of love" and not as part of an explicit
bargain. The official purpose is to create unity or good will
(sambanda kama) between the actors. A characteristic of friendship is that the partners do not publicly express concern over the
value or frequency of gifts exchanged. As we say about our Christ-
mas giving (even if we do not believe it), it is not the value but the
spirit that "counts." Täggas are exchanged between those, usually
kinsmen, who wish to maintain friendly, and more or less equal,
relations or between individuals who want to institute such a relationship. Dislike for a kinsman may be signified by ceasing to exchange gifts with him. Whenever visiting a friend one brings a
small gift (podi tägga) as an expression of cordiality; probably the
friend will return the visit during the same "social season." A
subtle form of reciprocity occurs, obviously. But that is not the
point. The emphasis in gift giving is always placed on the manifest
intention, which is to create good will by presenting something that
does not explicitly demand reciprocity. "It came from the heart,"
as we would say.

The purpose of giving bribes is the reverse of this. When an
individual desires a favor from someone in an advantageous position, a prestation is always sent along with the request or before
it. A bribe is like a visiting card that announces a petitioner.
There is no doubt in the Sinhalese mind that "money talks." It is,
in fact, called the younger brother of the gods (salli deviyangē
malli). Although man gives pūjāvas to deviyās, he has no sambanda
kama with them. Likewise, one does not give a bribe to a government official to foster a friendship. It is merely a part of a contractual agreement, a "give and take" (ganudenu).

A santōsaya (tip, fine) is given to an inferior person to send
him away "happy." When an outcaste beggar comes to the door it
is customary to give him a little something; otherwise he will curse
or shame the householder. One also gives a santōsaya to servants,
to tenants, and to elephants who perform tricks -- in fact, to anyone who is of lower status. It is precisely like the dola offerings
given to yakās so they will stop pestering people.

There are various elaborations or mannerisms associated

with these secular transactions to signify the intent of the prestation. When presenting something to a high status person, one must
use both hands; one hand is sufficient when presenting an object to
an individual of lower status. There are linguistic devices as well.
I recorded seven different colloquial second personal singular pro-
nouns, each carrying a different status connotation. There are five
ways to say "come here" (extremely contemptuously, very contemptuously, contemptuously, impersonally, respectfully), five
ways to say "go away," five ways to say "give me." Similar mannerisms are used in treating with Buddha and the spirits. The
principle is simple. The Sinhalese is an extraordinarily status
conscious individual. He likes to know where he stands, and he
wants to be certain others know it too. He assumes the supernaturals feel no differently.

But this discussion of secular transactions is an aside that
need not detain us. Religious transactions -- using a broad definition of religion to include Buddhism and the spirit cults -- are nonreciprocal ones that are considered meritorious and those reciprocal ones directed to supernatural beings.

By now you can see I am heading toward two basic distinctions
(see Table 4). On the one hand, I distinguished between religion
and society, and that need not concern us anymore. On the other
hand, I was making a distinction between two basic categories within the religious system -- between what anthropologists usually
call religion (Buddhism) and magic (spirit cults) and what I prefer
to call sacred and profane orientations. Both of these distinctions,
which are fundamental to the understanding of religion, were made
on the basis of a structural analysis of ritual transactions.

Table 4. Transactional Units Compared

	Nonreciprocal "gifts"	Reciprocal "bribes" and "fines"
Religious	dan dīma etc.	pūjāva balibili dola
Secular	tāgga	allasa dadaya

I will illustrate here some of the implications of the second
distinction with the help of yet another diagram (see Table 5). Just

by running your eyes down each of the two columns you will see
how practically everything that is important about Sinhalese religion can be included under one or the other of these two basic categories of nonreciprocal and reciprocal transactions. This is because, in my view, rituals are social devices that mediate between
ideologies, collectivities, and personal religious experiences: they
are the carriers of symbols and the media of collective action. If
you classify rituals, you have classified the elements of a religion.
The psychological dimension was not included in this table, although
it could have been. Under the nonreciprocal category we have the
experiences of "insight" or "gnosis" (pañña) and "spiritual joy"
(prītiya); under the other category we find references to the "pleasures of the five senses" (pas kam säpa). The two kinds of psychological experience are as opposed to one another as all the
other elements in the two lists.

You will notice we are here dealing with the basic opposition
in Sinhalese religion that is so much talked about; it is referred to
in Robert Knox's famous dictum that the Sinhalese have "Budu for
the soul and the gods for this world." To a certain extent it is the
relation between sacred and profane or church and magic in the
Durkheimian sense of those terms. It is also this opposition that
Leach and Yalman have emphasized, although they do not phrase
it the way I do. But the fact that everyone, including the Sinhalese,
stresses this dichotomy in their religion seems to me to be coinci-
dent with Durkheim's contention that "in all history of human
thought there exists no other example of two categories of things
so profoundly differentiated or so radically opposed to one another"
as the contrast between sacred and profane (1915: 38). In Sinhalese it is lokottara saranagänima, versus laukika saranagänima,
i.e. "taking refuge in the supramundane" (Buddhism) as opposed
to "taking refuge in the worldly" (magical-animism).

Table 5. Sinhalese Religious Categories

Ideology	Non-R Category	R Category
	Sacred (lokottara)	Profane (laukika)
	Salvation (nirvānaya)	Consolation (sänasilla)
	Self-purification (satpuruṣa) of mental defilements (kleśa)	Self-protection (āraksāva) from external defilements (kili)
	Merit-demerit (pina-pava)	Amoral actions

Table 5. (Continued)

Ideology (Continued)	Law of volitional action (karmaya) Rebirth (sañsāraya)	Science of spirits (bhuta vidyāva)
Ritual	Nonreciprocal or merit-making transactions (pinkama)	Reciprocal or magic transactions
	Unit acts:	Unit acts:
	- homage to Buddha (vändima-pidīma)	- offering to god (dēva pūjāva)
	- alms-giving (dan dīma)	- " to planetary deities (balibili)
	- etc.	- etc.
	Ritual sequences:	Ritual sequences:
	- vihāra pūjāva	- dēvāla pūjāva
	- other pinkama	- etc.
Organization	Moral community or "Buddhist church" (Buddhaśāsanaya) (moral relationship)	Magician and clientele (therapeutic relationship)

Note: The English words are only approximate translations or
glosses for the Sinhalese terms, most of which have been
given more elaborate treatment elsewhere (Ames 1964a).

III

This is not the whole story about Sinhalese religion. So far
I have been talking about distinctions, separate categories, oppositions; now I want to show how aspects of these different categories
and oppositions are combined to form patterns or sequences of
ritual action. What I have done up to now is isolate the various
basic structural units and ideas in Sinhalese religious life. We
find among other things certain oppositions. The next step is to
show how the structural units are combined in ongoing ritual sequences; here we see that in actual practice those oppositions are
resolved. The formula to remember is that structural units are

frequently fused, but never confused, with one another. This fusion is not ad hoc or accidental but one that reflects a very important functional interdependence. I will now describe several concrete examples of this fusion, show how there is a definite order
to the combination of unit acts, then argue that the Sinhalese pantheon (i. e. myths about spirits) also reflects this ordered arrangement.

The first example is usually called vihāra pūjāva or Buddha
pūjāva. It is centered at a Buddhist temple (vihāraya) and the
emphasis is on nonreciprocal prestation, although prestations of
the other type are also included. Vihāra pūjāva is performed every
night at the Buddhist temple, but on those nights marking the four
quarters of the moon a specially elaborate ceremony is held. It is
this latter ceremony that I wish to consider.

It begins in the morning with an alms-giving (dan dīma);
members of a household take a specially prepared meal or dan to
the monks in the temple. The next important event occurs the
same evening, about 8:30 or 9 p.m. when people of the village
gather at the temple. They first pay homage (vändīma-pidīma) to
the Buddha and his symbols (bōdhi tree, dāgoba, and the monks)
by offering flowers, incense, and honorific recitations. This may
take half an hour or more. Next both the laity and the monks offer
merit (pin dīma) to all beings. In addition they make a special
offering of merit, and perhaps also food (dēva pūjāva), to the two
deviyās, Vishnu and Kataragama, whose shrines are included within the vihāraya compound. They ask these spirits to bestow worldly blessings upon them. Finally the head monk delivers a sermon
(bana kiyavanavā) to the laity. Then everyone returns home and
the monks retire to their quarters. If it is an especially important
vihāra pūjāva commemorating some significant event, a second
alms-giving may be given the following day. But we need not
bother about that.

The basic unit acts that make up this ritual sequence (see
Table 6) are as follows: dan dīma, vändīma-pidīma, dēva pūjā
kirīma, and bana kīma (see 6a). The first three and last ones are
nonreciprocal transactions; the fourth act (dēva pūjā) is a reciprocal one, for it is an attempt to propitiate the spirits.

Table 6. Ritual Sequences

Transactional units	Ritual sequences
a. dan dīma	"vihāra pūjāva"
vändīma-pidīma	(dd + v-p + pd + dp + bk)
pin dīma	(Buddhist temple offering)
dēva pūjāva	
bana kīma	
b. Buddha vandanā	"dēvāla pūjāva"
dēva pūjāva	(Bv + dp)
	(deity offering)
c. Buddha vandanā	"graha sāntiya"
dēva pūjāva	(Bv + dp + bb + d)
balibili	(planetary deity offering)
dola	
d. Buddha vandanā	"yakuma"
dēva pūjāva	(Bv + dp + d)
dola	(goblin offering)

The next three examples (6b, c, and d) concern ritual sequences in which reciprocal transactions receive the primary emphasis and where spirits rather than the Buddha are the primary
foci. I call these "magical-animistic" because the intent is to propitiate spirits; Sinhalese class these acts as part of bhuta vidyāva,
the "science of spirits." It is necessary to give three examples
because reciprocal rituals are various and elaborate, whereas nonreciprocal rituals tend to be simple and uniform. The three examples refer to ceremonies usually called dēvala pūjāva, graha
sāntiya, and yakuma (or yakunnatanavā); each is primarily concerned with a different kind of spirit, the deviyā, graha-deviyā,
and yakā respectively.

Dēvāla pūjāvas are performed at spirit temples (dēvālayas)
or at spirit shrines attached to Buddhist temples. One makes a

vow (āpaya) to a deviyā that if a request is granted, a special offering (pūjāva) will be given him in return. The vow establishes a
contract with the deity. If the spirit responds by providing assistance, then the supplicant concludes the bargain by presenting the
offering; if the deity does not respond favorably, the supplicant is
not obliged to present any offering. In making the dēvāla pūjāva,
the individual customarily visits a Buddhist shrine first to pay
homage to Buddha (vandanā). With the merit thus earned, and a
tray of flowers and vegetables, he turns his back on Buddha and
goes to the dēvālaya to propitiate the deviyā (see 6b).

Graha sántiya and yakuma are night-long song-and-dance
festivals (nrta-gīta) in which balibili and dola are given to the
graha deviyās and yakās respectively. These tend to be the most
elaborate of all Sinhalese ceremonies. This, incidentally, illus-
trates a general (but not universal) structural principle of Sinhalese religion: the less pure the offering, the lower in status is the
spirit, the more malevolent he is, the more elaborate is the rite
to propitiate him, the more intricate and detailed are the techniques
demanded of the ritual specialist, the less this specialist is paid,
and the lower is his status in society. Flowers to the Buddha is
the purest of offerings; it is also the simplest to perform and requires no specialist intermediaries. The purpose of Buddha pūjāva
is to quiet the senses rather than to arouse them with ceremonial
fanfare; the offering may even be made in the seclusion of one's
home. Dola to yakās is one of the impurest offerings. Characteristically, it is performed with great elaboration, and highly skilled
dancers and magicians are invariably required. One kapurāla is
sufficient to propitiate all the deviyās; three magicians, two drummers, and several assistants will be used to exorcise one yakā.

In a graha sántiya various planetary deities are invoked on
behalf of a patient (āturayā) who is undergoing an inauspicious
astrological period. The procedure is to pay homage first to the
Buddha, next to the deviyās, then to the graha deviyās, and finally
to yakā assistants of the graha deviyās (see 6c).

A comparable procedure is followed in a yakuma, which is
an exorcist rite. Each of the major yakās is propitiated along
with his assistant yakās. Preceding every invocation, homage is
paid to the Buddha; during every invocation the deviyās are called
upon to help control the yakās (see 6d). This may be illustrated
by citing several stanzas taken from an invocation to the Blood
Goblin (Riri Yakā):

1. We pay homage to the Buddha, dhamma, and
   sangha. We take refuge in the Triple Gem.

2. After paying respects to the Triple Gem, we

now recite the history of Riri Yakā.

5. You came to Ceylon and when you saw God
Saman you paid homage to him.

7. According to the permission (varan) you received
from Saman, O Killer Goblin (Maru Yakā), you
can cause sickness to mankind until you receive
offerings.

After more hocus-pocus, Riri Yakā is eventually told that by
the orders of Buddha (Budu anin) and the power of the gods
(deviyangē balē) he must accept the dola and remove his curse
from the patient. He has no alternative but to oblige; he is bound
by a contract. If he did not obey he would accumulate even more
bad karmaya (it is a grievous sin to disobey the Buddha's orders)
and suffer the wrath of the gods.

In these three types of rituals (dēva pūjāva, graha šāntiya,
and yakuma) it is not necessary to make a material offering to
Buddha; but invariably homage is first paid to him in one symbolic
form or another. Most mantras or magical spells are begun with
"Ōm, namō!" ("Om, glory to Buddha!"). In a village fertility rite
(gam maduva) that I witnessed, the priest (kapurāla) began the
evening ceremonies by administering the three refuges (tun saranā)
and the five precepts (pan sīl) to the crowd. Only then did he proceed to invoke the gods.

In these three types of rituals we found the same sequence of
transactions as in the vihāra pūjāva. First the Buddha is venerated,
next the higher spirits, finally the lesser spirits. Even in a yakuma, where five or so major yakās must be propitiated, this sequence is repeated for each yakā: the Buddha is honored, flowers
are presented to the deviyās, then the yakā, reminded of his subordination to the laws of the Buddha and the power of the deviyās,
is told to pick up his offerings and leave the patient.

IV

The final part of my argument concerns the pantheon, or beliefs about the spirit world. Just as the society -- at least in
theory -- is organized in a hierarchy of ranked castes and differential privileges, so also the religious system is based on a hierarchy of privilege and status. It is therefore not surprising that
the Sinhalese pantheon should reflect this ordered arrangement or
hierarchy of ritual transactions outlined in the preceding sections.

As homage to the Buddha precedes all rituals, so the Buddha is believed to be the head of the Sinhalese pantheon. He is called the dēvātidēva ("god above the gods") or dēvadēvayā ("god of gods"). Prestations to Buddha are always of the purest kind -- special flowers, "soft" foods (bhojanama). The Buddha is the most virtuous and compassionate of beings. [5]

Dēva pūjāva is the next purest kind of offering and is the transaction that normally follows Buddha vandanā or is at least considered second in importance. Correspondingly, deviyās are second in the pantheon. They are benevolent spirits. The next transaction is pure-impure balibili; the next "status group" of spirits in the pantheon hierarchy is the class graha deviyā, recipient of balibili. Graha deviyās are benevolent and malevolent. Dola is the most impure offering to be made. The recipients -- the yakās -- stand at the bottom of the pantheon. They are wholly malevolent.

The principle here is that a spirit is what he is because of the prestation he receives. It is the ritual transaction that determines his status in the pantheon; it is the transaction that creates the image of the spirit in people's minds; it is through analysis of transactions that we may discover these spirit beliefs.

Most spirits are fixed in status, but some are not. The spirit Hūniyama, for example, when he is given dola during a yakuma, is referred to as a yakā. On other occasions and in different types of ritual he is given a pūjāva and consequently referred to as Hūniyam Dēvatā. (These are terms of reference not terms of address. Even when he is referred to as a yakā he may be called a dēvatā as a form of flattery. He is called massinā (cross-cousin, brother-in-law) for a similar reason. It is not only in kinship that one finds a distinction between terms of reference and address.)

So far in my pantheon I have listed four classes of spirits or supernaturals: Buddha, deviyās, graha deviyās, and yakās. They are distinguished from each other according to the different types of ritual prestations people give them. There are three further types of spirit I have not yet mentioned: Bōdhisatvayōs, dēvatās, and prētayās. Bōdhisatvayōs, or bōsats (future Buddhas), are thought to be higher deviyās. Dēvatās (like Hūniyama) are godlings or spirits interstitial between deviyās and yakās. Prētayās (ghosts) are at the very bottom of the pantheon. (It may be easier to keep these terms straight by referring to the right-hand column of Table 7.)

When Sinhalese wish to exalt a deviyā they call him a bōsat and may give him an extra pure offering to demonstrate their in-

44 AMES

tention. One god, Nāta Deviyā, has been so exalted in this fashion; he is said to be such a good Buddhist (the next Buddha, in fact) that he is seldom propitiated at all. Prestations to Nāta tend to be of a nonreciprocal character. It is argued that he is too busy meditating to respond to ritual propitiations. One informant explained that there is no sense in trying to propitiate Goddess Pattini either. She is anxious to earn merit and be reborn as a man, so she spends all her time listening to the sermons of Nāta. She has no time to respond to ritual petitions and no interest in worldly events.[6]

Table 7. The Sinhalese Pantheon

Sacred | Profane

I   vändīma-pidīma   =   Buddha

II   dēva pūjāva (+)   =   bōsats   (future Buddhas)

III   dēva pūjāva   =   deviyās (deities)

IV & V   balibili (or pūjā and dola) =   graha deviyās   dēvatās (godlings)

VI   dola   =   yakās (goblins)

VII   dola (-)   =   prētayās (ghosts)

II, III } Benevolent vegetarian deities

IV, V } Malevolent - benevolent meat-eating godlings

VI, VII } Malevolent flesh-and-blood-eating goblins and ghosts

Dēvatās refer to an ambiguous category of spirits, similar to the graha deviyās, who are neither all good nor all bad. They tend to be a more useful kind of spirit because they can both help you and wreak vengeance on your enemies. Deviyās can only do good; yakās can only do bad. This ambiguous status of the dēvatās is demonstrated in the offering they receive: a prestation that is both less pure than pūjāva and less polluting than dola.

Prētayās (ghosts) are the lowest of the low. They are given the remains of dola offerings that even yakās will not take. Wholly malevolent but incompetent, they are more annoying than danger- ous.

We have oppositions and we have transitions in this pantheon, all illustrated by different kinds, or grades, of transactional units (see Table 7). Deviyās and yakās are opposite to one another, and so are their prestations. Dēvatās, resembling both higher and lower spirits, just as their prestations are composed of pure and impure materials, represent a transition between the two category oppositions. Prētayās and bōsats, who lie at opposite ends of the spirit and transactional hierarchies, link the pantheon to the Bud- dhist world view. Prētayās are precisely what the virtuous Buddha is not: the anti-Buddha of greed, sloth, and ignorance. This is illustrated in their offerings. Dola means greed, craving; prētayās are so foolish they will even accept the droppings of yakās. Pious bōsats, on the other hand, exemplify those who strive to become Buddha-like: serene, passive -- and nonresponsive to reciprocal prestations.

V

Now I will try to summarize my argument. In their studies of Sinhalese religious symbolism, Leach (1962) and Yalman (1962) pointed to certain basic "binary oppositions" -- passivity and activ- ity, asexuality and sexuality, purity and impurity, death and life. Examining a similar body of material from the social structural point of view of ritual transactions, I perceive transitions as well as oppositions. I have suggested that contrasting types of trans- actions are usually fused in an actual ritual sequence: they become complementary rather than opposed -- or, as Dumont would say, "linked and opposed." In certain examples, unit transactions, and the spirit symbols that are reflections of these acts, symbolize an ideological opposition: nonreciprocal and reciprocal, meritorious and magical, sacred and profane. In other cases, transactions act as mediators between ideals. The magical and the meritorious are fused into one logical sequence in which the subordination of one to the other is ritually enacted. In both instances these trans-

actions and symbols reaffirm the basic ideology, either through
opposition (as in Christianity the Devil opposes Christ) or through
transition (as Mariolatry presupposes Christ or the deviyās pre-
suppose the dēvātidēva, the "god above the gods" who is Buddha).

I began by asking a few simple questions: What objects or
goods are transacted? What are the manifest intents or stated purposes of these transactions? This simple beginning has led to a
number of conclusions about Sinhalese religion:

1. The internal structure or division of labor within Sinhalese religion was briefly described, e.g. the distinction between
nonreciprocal (expressive) and reciprocal (instrumental) transactions, or meritorious versus magical patterns, or religion versus magic, or worship versus therapy.

2. Certain parallels were suggested between secular and religious patterns of interaction: (a) bribes, gifts, fines, and (b)
parallel hierarchies of status and privilege.

3. The existence of parallels between religious transactions
and the order of spirits in the pantheon was also established. The
hierarchy of spirits reflects the hierarchy of offerings, which in
turn is parallel to the hierarchy of castes.

4. Something not previously discussed is the relevance of
the method presented in this paper for the study of other religious
systems. I would say this much:

(a) If there are different spirits, they will be treated
differently; the patterns of interaction between man and
spirits will therefore indicate the structure of the pantheon.
This paper presents a methodological approach that focuses
on concrete interactions as a way to discover symbolic
fantasies.

(b) Differences between categories of spirits will be
more apparent and more elaborate in those societies where
the differences between people are more apparent and more
elaborate, e.g. in the caste-stratified societies of India
(Harper 1959; Singh 1961) and Ceylon, or in traditional,
feudal-like Roman Catholic societies.

5. Finally, reference was made to a certain number of
spirits in the Sinhalese pantheon. Leach in his paper on religious
syncretism in Ceylon deals with two main classes of spirits -- high
gods and intermediating gods -- whom he calls devas and dēvatās.
He shows how these two classes represent a fundamental opposition

in Sinhalese symbolism. Yalman talks about three levels of spirits
-- Buddha, deviyās, and the graha deviyās, with the deviyā category subdividing into deviyās and yakās. In my pantheon I find
seven different kinds of spirits! All three of us are talking about
the same pantheon but we each see something different. Leach
finds a dual opposition; Yalman finds a trinity of oppositions; I find
transitions as well as oppositions.

You may draw your own conclusions. There is one that im-
presses me. Anthropologists are always talking about how religious beliefs reflect patterns of kinship structure. In Ceylon, on
the other hand, we have a case where religious beliefs are beginning to reflect the methodological hocus-pocus of anthropologists!

NOTES

1. This paper is based on research carried out in Ceylon during
   1959 and 1960, sponsored by a fellowship from the Social
   Science Research Council. It was written in 1962 while I was
   a fellow on the Committees for the Comparative Study of New
   Nations and for Southern Asian Studies, University of Chicago.
   I am also gratefully indebted to a number of people, both in
   North America and Ceylon, for their helpful comments on the
   various versions of the paper.

2. Sinhalese, rather than Pali or Sanskrit, terms are used
   throughout this essay. Spelling is according to de Zoysa
   (1948-49) and transcription into English approximately according to Geiger (1938). Words are pluralized with the English "s. "

3. The terms reciprocal and nonreciprocal are likely to mislead
   the reader unless he pays close attention to the narrow defini-
   tions I give them. My usage is similar to Schneider's (1962:
   23) distinction between "a stipulated kind of reciprocity" and
   its opposite. Alternate and equally useful terms would be
   Parsons' (1951) "instrumental" (reciprocal) and "expressive"
   or "consummatory" (nonreciprocal) type activities.

4. The fact that individuals may not always live up to their ideals
   is another matter that I do not wish to consider in this paper
   -- except to mention that such failures are major sources of
   strain and therefore important foci of change (Ames 1964a).

5. Although the Buddha no longer exists himself, he continues to
   be represented as the supreme, even if absent, lord of the
   pantheon -- somewhat like the absentee lord of the land -- be-

cause his virtue and deeds are remembered. His influence remains even if he does not. Virtue, like sacredness or mana,
carries its own power. Ballads refer to <u>Budu guna</u> and <u>sīla</u>
<u>guna</u>, the energizing power of the Buddha, the power of his
virtue. Guna has fertility implications; it is the same term
used when you want to talk about multiplying one number by
another. Reference is also made to <u>Budu rës</u>, an electrifying
power that emanates from Buddha relics. In addition to the
Buddha's virtue, the power of his teachings (<u>dharma balē</u>) remains to influence the world. Another expression of the Buddha's suzerainty is the belief that during his lifetime he made
a contract (<u>varan</u>) with all spirits, ordering them to obey ritual petitions and to obey those spirits superior to themselves.
To break such a sacred contract would be a sin resulting in
tremendous misfortunes.

6. To avoid misunderstandings the reader is again reminded that
these statements, like all other factual ones in this paper, refer only to my Matara town and nearby village. The status of
Pattini is quite different in other parts of Ceylon, where her
temples abound. In other words, though the principles remain
the same, the names of the spirits concerned vary with each
local tradition -- and sometimes with each informant!

REFERENCES CITED

Ames, Michael M.

    1964a   "Magical-animism and Buddhism: A Structural
                Analysis of the Sinhalese Religious System," <u>Journal</u>
                <u>of Asian Studies</u>, <u>23</u>, 21-52.

    1964b   "Buddha and the Dancing Goblins: A Theory of
                Magic and Religion," <u>American Anthropologist</u>,
                <u>66</u>, 75-82.

Durkheim, Emile

    1915   <u>The Elementary Forms of the Religious Life</u>,
                London, Allen and Unwin.

Firth, R.

    1963   <u>Elements of Social Organization</u>, Boston, Beacon
                Press.

Geiger, W.

1938   A Grammar of the Sinhalese Language, Colombo, Royal Asiatic Society Ceylon Branch.

Harper, Edward B.

1959   "A Hindu Village Pantheon," Southwestern Journal of Anthropology, 15, 227-34.

Leach, Edmund R.

1958   "Magical Hair," Journal of the Royal Anthropological Institute, 88, Part II.

1961   "Lévi-Strauss in the Garden of Eden," Transactions of the N.Y. Academy of Sciences, 23, series II, 386-96.

1962   "Pulleyar and the Lord Buddha: An Aspect of Religious Syncretism in Ceylon," Psychoanalysis and Psychoanalytic Review, 49, 80-102.

Lévi-Stauss, C.

1955   "The Structural Study of Myth," Journal of American Folklore, 78 ("Myth: A Symposium," ed. T.A. Sebeok), 428-44. (Reprinted in Lévi-Strauss, Anthropologie structurale, Paris, 1958).

1958   "Structure et dialectique," Anthropologie structurale, Paris, Plon, pp. 252-66.

Oliver, Douglas

1958   "An Ethnographer's Method for Formulating Descriptions of 'Social Structure'," American Anthropologist, 60, 801-26.

Parsons, Talcott

1951   The Social System, Glencoe, Free Press.

Schneider, David M.

1962   "Double Descent on Yap," Journal of the Polynesian Society, 71, 1-24.

Singh, T.R.

1961   "The Hierarchy of Deities in an Andhra Village," in L.P. Vidyarthi, ed. Aspects of Religion in Indian Society, Meerut, India, Kedar Nath Ram Nath, pp. 166-71.

Yalman, Nur

    1962   "On Some Binary Categories in Sinhalese Religious
              Thought," Transactions of the N.Y. Academy of
              Sciences, 24, series II.

de Zoysa, A.P.

    1948-49   Sinhala sabda kosaya, 2 vols. Colombo, Dharma
              Samaya Yantralaya.

THE PRIEST ROLE IN CENTRAL VILLAGE THAILAND

Jasper Ingersoll

Catholic University of America

The concern of this chapter will be the general features of religious life in Thailand as these emerge from an analysis of the role
of the central figure in that religious life, the Buddhist priest.
Analysis of his role is divided into five parts: his main activities
in the performance of his duties, role relationships with other
priests and with laymen, the principal norms regulating his role,
the basic value concerns of his role, and the sources of his training for his role duties. While by no means comprehensive, an
examination of various aspects of community religious life is necessarily included since the priest role is such a pivotal one in Thai
Buddhist life. Despite the complexities of the priest role and the
limitations of the analytical concepts employed here, I regard the
role concept as a useful unit around which to organize the welter
of social and cultural behavior before us in terms that make for
significant comparisons with the other Buddhist societies discussed
in this volume.

Most of my observations for this analysis are drawn from
fifteen months' residence with my family during 1959 and 1960 in
the village of Sagatiam, ten miles west of the provincial capital of
Nakhonpathom and about fifty miles west of Bangkok. The headpriest of the village temple urged me to have our house built on
one corner of the temple compound -- a choice I never regretted
for the ready access the site gave us to temple and village activities. The temple and the government school in the temple compound serve a single settled area of about 1, 800 people in nine administrative hamlets, each with its own headman.

Several observers of village Buddhism have pointed out the
elaborate richness of the religious fabric: the diverse threads of
the Buddhist and Brahmanic traditions interwoven with the indigenous tradition of worship of spirits and a host of supernatural objects, the whole presenting a complex array of religious, magical,
and divinatory emphases. In such a rich social-cultural fabric,
we naturally find a large inventory of religious roles.

The most important religious figure in Thai society is the
Buddhist priest (phra), whose social status has the most highly
elaborated and formalized role expectations in Thai culture. Although this analysis will deal mainly with the priest's role activities and role relationships with the laity, we must also take note
of other religious specialists. Several types of healing and divination have religious associations and specialists in one or another

of these healing or divining activities occupy definite statuses with
distinct role expectations. Yet other people similarly engaged do
not have very fully patterned positions or expectations. Indeed,
some of these activities scarcely lend themselves to neat role
classification since the actors tend to mix the various types of
healing and divination practices in different combinations. Further
complicating classification is the wide range from those who spend
full time in one or more of these activities to those who serve as
specialists on only a few occasions a year.

In his penetrating study of supernatural objects in Central
Thailand, Textor (1960) has abstracted several human and supernatural roles, as follows. In seeking to gain new benefits, maintain present ones, and avoid punishments from the realm of the
supernatural, an actor may interact with one or more of some 118
supernatural objects. He may also have role relations with a dead
person who is the source of the supernatural object and with a live
person who constitutes a victim over whom ego wishes to gain some
sort of control. When his own occult knowledge and skills are inadequate, ego seeks a religious-magical specialist (called generi-
cally a maw) to intervene in his behalf. The maw is often a priest
or an ex-priest who learned his occult specialty while in the priesthood. Some of these types of maw are discussed below under priest
role behavior.

One main type of occult specialist not particularly associated
with the priesthood who deserves mention here is the medium or
shaman who goes into trance. The death some years ago of the
Sagatiam headpriest's mother removed the last person in the village who could become possessed by spirits. Quite similar to the
natkadaw of Burma, this woman became possessed by a spirit
called Lord of the Place. Several writers describe the same phenomenon for Central and Northern Thailand (Textor 1960; Kaufman
1960; Kingshill 1960). Some villagers now consult several shamans
or mediums outside the village variously called khon klaang (medium), maw khaosong, and khon song mae cao. These people, of both
sexes, become possessed by a "shrine lord" (Textor 1960) usually
of the opposite sex, who speaks through the possessed medium,
giving predictions of the future to clients and sometimes suggesting
cures for predicted illnesses or solutions to predicted difficulties.
The village headpriest consulted in a nearby town a male shaman,
who was possessed by a female shrine lord, for an auspicious day
on which to dedicate the new school. To give me an opportunity,
he said, to meet a shaman the headpriest took me along. When we
arrived the male shaman was already in trance, speaking to a
client in a high, strained voice: that of the female shrine lord by
whom he was possessed. Compared to most of the people who had
come to consult the shaman, the priest seemed so casual and de-

tached from the proceedings that I was surprised to see him finally seat himself across the small table from the shaman and consult the shrine lord about the new secondary school building he was
planning in the Sagatiam temple. His seemingly relaxed smile
faded quickly as the shrine lord informed him, through the shaman,
that trouble lay ahead in the building of the school because one of
the priests was not good. We leaned forward anxiously but did not
learn the identity of the priest in question. After shaking convul-
sively and briefly resting his head on the table, the shaman came
out of trance and spoke to us in his normal masculine voice. He
expressed surprise at seeing the headpriest who had not been there
when he entered trance. The headpriest explained that this Chinese
shaman, a fairly close friend of his, contributes generously to several temples. Although quite outside Buddhist doctrine, shamans
like this man are quite within the experience of Buddhist priests
and laymen, who consult them frequently.

Another type of maw not associated with the Buddhist clergy
is the man who calls the khwan (life-essence or soul) of a client.
The khwan enters the body at birth and leaves the body permanently
at death. Although beneficial to a person, the khwan may depart at
times and wander about. Most villagers have only a vague notion
of the nature of this elusive spiritual essence. A specialist, a maw
khwan, serves to call back the khwan at life-cycle rituals, e. g. at
entry into the priesthood and marriage and in case of serious illness. At such times a person is thought to benefit by the reintegra-
tive experience of having his khwan called back and secured within
his person. Commanding an elaborate chant, a peculiar and rapid
style of delivery, and a rich pageantry of activity, a skillful maw
khwan can achieve a remarkable state of dramatic tension and
climax with his ancient performance.

A final segment of magical activity in which priests do not
play so active a role as lay specialists is that pertaining to the
spirits (phii). Though priests may give ritual treatments to people
diagnosed as suffering from troubles inflicted by a spirit, they do
not normally deal so directly with the spirits as do a few traditional
specialists, notably the spirit doctor (maw phii). A spirit doctor
may induce a spirit to leave the body of a patient by chanting the
efficacious, sacred texts or resort to beating a spirit out, using a
leafy branch dipped in holy water (nammon). He also makes a medicine of oil (namman) and herbs which he sacralizes for greater potency against spirit-caused diseases. One or two local villagers
had reputations for curing spirit disorders and for tying the offending ghosts securely in trees to preclude their causing further harm.
Though technically free of any concern for the spirits, members of
the Buddhist Sangha rarely speak out against the local notions about
ghosts. Having grown up in the village milieu, many priests and

novices are quite fearful of ghosts, especially at night, though the
Sagatiam headpriest and his assistant expressed or displayed very
little such fear.

All of these types of magical specialist in village Thailand --
the shaman, the khwan specialist, the spirit doctor -- are credited
by the villagers with special knowledge and power to cure, but the
villagers judge the extent of this special power by the apparent
amount of success each practitioner has in dealing with his patients'
ailments. A traditional practitioner who has been engaged for
some sort of service is usually treated with ritual respect and deference.

Let us turn now to the role of the Buddhist priest in Central
Thai village life, after a preliminary glance at the temple population and the two major sects in Thailand. The 1,8000 people of
Sagatiam support a large clergy, though the number of people inhabiting the temple fluctuates considerably during the year. During
the Buddhist monsoon holy season (Phansaa), roughly from July
until October, the temple in Sagatiam may have twenty or more
ordained priests following the full discipline of the order and under
the authority of the headpriest and his deputy, but the number of
priests may drop as low as five during the winter and hot seasons.
The number of novices varies from about fifteen to as few as five,
the largest number not necessarily coinciding with Phansaa. As
many as forty temple boys may be helping the priests and novices
during Phansaa, some going home at night to sleep, but about twenty
is typical later in the year. I have seen many rural temples with
roughly the same population as the Sagatiam temple. In Northern
Thailand, as in Burma, the proportion of priests and novices is
reversed, with novices far outnumbering priests.

For the past century the Buddhist Sangha in Thailand has been
divided in two sects. From a series of reforms and purifications
of practice instituted by King Mongkut in the 1830s while he was
still in the priesthood, a reformed sect gradually emerged (Dhaninivat 1960: 32-39). The traditional order, known as Mahaanigaai,
is much larger than the reformed group, the Tamayud, which
places a stricter interpretation on the doctrine. Beliefs and practices are broadly the same in the two sects, but the actual role
activities and relationships of the Tamayud priests are different in
particulars from the Mahaanigaai priests because of the more strin-
gent Tamayud conformity to doctrinal role norms. These role differences seem important to some of the senior Tamayud priests
but not to Mahaanigaai priests, or to laymen whichever their sect.
The village temple in Sagatiam belongs to this smaller Tamayud
sect.

The villager regards the life of the priest as the highest possible human response to the teachings of the Lord Buddha about the
meaning of life and suffering and the achievement of happiness.
The priest role idealizes both the diligent pursuit of virtue by the
priest through monastic asceticism and the beneficent provision of
pastoral services for the laity through the virtue acquired by the
members of the priesthood. The role of the Buddhist Sangha thus
has a dual orientation: monastic and parish. Only a very few men
wearing the yellow robe in Thailand are forest or mountain re-
cluses. As the great majority of the members of the order in Thailand live in temples located within settled rural or urban areas,
the priest exists in close proximity to the strivings of the secular
world, if at the same time somewhat withdrawn, and his role performance reveals his constant dual orientation to monklike purification of self and to priestlike services for the spiritual welfare of
laymen.

A further complexity in the priest role is that it comprises
men with vastly different depths of experience in the role and of
commitment. The senior leaders of the Sangha, who spend their
entire lives in the order, have developed a role of great cultural
complexity. But the great bulk of the actors in the priest role at
any given time are young farmers and workers in their twenties,
who have almost no grasp of this rich cultural tradition and who
will probably spend only a few months in the order. Most priests
enter for the three-month monsoon holy season (Phansaa), leaving
a few weeks or months afterward. The same priest role includes
Everyman, in a sense, and also a venerated elite. This extreme
variety of commitment and experience in the priest role clearly
has its embarrassing hazards for role analysis. The headpriest
of the Sagatiam temple, in his mid-forties, has been a priest for
over twenty years; his assistant, in his early thirties, has been a
priest for over twelve years. Both men are quite free to leave the
order at any time, and both are quite unlikely to do so. The other
priests -- some in the order only a few weeks but several up to
four years -- are much more likely to decide to return to secular
life sooner or later, having acquired a highly valued moral and
spiritual training and an enhanced status.

We will now turn to the five aspects of the priest role: behavior, relationships, norms, values, and learning.

Role Behavior

Most of the organized activities in the daily lives of the
priests and novices express their monastic role orientation. Arising between 5 and 6 a.m., they have an hour or less for studying
lessons, practicing a chant not yet learned, or for sweeping up

the temple compound. Between 6 and 6:30 the priests and novices
go through the village to collect rice from the villagers who are
waiting to make merit by placing a large spoon or two of rice in
the bowl of each priest and novice.

Immediately upon their return, the priests and novices eat
breakfast served by the temple boys, who eat later. Shortly after
breakfast, the headpriest leads the priests and novices to the sanctuary (bood) for the morning chanting (thamwadchao) of several
Pali chants which review the purposes and methods of the priesthood. First comes acknowledgment of their obeisance to the Buddha, his doctrine, and his Sangha (Phraphud, Phratham, Phrasong).
This is followed by a reaffirmation of the importance of doing good
and avoiding evil before death, as all of us must die. Then several
aspects of the priest's duties are reviewed: a priest's robes are
for covering, not beauty (though countless Western photographers
disagree); a priest should eat a suitable amount of food, according
to what is given; he should use medicine only as really needed; and
he should be satisfied with his living quarters wherever he may be
assigned. After the morning chanting the headpriest, especially
during Phansaa, may read passages of the priests' discipline
(Winai) from the Tripitaka. Adherence to this daily routine is
more rigorous during Phansaa than at other times of the year. The
morning chanting, for example, is supposedly an everyday re-
quirement, but "we are apt to forget," as the assistant headpriest
disarmingly expressed it, in the press of other things to do around
the temple and in the village.

The rest of the morning and the midafternoon are devoted to
study in the temple ecclesiastical school (rong rian nagtham). New
priests and novices entering the temple at the beginning of Phansaa
study the discipline of the order and some of the doctrine in addition to memorizing the Pali chants. The headpriest supervises
this instruction but leaves the greater part of daily teaching to his
assistant headpriest. Both of these men passed the first three
grades of elementary ecclesiastical study but did not continue with
the next seven grades of advanced study of the doctrine and of the
Pali language. Young men entering the temple for a single Phansaa
season study in the lowest grade of elementary studies, but many
leave the order before the examination in December or January.
Those who do remain do not engage in organized study again until
the next July, instead spending the mornings and afternoons during
the first six months of the year in a variety of small tasks, e.g.
laundering and dyeing their robes, cleaning up the buildings and
grounds of the temple, and continuing to memorize the chants.
There are also frequent trips to other temples, especially the provincial head temple in the town of Nakhonpathom. Men entering
the order late in life may do no more than memorize a few Pali
chants.

About 11:00 a.m. the temple boys and perhaps a few laymen prepare another meal for the priests and novices, who must finish eating by noon and abstain from solid foods until breakfast the next day. The priests often retire for a brief siesta after the noon meal, though the headpriest is likely to have some visitors who have come for various purposes.

Study resumes in midafternoon. In 1960 the assistant head-priest taught twenty-one students in the beginning grade in the morning and five students in the second grade in the afternoon, leaving each grade free to study individually while not in class. The two students studying for the third level worked individually with occasional consultation of the headpriest or the assistant head-priest.

Late afternoon is apt to find some of the priests and novices tending the flower gardens in the temple. As a rule, the temple is the most attractive and best maintained part of any rural village. Using a bamboo tube with a cloth to strain out and avoid killing any living creatures, the priests water the flowers and plants each day but, because of their discipline, the priests leave the murderous task of weeding to the novices and laymen. (Just as no priests push the recently donated lawn mower!) It is a time for relaxation. The boisterous school children have ended their lusty-voiced les-sons for the day and departed. The temple is relatively serene. After taking a bath (filtering the water against any small forms of life), priests and novices cluster for friendly chats or leisurely walks around the spacious temple area. The assistant headpriest said that those who are free at this time often discuss their studies in the doctrine and texts, but this is a rather idealized picture of the normally idle conversation.

Before sundown the priests and novices return to the sanc-tuary for the late afternoon chanting (thamwadjen), the procedures and chants of which are much the same as in the morning. Evening is a time for further study or for practicing new chants. A few priests may gather in the assistant headpriest's room to listen to the radio or, since the advent of community development activities in Sagatiam, go to the temple school for a private viewing of the village television set, which villagers watch outside the school two or three times a week! The headpriest often calls a meeting of the priests and novices during Phansaa to talk to them about proper priestly conduct and to check the newcomers' progress in chanting.

With the important exception of the morning gathering of rice, the organized daily behavior of the priests and novices tends to em-phasize the monastic aspect of their role. This emphasis changes markedly as we turn now from daily to weekly patterned behavior.

The Thai Buddhist sabbath (<u>Wan</u> <u>Phra</u>) occurs four times in
a lunar month, viz. on the eighth ana fifteenth days of the waxing
and waning phases of the moon. The morning of the sabbath the
priests remain in the temple as the villagers gather for the weekly
service in the spacious meeting hall (<u>saalaa</u>). When most of the
villagers are assembled, the headpriest leads the priests and novices into the meeting hall where, after kneeling and bowing their
heads to the floor three times in front of the Buddha image, they
seat themselves in a line on the low dais along one side of the meeting hall. A temple leader, a former priest, requests the recitation
of the five vows and the three refuges. One of the priests leads the
congregation in the familiar Pali chants expressing commitment to
the Buddha, his doctrine, and his priesthood and to the renewal of
their efforts to avoid the evils of killing, stealing, lying, enjoying
improper sensuous pleasures, and indulging in intoxicants. As the
people then fill the rice bowls of the clergy, the latter recite a
series of chants (<u>thawaaj</u> <u>pawn</u>) to help make the congregation
better people by giving them knowledge of the Buddha's achievements. None of the village clergy or laity in Sagatiam could translate the words of the Pali chants, but everyone understood the
merit acquired by being present and by sharing merit in this way
with their ancestors and with other people. The priests then recite a final chant invoking a blessing of good fortune (<u>haj</u> <u>pawn</u>) for
the laymen.

At this point the more pious laymen, usually the older people,
withdraw from the large meeting hall to the small sanctuary to receive the eight vows from one of the priests, the additional vows
being to abstain from eating food after noon, enjoying entertainment or bodily adornment, and using any soft or luxurious seat or
bed for the day and night of the sabbath. Seated in a special preaching chair, a priest then reads a sermon from long, slender palm
leaves. The clergy and the laity observing the eight vows must eat
before noon and the rest of the laity may stay to help serve the
priests and chat. Laymen observing the eight vows often remain
in the temple for the day and sleep there overnight.

During the monsoon holy season the priests and people return
in the afternoon to the large meeting hall where the priests again
chant for the people. People from one of the nine hamlets serve
the priests and the congregation with black coffee, at the same
time presenting gifts to each priest and some useful equipment to
the temple. A priest then mounts an ornate pulpit and reads a
second sermon to the people.

The priests thus spend a major part of the sabbath in the
company of the laity, with most of their activities directed toward
the laymen's spiritual benefit. Clearly, their role performance
on the weekly sabbath has a much stronger emphasis on the parish

orientation than does their daily regimen.

The priests have some additional fortnightly and monthly role duties which are purely monastic. On the sabbath of the fifteenth day of each phase of the moon, the priests pair off to confess to each other any violations of the discipline committed in the preceding two weeks. Afterward all the priests retire to the sanctuary where, in the early evening, one capable member of the order (often the assistant headpriest) recites in Pali the 227 <u>Winai</u> rules of priestly conduct while the headpriest, seated to one side, follows the written text to correct the recitation at any point where it is not word-perfect. Each month on the day before the full-moon sabbath, the priests shave their heads and eyebrows to reinforce their disciplined effort to reduce their attachment to personal vanity and even to personal identity.

Several special days in the Buddhist calendar involve special patterns of activity for the members of the clergy. Two particularly demanding holidays are Maaka Buuchaa on the full-moon sabbath of the second lunar month (February), celebrating the miraculous meeting of Buddha with 1,250 of his followers, and Wisaak Buuchaa on the full-moon sabbath of the sixth lunar month (May), celebrating the birth, enlightenment, and death of the Buddha. The priests lead laymen bearing candles, incense sticks, and flowers in a gala procession three times clockwise around the sanctuary. After placing their candles, incense sticks, and flowers along the outside wall, the priests and people enter the sanctuary for a series of chants and sermons which continue until dawn.

Thus far we have seen a pronounced monastic orientation in the daily regimen, as well as in a few fortnightly scheduled activities of the clergy, and a clear parish orientation in most of their activities on the sabbath and on several Buddhist holidays. The priests also perform a number of other services for the laymen, as requested. Of these the most general, frequent, and important is the conduct of home rituals.

In addition to the weekly and seasonal ceremonial cycle, the clergy conducts a great many rituals for families at home. (The ceremonial cycle shows many similarities to that for Burma described below by Manning Nash.) Several life-cycle events -- such as weddings, housewarmings, ordinations, cremations, and merit-making for kinsmen recently dead -- involve ritual participation by the priests. From the completion of the rice harvest in February or March until the beginning of the new rice season in late May or June, the priests can expect numerous invitations to private ceremonies. The family observing one of these events invites the headpriest, who selects a group of priests and novices -- usually five or seven but an even number is standard for death ceremonies.

The family offers the priests an elaborate breakfast (good form socially and good merit spiritually). The priests perform the ritual by reciting the Pali chants appropriate to the occasion and generally beneficial to the family and participants. The water made holy during the sacred chants also has beneficent qualities for the laity.

Only one family ritual, ordination, entails a monastic as well as a parish role orientation for the priests. In the ritual conducted at home, the priests are essentially blessing the family and its son who is about to enter the Sangha; the following day, assembled with the same family in the sanctuary, the priests are oriented toward their own order and the recruitment of a new member.

In addition to these family and kindred rituals, the priests perform occasional rituals on request for some larger segments of the village community. An ancient custom was revived in 1960 when an elderly lady who had led the digging of a new well asked the priests to chant at a merit-making ceremony to inaugurate the well. Villagers from the fairly large area the well was to serve attended this ceremony, which no longer retained what some villagers recalled of the earlier animistic associations.

Two other syncretic rituals for the village community both concern fertility and rainfall. The animistic rite of supplicating the spirits by offering them food along with small clay figures of the people and draft animals in one's family (song krabaan) is now coupled with a communal merit-making ritual (thambun klaang baan) in which the priests come to a central location in each neighborhood in the village and recite chants blessing the merit-makers. Some villagers thought that this merit-making ceremony was also a supplication for rain, a suggestion of a transfer of propitiatory associations from the old magical rite of song krabaan to the moral associations of this Buddhist merit-making rite.

The third syncretic rite was the chanting by the priests out in the fields in the dry season to call down rain for the village, as the Buddha is said to have done. Their appeal was directed to Phra Phirun, the deity associated with rainfall. While the priests were chanting in the parched fields, some of the villagers were enacting the magical rite of placing two little clay figures in a posture of sexual intercourse. Heaven (male) is asked to drop its rain (semen) and fertilize earth (female). All three of these rituals -- the only ones I found which the priests perform outside the temple for a neighborhood or for the village as a whole -- are syncretically associated with animistic rituals. I am struck by the apparent connection between communal and animistic rites but have no explanation at present.

All these activities -- monastic or parish, strictly Buddhist
or syncretic -- are part of the role behavior common to all the
priests in the temple. The priesthood and the laity expect every
priest to participate in these activities and the novices take part in
most of them. But the role of the priest with some years of experience includes additional activities and skills which laymen -- rural
and urban -- consider to be of vital importance though representing
a compromise between what laymen value or desire from the priesthood and what an individual priest chooses to add to his role performance. These additional role activities concern healing and
counseling lay clients and exerting community leadership.

A priest with the inclination to become skilled in the occult
arts of healing must attach himself to a healer-priest who will gradually instruct him. The cultural inventory of illnesses and treatments in the realm of magical healing (sajjsaad) is staggering.
This tradition of magical healing does not depend entirely on the
priesthood for its transmission but most of the healers I have met
practiced healing as a priest and learned the art while in the temple.

The reformed Tamayud sect is less sympathetic than the
majority Mahaanigaai sect to magical healing among the priests.
While this is not uniformly true of Tamayud temples (cf. Kaufman
1960), none of the priests in Sagatiam has developed many magical
healing skills. Villagers do come to the headpriest for such services as a blessing involving sacred Pali incantations (kaataa) and
holy water or the tying of the white strings around the wrist as a
means of securing the client's khwan-soul. The headpriest can make
helpful suggestions about effective herbs to take for some ailments
but shows no interest in developing a reputation for such diagnoses.

Other priests, however, have acquired extensive reputations
as magical healers. A Bangkok priest who visited a nearby temple
for a week drew clients from many surrounding villages. This
priest relied on a wide variety of healing techniques: Pali incantations (kaataa); pointing at the location of an ailment while staring
at it and thinking intensely of nothing else; spitting holy water three
times at an injured spot and mumbling a kaataa while his mouth was
full; moving his hand along the patient's body toward head or feet
and often tapping the floor near the patient to draw afflicting ghosts
out of the body; rubbing a sacralized oil on ailing parts; giving people medicine to take home and boil while repeating the proper incantation; amulets of different sorts to render one safe from bullets
or knife blades (or to help a merchant promote sales); and love
potions made of sacred materials. This man did not usually release a patient until the patient claimed some relief from his ailment. Villagers expressed a mixture of pious and pragmatic cre-
dence in the priest's apparent success along with some skepticism

of his results. Most agreed that any special supernatural power he
was able to use was partly a function of his devotion to priestly
discipline and that such power would disappear with any improper
conduct.

The role behavior of the Sagatiam headpriest includes a greater emphasis on counseling, in a broad sense, than on healing. On
my frequent visits to the priests' residence hall I normally found
the headpriest talking with someone or with a group of people who
had come for advice. The request might be for an auspicious date
to raise house pillars, to hold a wedding or a housewarming, to
have a son leave the priesthood, to undertake some new task, or to
begin a journey. The headpriest consulted a manual for answers
to their questions but seemed to place rather little confidence in
such information, clearly convinced that more learned priests or
astrologers in town could provide better information of this kind.
Villagers also brought their cares and worries to the headpriest,
but with some restraint: it is not proper to involve a priest directly
in violence or hostile conflict. People frequently talked with the
headpriest about their farming difficulties, for which he had a deep
concern. Many people came just to visit the priest and make a
little merit by paying their respects and having a chat. In this
conversational situation, the headpriest offered a good deal of restrained pastoral counsel -- sage, practical advice given with a
feeling for the Buddha's teaching.

Sometimes this informal counsel fell into the other role activity the headpriest had strongly emphasized, community leadership.
Gradually and quietly the headpriest had become a strong village
leader by expressing genuine concern for the well-being of the villagers, by undertaking energetic improvements in the temple which
were of importance to the village as a whole, and by responding
vigorously to the recent program of community development introduced by government officers. These were largely personal
choices as to style in performing his role. The headpriest's opinion was asked on such questions as the digging of a new canal,
plans for raising more funds for the new school, the next temple
fair, the repair of the gasoline generator supplying electricity to
the temple, the district officer's plan to invite Bangkok officials to
visit the village, and the like.

As he sought to develop the buildings and grounds of the temple, the headpriest assumed leadership of an essentially community enterprise. Built and enlarged by almost everyone in the village, the temple belongs to the whole community as do no other
buildings or institutions. The headpriest had recently presided
over the completion of a modern building for the priests' study but
villagers were using it as a communal hall, a place to gather for
casual chats or for meetings with government officials. The head-

priest also got the temple pond deepened so that the villagers'
supply of water would extend longer into the dry season.

With the coming of government community development activities, the headpriest gradually acquired much greater community
leadership responsibilities. Practically every official who visited
the village went to see the headpriest to explain his program and
hopefully win the priest's endorsement. The priest actively supported many of these programs, often using family ritual gatherings to help promote some new scheme. At one cremation, for
example, after the priests had finished reciting the chants and
while the coffin and the corpse were ablaze, the headpriest gently
began a quiet, earnest conversation with a circle of villagers to
advocate moving ahead with the water improvement program!

One final observation on role performance: I did not have the
general impression of a group of men living with endless time on
their hands. I was more impressed with the continuing pace of
their activities and duties. Frequently priests and novices were
hurrying to finish some job by some certain time. The pace of
activities very much depends on the headpriest, and in Sagatiam
this man, for all his unaggressive demeanor, drove himself and
his fellow priests at a very vigorous pace.

Role Relationships

Living together in the same temple, the priests must relate
to each other constantly, with a high degree of intimacy and con-
straint in their behavior and in accord with an elaborate set of
norms. Although some of their interaction and control of material
goods shows a stress on equality, the principal emphasis in their
relations is hierarchical. In temple affairs and in the discipline
the headpriest has a dominant position over the other priests, especially the young ones. In material matters, too, whereas each
priest and novice must receive the same gift in money or equipment from laymen making merit at a home or temple ritual, the
headpriest necessarily attends more home rituals and therefore
enjoys a greater yearly income from such gifts.

The priests always file in and out of temple and home rituals
and seat themselves for chanting in order of their seniority in the
order. The few men remaining for many years in the priesthood
teach the doctrine in the temple school and receive deference as
respected teachers from the new priests who are their students.
The senior, permanent priests enjoy a very high status in the village that is almost outside the normal dominance hierarchy. But
the young men in the robes for a single monsoon holy season,
though they command ritual deference from the laity, hardly occupy
a prominent status. Only after these young men leave the temple

and return to secular life does their status become established.
(For an elaboration of this point see report on Thailand by Michael
Moerman below.) The hierarchical terms of address and response
between senior and junior priests are fairly similar to the terms
between actors in senior and junior statuses in the society at large.

Very few indications of egalitarian role relations are discernible between priests and novices. The novices study in the
same temple school with the younger priests and learn to recite
the same Pali chants. In fact, novices with a few years' experience in the temple will have acquired far more of the role skills
of the priest than the newly ordained priest. Yet despite their
greater familiarity with the Sangha, the novices are younger than
the priests and are not considered responsible for observing the
detailed norms to which the priests must conform. The priests
treat the novices as younger brothers with less sacred responsibilities. Novices, who may help themselves to food, frequently
help serve meals to the priests, who cannot touch food until it is
ritually offered to them (prakheen). Like the priests, novices eat
only two meals a day, taking their meals at the same time the
priests do whether in the temple or in a home ritual. Aside from
the headpriest, who eats alone, the priests gather in small circles
of about five for meals. The novices do likewise, but not in the
same circle with priests. Priests may eat only with other priests.

The members of the Sangha interact with laymen in a large
number of situations. The layman with whom a priest has the most
constant association is his temple boy, often a younger relative
who acts as a personal assistant to his older relative in the priesthood. Temple boys spend most of their day, aside from attending
school, near the priests' residence. The priests also meet the
laymen who come daily to assist with the preparation and serving
of meals and with other tasks. Regular contact with a larger segment of the village laity arises in morning rounds collecting rice.

The members of the Sangha have weekly and periodic role
encounters with laymen who come to the sabbath rituals at the
temple. During the monsoon holy season (Phansaa) the number of
laymen is considerably greater than during the rest of the year.
Gearing's concept of "structural poses," i.e. changing patterns of
a social structure through time, directs our attention to seasonal
shifts in the locations and nature of priest-lay role relations (Gearing 1958). During the monsoon months, the priests tend to stay in
the temple, and the laymen come in greater numbers to the temple
for large congregational interaction with the priests in sabbath rituals. During the cold and hot seasons, the structure of relations
alters somewhat as the laity comes to the temple in smaller numbers but invites priests to conduct family rituals throughout the

village. During these months the priests also spend more time
away from the temple overnight and therefore encounter laymen
more often in the secular world. This view of the shifting structure of social relations through the year further points up mild
seasonal changes in emphasis on the dual orientations, monastic
and parish, in the priests' role behavior and their role relations
with laymen. Priestly healing and counseling services remain at
relatively more constant levels throughout the year.

There is an observable duality in the characteristic relationship between clergy and laity: an intimate social interaction and
interdependence side by side with a marked cultural distance between priest and layman. This general pattern, which is a function
of the dual monastic and parish orientations of the priest role,
changes only superficially as the situations and types of interaction
between priest and layman shift during the year. The need of
priest and layman for each other's role performance produces a
close and constant role association. The priest depends on the
layman for his food, clothing, and other material needs -- and he
cannot even make use of these things until a layman has ritually
presented them to him (prakheen). The whole monastic life of
purification through abstention depends on continuing material services from laymen. The Buddhist layman may legitimately involve
himself much more than the priest in worldly activities, but he
must then seek, through the priesthood, to improve his spiritual
condition.

Despite their interdependence, the priest and layman live
quite apart in some respects. A priest has no physical contact
and only limited social contact with women. The priest should not
be exposed to secular violence or undue gaiety. During a temple
festival, the headpriest normally conducts the priests and novices
into their monastic dwellings after the chanting and before the laymen's supper and gala entertainment begin. A priest who must go
someplace seeks permission to leave the temple area and normally
goes only in the company of another priest or male layman. When
talking with priests, laymen customarily sit in postures of formal
respect and on a slightly lower level. Laymen walk behind rather
than beside priests and use a special vocabulary of honorific terms
for addressing priests. The language has a set of separate terms
for priests and laity for such things as eating, sleeping, and bathing. More generally, both priests and laymen refer frequently to
"the way of the priest" and "the way of the world" as two distinct
and somewhat mutually isolated realms of existence. Thus, priests
and laymen maintain intimate social role interactions, close social-
cultural role interdependence, and rather distinct and mutually
distant cultural role orientations.

This complex pattern of interdependence and distance between priest and laity offers some perspective on two final aspects of village role relationships: social hierarchy and the economic base of the temple. By withdrawing, in some respects, from the normal ambitions and gratifications of men, the priest eventually acquires a very high social status and great prestige. By abstaining from secular life and thereby gaining in holiness, the priest offers the layman his major opportunity to make merit, i.e. through support of the priest and the temple. The performance of both roles entails generous economic support of the priesthood by the laity.

We have already seen several indications of the high status of the priesthood in central Thai village society, notably the large number of villagers and officials who consult the skilled senior priests for a great variety of reasons, the special terms used in addressing or responding to priests, the special vocabulary to distinguish priest and lay behavior, and the postures of deference laymen assume when walking, sitting, and talking with priests. Depending on how formally a layman defines a situation, he prostrates himself in front of a priest when beginning a conversation and when about to leave. Numerous village studies have reported the high respect in which most villagers hold the priests, especially the headpriest, as gauged by their answers to sociometric questions. Villagers are usually loath to do anything about ineffective or senile headpriests.

The high status of the priest is different from the high status of any layman. Although an active headpriest may exert influence in a great many ways, his high status consists in part of his conformity to role norms that preclude his attainment of status and influence in a secular manner. A priest's status is high in the social hierarchy but somewhat outside it.

A basic aspect of the role of Thai laymen is providing material support for their temple and priests. I shall attempt only a few summary observations.

The contributions are so numerous, so frequent, and so varied in size and content (cash, food, clothing, utensils, or labor) that it is very difficult to determine how much of its income a family may contribute in a year. The morning feeding of rice and curries to the priests; the weekly sabbath and frequent special occasions on which people present food to the priests; the weekly and special donations of money to the temple; contributions of labor to help build a new priests' residence, to deepen the temple pond, or to help prepare and clean up after a large temple fair; small donations to fund-raising for other temples outside the village; money and gifts to priests who have chanted at a family ritual -- all these

expenses and more constitute a substantial outlay for most village
families. But villagers could not remember all of these occasions
or the amounts spent during the course of a year.

The fairly frequent solicitations for money are for a temple,
not for priests. People are often asked to make merit by contributing to some fund for their own or for some other temple, but
they present gifts to priests only after certain rituals or when they
wish to make merit individually.

Despite frequent appeals for funds, the village temple must
depend on wealthy urban Thai and Chinese benefactors. Pictures
of donors on the walls of temple buildings and lists of names on
plaques (ranked by the amount of the gift) are not faces and names
of villagers but of rich urban donors. For the building of the new
priests' school in the temple, the largest donation from a villager
was 100 baht, while one old widow in town contributed 20, 000 baht.
Rather than thinking of exchange rates we may more usefully keep
in mind that an unskilled laborer can earn about 10 baht a day:
roughly the same number of dollars that an unskilled worker in
America might earn in a day. The annual temple budget showed
expenses of about 25, 000 baht, most of which went into building a
new residence hall for the priests. The temple had a total regular
income of about 27, 000 baht, of which 10, 000 was raised for the
new residence hall. The village temple was also fortunate to be
chosen to receive the annual Gatin merit-making contribution collected from the entire province. This Gatin contribution added almost 50, 000 baht to the temple income, and it was put in the temple
bank account toward the building of the new government secondary
school on the temple grounds. This is another instance of the dependence of the temple on sources outside the village for really
substantial donations.

The temple budget did not list the items very precisely.
There was no indication of some sources of income such as the
rent for the rice fields the temple owns or the contributions made
by peddlers for space to sell their wares during temple fairs. My
feeling is that the money is scrupulously handled by the priests and
lay leaders but that the accounting is rather makeshift and vague.

Such gifts and money as the priests receive for their services come entirely from the village people. A group of young
men about to leave the priesthood at the end of their three months
estimated the cash income of the headpriest during the monsoon
holy season to have been about 500 baht, of the regular priests
between 300 and 400 baht, and of the novices about 100 baht. Income from ritual services would be much higher during the hot
season. Permanent priests could probably accumulate several

thousand baht a year, but probably less than the village headpriest in Kaufman's study (1960) who received almost 8,000 baht.

The economic base of the temple and the priesthood, though largely a function of the nature of merit-making for the priest and lay roles, is also a function of the temple as a basic expression of the community itself. By their contribution of labor and funds toward the improvement of their temple, the villagers are not only making merit for themselves but also developing the village institution with which all most fully identify. As a place name, as the location of a series of significant personal and communal experiences, as the embodiment of a tradition of aspirations toward the good life, the temple is the heart of the Thai village community. The temple characteristically has the best buildings and best landscaping of any area in the village. Local village pride has no greater expression than the villagers' achievements in their temple.

Role Norms

Conformity to a very elaborate set of norms and proper procedures is a central attribute of the priest role. To be a priest is to observe the rigors of the discipline of the Sangha. This discipline is stated mainly in the form of proscriptions against unacceptable behavior, the most formalized statement being the 227 Pāti-mokkha rules in the Winai section of the Tripitaka, or Pali Buddhist canon. Violations of rules in various sections are considered as "heavy," "medium," or "light" offenses.

The rules of the first section, against which offenses are considered "heavy" and which call for immediate expulsion from the order, are: having sexual intercourse with any person or animal; taking anything that is not given; killing a person or in any way causing a person's death; deliberately lying or speaking deceitfully.

Offenses against rules of the second section are considered "medium" and bear the punishment of a probationary period of living alone in a hut for as long as the offender was knowingly at fault plus six extra days of penance. These rules include such offenses as deliberate emission of semen, bodily contact or provocative talk with a woman, acting as a go-between for a man and woman, and causing conflict among the priests.

The final sections are "light" offenses which require only that an offender confess them. These sections concern such issues as proper handling of the robes and alms bowl, requesting needed things from the laity, refraining from touching money, and sleeping

and eating in a layman's house. Restrictions exist against digging
in the ground and cutting plants, watching soldiers preparing for
war, killing any sort of animal, and becoming ordained before the
age of twenty. Rules against improper conduct toward other priests,
novices, nuns, laymen, and laywomen appear with a great variety
of particular emphases throughout these final sections.

The Pātimokkha constitutes an extraordinarily comprehensive inventory of official norms for the priest and has both provided
the discipline for his principal role activities and fostered a monastic cultural tradition that has generated a set of further norms
related to the stated ones in the scriptures. Some of the most
conspicuous normative conduct I observed among village priests
concerns eating, killing, circumscribed relations with the laity
(especially women), proper dress, handling money, and special
conduct during Phansaa.

In referring to the rigors of monastic life, most villagers
begin with the same point: the proscription on any solid food after
noon. Before a long afternoon sermon the villagers serve coffee
to their priests, putting no milk in it since this is considered a
"food." Because a priest may never help himself to any food, a
few laymen are always on hand to present the food to a priest at
the eating circle, who then carefully places each dish of food received within the circle on behalf of the other priests.

One of the most serious concerns for a priest is to avoid
taking life. When the village was rushing to complete a new residence hall in the temple before the celebration of the recently won
honorific titles (for good pastoral service) of the headpriest and
his assistant, the priests and novices worked tirelessly into the
night on the heavy construction work. Only the novices, however,
could dig the old pillars out of the ground and dig holes for the new
pillars. Though forbidden to dig in the soil, the priests could mix
concrete because the building sand was not thought to harbor any
life. A priest must even be attentive to the foliage when he spits
or urinates.

The correct manner of priestly dress for various situations
is subject to innumerable regulations. The uncovering of the right
shoulder while in the temple area, the removal of the priest's sandals while in a layman's yard, the proscription on covering the
head while among the laity -- all are carefully observed. When we
went to see a new irrigation ditch outside the village, the headpriest wore his sandals but slipped these off as we entered a villager's yard, motioning silently for his temple boy to carry them
until we had passed through to the other side.

The rule against handling money is a subtle issue with priests. At times the headpriest is responsible for allocating large sums for temple festivals or for new school equipment and it is his duty to review problems concerning the temple budget and the new school building fund. His is a major voice in dispersing these funds and often the headpriest actually makes the purchases -- with a little temple boy carrying the money in his pocket to be paid out as directed. The headpriest keeps some of the temple funds, as well as his own money, in his room in the temple but to avoid direct handling will take a male villager into his room to bring out the cash as need arises.

The life of a priest involves constant abstention from secular activities and associations with the secular world. The role norms are demanding, and it would be mistaken to suppose that most village priests conform to them entirely. It is not so much that the priests violate the rules as that the rules, like life in general, tend to be regarded in a gentle, mild way. Their conformity to the norms has an asceticism that is amiably moderate rather than grimly dedicated.

This facet of Thai culture is perhaps best illustrated by noting some of the deviations from several of the types of normative behavior discussed above. The priests and novices in Sagatiam seem to conform with surprising success to the rules on eating. I found no instance of clandestine snacks, even among the husky young priests and novices. The deviation I did observe concerned the ruling against a priest's evincing any interest in the food offered to him. Many priests and novices ate with apparent relish, making appreciative remarks about some especially delicious food.

The strictures on taking life in any form seem to exact quite thorough conformity. Yet, though refraining wholly from killing any animals, the priests readily eat the succulent products of the sinful slaughter house in town. No norms exist against smoking and most of the priests smoke regularly.

The assistant headpriest said that detailed procedure for proper dressing and for handling of the robes is the sort of norm village priests most frequently fail to observe correctly. Procedural errors, confessed quite often, are not considered very serious.

A major departure from a strict interpretation of monastic discipline is the common fear of the spirits (phii). Two elderly laymen who were unusually learned in religious matters said very succinctly that some priests fear spirits, though to do so is not really to follow the doctrine since priests who are earnest should

not have any regard for ghosts. But the ancient association of
Buddhist doctrine with indigenous belief in spirits and the encul-
turation experiences of Thai village priests place the austere view
of my two informants beyond the attainment of most priests. Concern with spirits, though still strong in Sagatiam, is distinctly
less pervasive, less closely associated with Buddhism, and de-
clining more rapidly in comparison with the Lue of Northern Thailand described elsewhere in this volume by Moerman.

After considering the priests' conformity to and deviations
from their role norms it seems reasonable to conclude that, despite the demanding nature of these norms, the priests tend to conform to them to a remarkable degree. This relatively impressive
enactment of the priestly norm seems to be a psychosocial mixture
of internalized standards, awareness that others hold the same
standards, and consideration of the social deprivations for deviance as well as the rewards for conformity to these norms.

Internalization of priestly norms begins at an early age as a
boy gradually notices that everyone regards the priesthood as the
highest form of goodness possible in this life. It is difficult for a
villager who enters the priesthood to reject the normative expectations placed upon a priest inasmuch as these expectations are
spiritually ennobling and thus the effective means to great merit
for himself and for his grateful parents. True, the very importance of the priestly norms makes for their idealization and Thai
literature is generous with examples of cynicism as to the actual
conduct of the Sangha. But the conscientious efforts of the young
village men to pattern their behavior after the rules and their lack
of criticism of the numerous strictures seem to affirm their acceptance of the norms as good -- at least for the period they serve
in the Sangha.

It would be inappropriate, however, to regard these conscientious efforts as predominantly inner-directed in Riesman's
sense (1953: 28-32). In his role relations with other priests and
with laymen, a priest knows that others expect him to conform to
his role norms just as he expects them to conform to theirs. These
perceptions about expectations from other actors, the "role sanctions" as Parsons (1951: 38) labels them, also help the priest follow his required path. The priest is, first of all, in practically
constant association with other priests and is further reinforced
in his role by his contact with laymen, who reward his restrained
clerical behavior by their show of decorum and reverence. The
priest is part of a system of constant, informal social inspection.

In addition to this informal social control, two formal mechanisms operate within the Sangha: the discipline itself and the reg-

ular confession. Many people refer to the priests as being "in the discipline. " Noticing a young village carpenter, who had recently been a priest, doing a poor job, the community development worker commented wryly that the young man was more careless now that he had left the priesthood and its discipline.

In Sagatiam the priests perform the rite of the confessional twice a month and it is a serious matter of demerit (baab) to neglect any infractions. Yet any priest is quite free to tell other priests information received from a fellow priest's confession. The confession pattern is thus a particularly strong social control mechanism in view of the danger of demerit for failing to confess and of the threat of ridicule from other priests if one's transgressions become known after confession.

An observation made by Mosel (1964: 14) of the urban Thai administrator seems relevant here:

> One gets the impression that he does not internalize the role, but rather internalizes the values and beliefs which prescribe that he should play the role, whatever it is . . . Thus when he shifts roles, he can turn off the behavior and the emotional involvement that he has in it, and thus easily don another role.

Without calling into question the diligence and sincerity with which young villagers enact the priest role in Sagatiam, I can record the impression that, however fully they internalize the norms of their role, their conduct betokens strong acceptance of the general norm that they should act like priests while they are priests. The ease with which they appear to move into and later out of this complex role performance further suggests that conformity seems important to them somewhat apart from their own personal understanding of, or reaction to, the role norms.

The rewards for conformity to role norms appear to correspond, naturally enough, to the main role values for the priest role.

Role Values

Merit is the central value and makes possible the attainment of all others. The complex doctrine of merit is a Buddhist modification of the Hindu doctrine of karma. The provincial abbot once explained: "Our merit is the result of what we do, say, and feel. The good that we may do and the reward we receive is merit (bun). Evil choices and the punishment they bring us is demerit (baab). " This moral process of receiving rewards and punishments continues throughout the endless karmic cycle of rebirths.

Untutored in the complexities of the greater tradition of Buddhism, the villagers nevertheless understand merit in direct personal terms. At a housewarming breakfast several village teachers were talking about merit when one turned to Headman Chom, the white-haired temple leader, and asked a question villagers would rarely pose explicitly: what does merit mean? With the assurance of a long life devoted to an ancient tradition, Headman Chom did not even interrupt his breakfast in replying, "Merit means happiness (khwaamsug)." In this brief statement, Chom was recognizing the importance of merit as a spiritual value and as a means to the inevitable attainment of a further value, happiness.

Merit is a value important to both priest and layman. A key to the nature of the priest's role is that he is considered the most meritful person in the village. Being in the discipline of the order makes it possible for him to accrue merit for himself and for his family and for the laity generally. Priests speak about merit less than laymen do. Though both feel the constant need for adding to their merit, the priest can feel a certain security in the special store acquired by the fact of being a priest. By extension, the more permanent priest gains an additional sense of well-being, believing that his merit continues to grow as long as his robes do not become "too hot" and no strong inner compulsion to leave the order arises.

The element of reciprocity is apparent here as it is in many Thai relationships. The priest acquires merit primarily through his monastic activities, made possible by the layman's complete material support, the supplying of which is the layman's chief means of acquiring merit. The priest in his parish activities too acquires merit by offering the layman opportunities for greater merit through temple and home rituals and by receiving the layman's merit-making material offerings in return. Whether priest or layman, the individual invariably acquires merit in exchange for some valued good, service, or sentiment offered to another person or persons.

More broadly, the value of merit has both an individual and a social aspect. Buddhists view the workings of karma as deeply personal. Individuals must make their choices in life and receive their subsequent rewards and punishments as individuals. This personal emphasis appears both in the written tradition and in daily life. Yet, while only individuals can acquire and possess merit, the means for doing so is very largely cooperation with other individuals in social situations of patterned role relationships.

   Like the layman, the priest realizes other role values as a
consequence of his merit. The priest's role norms do not generally permit him the layman's sort of direct action to improve his
value position. But the priest's special merit makes such direct
action unnecessary. Sacred knowledge and spiritual wisdom may
be pursued directly, such values as respect and power only passively and indirectly through accumulation of merit and its recognition by laymen and other priests. But this recognition of his
merit by others validates it and enables the priest to attain through
it other valued ends in life.

Role Learning

   Asked how their knowledge of priestly duties and conduct had
been acquired, a group of young men who had just left the priesthood listed these sources of information: about a week of living
and working in the temple as laymen before their ordination in order to memorize the Pali chants of the ordination ritual; some instruction from the bishop during the ordination ceremonies; individual help from older priests during the first few days in matters
of robe handling and temple duties; study of the doctrine in the
priests' school; the frequent brief instruction by the headpriest
after morning or evening chanting in the sanctuary; the headpriest's
special evening meetings for fuller instruction or for practice of
unfamiliar Pali chants; and general observation of the system together with the older priests' answers to their specific questions
about the system.

   These men overlooked their earlier learning experiences.
Had not some of them once been in the position of the little temple
boy standing in the doorway watching intently the ordination ceremony of which he might some day be the central figure? The temple boy and later the novice have a very broad exposure to the life
of a priest long before their own day comes.

   These young men also neglected to mention the rich pageantry
and drama at the time of the family ceremony at home the night before their entry into the priesthood. The elegant dress of the candidate betokened the palace life of the Buddha before he forsook the
world. The doctor who called back his khwan-soul reviewed the
Buddha's entire life story and his entry into the new life in the temple. Any young man growing up in the village has ample opportunity
to acquire a good deal of latent learning about the priest role before
he dons the yellow robes. Once in the order, most of the young
neophytes seemed to switch easily to the new forms of address and
self-reference.

   A central aspect of role behavior for young priests or novices is learning and study. Many do not go on to secondary school in the town but instead remain in the temple as long as they are able to pass the annual priests' exams. A number of young village priests have gone on to Pali studies and a very few even to the Buddhist University in Bangkok.

Conclusions

What, finally, is the essential place of the man in the yellow robes in central Thai culture? From this brief examination of five aspects of his role, we see a figure who stands for both monastic withdrawal from the sensate world and compassionate spiritual or parish service to those who toil and suffer in that very world. His binary orientation has appeared in all five aspects of the priest role. During the course of the year and during the course of a man's career in the Sangha, a series of shifts are discernible between these two contrary yet complementary emphases of his role: the daily round of temple activities is predominantly monastic, the weekly and several annual holy days show a greater parish emphasis in both activities and relations with the laity.

The Phansaa season is basically a time for turning inward toward a more monastic regimen, although it is also a time for more extensive weekly relations with laymen coming to make merit at the temple. The hot season after the rice harvest brings the most pronounced parish activity and is a period of frequent home rituals. The monastic norms guiding the priest's behavior also regulate his relations with the laity in a way that enhances his sacerdotal worth to them. His basic role value of merit, deriving from his monastic normative conduct, is more fully realized as he enables laymen to make merit through his priestly role. A new priest or novice emphasizes the monastic aspect of his role in his earnest study of the Dharma, while his study of the chants is both monastic and parish. As he remains in the order for some years and assumes more importance to the laity as a holy man, a priest has to learn more of the parish duties of ministering to the laity and running the temple.

The varied expectations on the Thai phra in the yellow robe constitute a sort of compound role. Individuals of different seniority in the Sangha and the same individuals at different times emphasize distinct parish and monastic orientations. The monastic aspect of the role seems the primary one in establishing the identity of the phra in Thai society. But his very identity seems to serve the ultimate cultural reason for his being: cultivating merit in his special way of life so that otherwise hapless laymen may also improve their lives with merit. These Theravada villagers are unacquainted with the Mahayana ideal of the Bodhisattva who compassionately remains in the world to assist mortals toward Nirvana.

These Thai villagers, however, regard the holiness of the phra so highly precisely because his special merit assists them to inch their way forward along the great Karmic Path.

REFERENCES CITED

Dhaninivat, Prince

    1960   A History of Buddhism in Siam, Bangkok, Asia
             Foundation. (Reprint of article submitted to the
             Encyclopaedia of Buddhism of the Government of
             Ceylon.)

Gearing, Fred

    1958   "The Structural Poses of the 18th Century Cherokee
             Villages," American Anthropologist, 60, 1148-57.

Kaufman, Howard

    1960   Bangkhuad: A Community Study in Thailand, Locust
             Valley, New York, J.J. Augustin for the Association
             for Asian Studies.

Kingshill, Konrad

    1960   Ku Daeng: The Red Tomb, Chiengmai, Prince
             Royal's College.

Mosel, James

    1964   "Self, Role, and Role Behavior of Supervisors in the
             Thai Bureaucracy," paper read at meetings of the
             Eastern Psychological Association.

Parsons, Talcott

    1951   The Social System, Glencoe, Illinois, Free Press.

Riesman, David, Reuel Denney, and Nathan Glazer

    1953   The Lonely Crowd, Garden City, New York,
             Doubleday.

Textor, Robert

    1960   "An Inventory of Non-Buddhist Supernatural Objects in
             a Central Thai Village," Ph.D. dissertation, Cornell
             University.

THE BUDDHIST MONK IN RURAL BURMESE SOCIETY

David E. Pfanner

The Ford Foundation

Of the two elements making up the syncretic religion of Burma --
Buddhism and animism -- Buddhism is by far the more formal and
institutionalized with its system of loosely federated monasteries
and its abundance of sacred literature. The principal religious
role in Burmese society therefore falls to the Buddhist monk and
it is on his role that the following discussion will focus. In addition to brief background material on the area of research, there
will be a detailed examination of the Buddhist monk's pivotal role
characteristics, activities, social relationships, values, norms,
and recruitment. In the concluding remarks an attempt will be
made to give an overall assessment of his role in Burmese society
together with a synoptic comparison of his role and that of the nat
(spirit) specialist.

Data is drawn largely from field research in villages of the
Pegu district of Lower Burma, one of the principal rice producing
districts in the country. The area lying between the Sittang river
on the east and the Pegu Yoma on the west is an enormous rice
plain resembling the delta of the Irrawaddy in many respects. At
one time this area was included within the ancient Mon empire with
its capital at Pegu, but a series of disastrous wars with the Burmese, and later Burmese migration into the area, resulted in the
virtual elimination or assimilation of the Mons in this district.
Burmese migrants from Upper Burma resettled the area after the
establishment of the British colonial administration in the early
nineteenth century.

The village of Mayin is located eight miles north of the district headquarters at Pegu, a city of 45,000 people, and is three-
quarters of a mile from the Rangoon-Mandalay road. There is no
all-weather road serving the village and no regular vehicular traf-
fic. A village of 698 people living in 150 houses, Mayin is one of
four making up a village tract under the jurisdiction of a single
headman or village council. The four villages are within a two-
mile radius of one another.

The Village Monasteries

The collection of buildings where Buddhist monks reside,
study, and teach, and where the laity observe the sabbaths or duty
days, is called the pongyi kyaung, which could be freely translated
as "monastic school" and is comparable to the wat in Thailand. Individual buildings within this compound are the sermon hall (dham-

mayone), ordination hall (thein), school (kyaung), and rest house
(zayat). The monastic compound is frequently geographically
separate from the rest of the village, a separation that is symbolic
of the isolation of the monks from the day to day concerns of the
villagers. The sanctity of the entire area is marked by the removal
of footwear before entering.

The residents of the village monasteries, of which there are
two, consist of a brotherhood of monks hierarchically ranked according to the number of consecutive years passed as a monk. At
the head of each monastic school is a senior monk whose role is
analogous to that of an abbot, usually known as the sayadaw or
venerable teacher. Ordained monks with less seniority (upazin)
and novices who have been initiated but not ordained make up the
usual complement of monastic inmates.

Monks of all ages constitute 2.5 to 3 per cent of the total
Buddhist male population of an area north of Pegu containing 47
villages. At least half of these are novices who do not remain permanently in the monasteries. In this same area of the Pegu district, there is an average of one monastery for every 162 houses,
the average number of houses per village being 172. Of the 47 villages, 83 per cent had at least one monastery in 1954.

By village standards, the monks of Lower Burma are well
fed and well housed. The two monasteries in the village studied
were rebuilt of wood with corrugated iron roofs after being completely destroyed during World War II. No building within either
of the monastic compounds displays any great evidence of wealth
in construction or furnishings, but the main buildings are well built
and sturdy. Most of the buildings are somewhat shabby in appearance and are in poor repair, particularly the infrequently visited
and little used ordination halls, which are only partially walled.

The monks are supported entirely by voluntary contributions
from the laity. Neither monastic school possesses any land from
which it earns an income, nor does either have any other source of
income apart from these contributions. In addition to the rice collected during the daily morning circuit of the village by the younger
monks and novices, certain families regularly send curries and
other foodstuffs to the monasteries for the support of the monks.
The village is organized into neighborhoods which cooperate in the
supply and preparation of special food on sabbaths, notably those
during the three-month period of intensified religious activity from
June to October, sometimes referred to as the Buddhist Lent.

Financial and other support for the monks is collected mainly
in villagewide subscriptions to an annual alms-presentation cere-

mony at each monastery and at the initiation ceremonies in which
a number of youths may be simultaneously initiated. At other less
elaborate and less public ceremonies, which often center around
some point in the life-cycle, monks may be invited to a home where
they are presented with gifts which may include a cash contribution.
This rarely amounts to more than K10/ - or about $2.10 per monk.

During the period 1959 to 1960 there were two large celebrations in the village with the monastic school as the focus and two
initiation ceremonies. At these four events alone, a total of
K10,757 or about $2,300 was spent. Of this, 38 per cent was
devoted to gifts for the monks -- robes, light blankets, sandals,
umbrellas, etc. -- and 51 per cent went for the purchase of food,
tobacco, and betel for the guests, who numbered in the thousands.
It is estimated by the author that from 6 to 8 per cent of net dispos-
able cash income is devoted to religious purposes, including the
support of the monks.

Apart from food, the financial base of the two monasteries
is more a matter of many small contributions than of a few contributions from relatively wealthy households. There are few
great differences among household incomes since over 90 per cent
of the villagers depend upon agriculture for their livelihood, use
an identical technology, and, after land nationalization, have family holdings of a generally equalized size.

The two monasteries of Mayin village represent the two
largest divisions of the Burmese Sangha: the Thudhamma order
and the Shwegyin order. The latter arose from a controversy that
developed within the Sangha during the reign of King Mindon in the
mid-nineteenth century (1852-77). As the younger and stricter of
the two sects, the Shwegyin order can be thought of as a reformed
order of monks. The two sects do not differ in their interpretation
or acceptance of the basic doctrine drawn from the Pali canon but
differ sharply in their adherence to or interpretation of the rules
governing the conduct of monks both within and without the monastic compound.

The disciplinary differences that divide these two groups
should not obscure the fact that, in most important respects, they
are alike: the religious role performance and expectations of the
monks are almost identical except for minor variations in dress
and conduct. Nor should these minor differences cloud the more
important sociological difference between them, that being that the
Thudhamma order of monks is the more liberal of the two, placing
fewer restrictions on the movement and communication of monks
with the laity. Therefore, Thudhamma monks are in many ways
closer to village affairs and to affairs in the world outside the

village. Briefly, the differences between the Shwegyin and Thudhamma monks are these: Shwegyin monks are strictly prohibited
from attending performances of dramatic entertainment, chewing
betel after noon, smoking tobacco, riding in horse or bullock carts,
telling fortunes, making astrological predictions, practicing medicine, or wearing robes in an informal style when outside the compound. In the village studied, villagers were equally divided in
their support of these two monasteries.

Role Characteristics

The high status of the monk is reflected in the role name and
in other linguistic behavior. The term commonly applied to fully
ordained members of the Sangha, pongyi, literally means "great
glory, " "great nobility, " or "great holiness. " An alternate form,
yahan, is usually translated as "perfect one. " The ceremony of
initiation in which a young Burmese boy is formally made a part of
the monkhood is known as a shinbyu, which means to "make a lord"
or to "make a holy one. "

The referential terms applied to monks -- pongyi, yahan,
thanga -- divide Burmese society into two distinct categories,
clergy and laity. The role norms separating these two categories
are as sharp as those dividing any two roles in Burmese society,
for the norms creating barriers to social interaction between the
clergy and laity apply to dress, residence, language, patterns of
food consumption, and social relations.

The pivotal role characteristics of the monk are to be found
in the areas of dress, possessions, residence, sustenance, and
conduct. All members of the Buddhist clergy are immediately
identifiable by their saffron robes and shaven heads. No member
of the laity dresses thus, and no monk may adopt the dress of a
layman and still retain his status as monk. The material property
associated with the role of a monk has been traditionally restricted
to a limited number of articles allowed by the monastic vows of
poverty: the three pieces of cloth making up the robes, an alms
bowl, a needle, a razor, a water strainer, and a short-handled
axe. Modern practice is somewhat at variance with this, however,
and most monks have some personal property such as open-toed
sandals, umbrellas, pens, pencils, reading glasses, paper, and
books -- but not rings, watches, or any other items of jewelry or
bodily adornment.

A monk may live in a separate residence if a benefactor is
willing to build it for him, but the usual pattern in the village of
Lower Burma is for all monks to live in dormitory style at the
pongyi kyaung or in separate quarters in a nearby building within

the compound. In all cases, however, the monks must live within
the monastic compound, which is generally insulated from the village.

   The food eaten by monks must meet numerous monastic regulations concerning its source, its composition, and the manner
and timing of its consumption. Although the role of monk cannot
be definitely regarded as a relational-type role, the monks are
completely dependent upon the laity for their support since they
are forbidden to work. Monks are forbidden by their monastic
vows to eat solid food after 12:00 noon. They may eat anything
which is offered to them in their alms bowl or that is sent separately to the monastery each day by a donor, but if it is known that the
life of an animal has been taken specifically for their nourishment
the monks should refuse the food. The offering of alms to the
monks is one of the highest forms of merit-making, and the daily
offering of rice by householders to the procession of monks who
each receive a large spoonful of rice in each of their alms bowls
must be considered ritual as much as a means of support. At no
time is the food requested, nor is there any recognition made when
receiving it. It is the layman who is in the debt of the monk for
accepting the offering, not the monk who is in debt to the layman
for providing him with nourishment.

   The shaven head and yellow robes of the monk are but the
outward visible signs of a life dedicated, however temporarily, to
the way of the Buddha. In order to understand the norms governing
the conduct of monks, it is necessary to have some knowledge of
the precepts governing the conduct of all Buddhists. The five familiar precepts incumbent upon all Buddhists require abstention from
taking life, from taking anything belonging to another without consent, from engaging in any impure act, from telling falsehoods,
and from the consumption of intoxicants. In addition to these five
precepts, which constitute the essential minimum of the Buddhist
ethic, laymen undertake to observe three additional vows on Buddhist sabbaths: to refrain from taking food after midday, to refrain from dancing, singing, playing instruments, witnessing un-
seemly shows, or using bodily adornment or perfume, and to refrain from the use of high seats or beds.

   The spiritual purity and moral superiority of the monks
originate partly in the merit earned by daily observance of these
and other vows. The novice is obliged to observe a total of ten
precepts with a redivision of those mentioned above to account for
nine plus the additional promise not to use or touch any form of
gold, silver, paper currency, or precious stones. The conduct
for ordained monks is specified in the 227 precepts contained in
the Patimauk or Book of Enfranchisement, a section of the Vinaya

or Wini basket of the Tipitaka, which defines pardonable and unpardonable actions on the part of the monks. Four cardinal sins result in expulsion from the Sangha: breaking the vow of chastity, taking human life, theft, or making false claims of supernatural power. All other infractions may be repented and absolved, but the commission of these results in disgrace and expulsion from the kyaung, the Sangha, and the village.

Monks do not adhere strictly to all 227 regulations, but they do observe the ten precepts (with one exception by Thudhamma monks, who may attend musical and dance entertainment). If the conduct of the monks was not beyond doubt in most important aspects of their lives, they could not be held in the high esteem they are in the village. All male village household heads have had firsthand experience in the monastery, both as lay students and as novices, and know the difficulties involved in the lives of the monks -- and the degree to which the vows are observed. The reverence in which the senior monks are held is testimony to their relatively blameless conduct.

Recruitment, Training, and Duration of Role Performance

Admission to the fraternity of monks in Burma is open to any male who is twenty years of age, who has his parents' consent, who is free of debt and of contagious diseases, and who has been provided with the eight requisities by a sponsor. The actual ordination ceremony (which did not take place in the village during the period of fieldwork) must be held in an ordination hall of a specified minimum size and in the presence of a specified number of ordained monks. The ceremony itself consists of a number of questions put to the candidate to which he must respond. The ten precepts are formally accepted, warnings are given concerning the four cardinal sins, and the candidate pledges observance of the monastic duties and precepts.

The candidate for initiation as a novice must be provided with robes and other articles and must be able to recite the Three Jewels in Pali in order to be admitted to the kyaung -- though the stipulation regarding the Pali formulae is relaxed in actual practice and it is unlikely that any boy is ever refused admission because he forgets his lines.

By the time a boy has spent months, and probably years, in the monastery as a lay student, he has learned much of what he is required to know as either novice or monk. He has been able to observe the behavior of monks under all possible circumstances, so there are few surprises in store for him. There is thus a long

period of anticipatory socialization for the roles of novice and ordained monk. The transition from the role of layman to novice or
from novice to ordained monk does not involve great anxiety or
trauma even though it marks an abrupt change in status.

From a sociological point of view, the most significant aspect of the recruitment of monks is the fact that, although they are
drawn from every level of society, status in the kyaung and as a
monk depends upon the consecutive number of years spent in the
kyaung and the intellectual prowess exhibited in command over the
sacred literature. In no way does status achieved outside the
kyaung affect the status of the individual monk.

If a monk who has been ordained wants to leave one monastery
and join another or if the villagers want to have a particular monk
take up residence in their monastary, they can contact the headquarters of the order where arrangements will be made for the appointment. In Mayin, a factor which appeared important in drawing monks to the village was the desire to study with, or be of service to, the abbot there.

The role of the monk in Burmese society is one which denies
the simultaneous performance of any other role; the role norms of
the monk make it incompatible as a multiple role. All occupational,
family, and kinship roles are denied a monk since he is restricted
from fulfilling the normative behavior expected or demanded by
these roles. His is a role calling for complete daily fulfillment of
various mandatory role norms to the exclusion of any others as
long as the yellow robe is worn. It cannot be dropped without vio-
lating these norms.

Every male in the village spends some period during his early life as a novice. Mayin male household heads have spent an
average of six years as lay students, and 45 per cent of them have
spent two or more years wearing the yellow robe. A total of 14
per cent have at one time been ordained as monks. Of these, 53
per cent remained in the monastery for less than a full calendar
year, 26 per cent for a year, and 21 per cent for more than a year.
Few men have been ordained in recent years, but most, if not all,
boys have been initiated as novices.

The practice of remaining in the monastery for a number of
years and then returning to the life of a layman is not uncommon.
Some of the present monks of the village cannot say with assurance
that they plan or intend to remain monks throughout their lives even
though they may have been monks for as long as six years. The far
more common practice, however, is to remain an ordained monk
for a relatively short time.

Young men eighteen or twenty years of age who responded to
a questionnaire concerning occupational preferences clearly indicated that, although the life of a monk meant one of merit and the
quicker attainment of a higher form of life in the next existence,
the difficulty of observing the monastic vows was a serious obstacle.
There was a real concern over the possible infraction of monastic
precepts which would then result in rebirth in a lower form or in
hell. Particular restrictions the respondents most often cited as
being difficult were the enforced seclusion in the kyaung, the lack
of an evening meal, and the vow of celibacy.

Role Activities

The role activities of the monk are performed almost exclusively within the compound of the monastery and are concerned almost entirely with religious self-education or the education of
others. Monks are expected to show their compassion toward laymen by teaching them the Dhamma, but this is not a duty incumbent
upon all monks and thus must be regarded as a secondary role
characteristic or duty. A number of young ordained monks in
Mayin have no responsibility whatever in enlightening the laity but
are not regarded as remiss in their duty because of it. As Scott
has written of the duties assumed by the monk at his ordination, he
"takes upon himself no burden in the shape of a curer of souls. He
is not a priest like a Christian minister, who undertakes to guide
others to salvation. . . . He is not a minister of religion, and all
he has to do is seek his own deliverance and salvation" (Scott 1910:
111).

Inmates of the monastery rise between 4:00 and 5:00 a.m. to
begin their day by making obeisance to the image of the Buddha and
reciting prayers and hymns of praise. The monks are relatively
free to do as they like until the young lay students arrive and begin
preparing the first meal of the morning. This meal is over about
7:30 when all novices and a few young monks of one of the kyaungs
file through the village paths in separate processions on their morning round of collecting the alms food of the villagers. While this is
taking place, the remaining monks begin teaching the students, who
may have cleaned the kyaung or compound before class. The second and last meal of the day is eaten about 10:30 a.m. first by the
abbot and senior monks, then by the novices, then by the lay students. The remainder is thrown to the dogs and crows, which are
supported in large numbers. Monks do not participate in the preparation of food or in the custodial care of the kyaung.

The period from about noon to late afternoon is largely devoted to study and teaching, with two breaks for rest or play by
the younger members. Students at one monastic school number

about twenty -- all between the ages of about six and ten. They
are divided into three groups depending on their level of attainment, and the monk with the main teaching responsibility circu-
lates among these groups from time to time writing lessons on
blackboards. He first reads the lesson aloud, then has the class
repeat it. What appears as utter confusion to the observer is the
result of these three classes shouting their lessons simultaneously
at the top of their lungs in a somewhat confined area. During the
time that the students are thus committing their lessons to memory, the monks seem indifferent to their progress and may engage
in their own studies or conversation.

     It is also during this period of the afternoon that the abbot or
a senior monk instructs the younger monks and older novices in
Pali. The language is widely believed to be the language spoken by
the Buddha in his lifetime and this is the rationale given for its use
in religious contexts. It is not taught as a language per se, but
rather passages are memorized and then the meanings explained
in Burmese. Only a monk who has advanced fairly far in his studies can actually translate an unfamiliar passage of Pali into Burmese at sight. The works studied in the village are the Mingalathok,
the Mahamangala Sutta from the Sutta Pitaka, selections from a
work called the Payeitkyi (Paritta), and abridgments of the Abhid-
hamma called Thingyo and Thada. Memorization rather than critical review or creative commentary forms the basis of much of the
advanced study of the Burmese Sangha.

     Lessons are over by about 4:30 in the afternoon, when the
lay students leave for home. The monks spend their evenings in
conversation, study, or prayer and are rarely to be found outside
the monastic compound. Formal religious observances within the
monastery are relatively few, consisting largely of Pali stanzas
chanted in the morning and evening. There is also a confessional
and recitation of parts of the Vinaya in the ordination hall on full-
moon and half-moon sabbaths in which only fully ordained monks
participate.

     During the course of the average day there are no specific
times or occasions at which laymen come to the kyaung except on
an individual basis. Monks perform no ceremonies, rituals, or
services for laymen except on the sabbaths. There are a number
of religious, semireligious, and secular events throughout the year
which involve the participation of the monks. These can be cate-
gorized as (1) Buddhist sabbaths and holidays which occur as part
of the annual ritual and ceremonial cycle, (2) communitywide but
privately sponsored religious events, (3) privately sponsored ceremonies to which monks are invited, and (4) secular national holidays. It is not my purpose to outline these here (see Manning Nash

elsewhere in this volume) but merely to indicate the type of activities in which monks participate.

The main occasions on which laymen come to the monastery
in large numbers are the Buddhist sabbaths, which are marked
according to the lunar calendar. On these days the abbot or senior
monk recites the Three Jewels and the eight precepts which are
recited responsively and pledged by the laity. It is also on these
occasions, which occur particularly during the lenten period, that
a sermon (tayabwè) may be preached. In general only a single
monk has any responsibility during the ceremony, which usually
lasts about an hour and a half. Other monks and novices are usually present but take little or no active part in the proceedings. On
certain occasions all may chant in unison. Following the sermon, a
libation of water is poured by one of the elders, the laity performs
shikkos before the Buddha, and monks intone the phrase "thadu,
thadu, thadu (well done). " The meeting then breaks up and the
women return home to finish their morning cooking. They return
by 10:30 a. m. when the monks are fed and, after the monks have
finished, the laity begin their meal. Those keeping the sabbath,
i. e. observing the eight vows throughout the day, remain in the
monastery until dusk.

The pattern of coming together either in the monastery or
elsewhere to feed the monks (hsungywè) and to hear a portion of
the law recited (taya-haw) is the commonest form of formal religious activity that brings monks and laity together. It provides
both with an opportunity to improve their karma by making merit
-- the laity by feeding the monks and the monks by enlightening the
laity. Such a ceremony can be held at almost any time on an occasion to which the sponsors want to lend the auspicious dignity
and sanctity that the presence of monks always brings. In some
villages on national holidays such as Independence Day the monks
are fed at the government public school. Monks are ritually fed
during certain points in the life cycle of the individual such as a
child-naming, housewarming, or death but do not take part in the
marriage ceremony, which is entirely secular.

Few villagers could be said to have a very informal or intimate relationship with any monk, and monks are generally not
asked for advice concerning personal problems. It is generally
held that people go to the headman with their personal problems.

One of the major differences between the Shwegyin and Thudhamma monks regards the activities of the latter in the practice of
medicine, tattooing, and the making of charms and amulets said
to have the power to protect the wearer from the influence of evil
spirits, demons, and witches. The Shwegyin monks are forbidden

to engage in such activities and have a somewhat indifferent attitude toward evil spirits, although they recognize their existence.
These activities are not essential to the role performance of the
monks and can also be performed by laymen with the requisite
knowledge of the designs and formulae. Monks have the leisure
in which to develop this knowledge and have a spiritual potency of
their own. It is not known how widespread this practice is among
the monks, but it is significant in illustrating the mutual compati-
bility of Buddhist and animist beliefs and practices among a group
in which one might least expect to find it.

Not all the role activities of the monks take place in the village of residence. On certain occasions, such as funerals, pagoda
festivals, and almsgiving ceremonies at neighboring monasteries,
village monks are invited to attend. These visits are partly reciprocal and the pattern should be considered one of the main links
between villages in the area. At a large annual ceremony at one
of the monasteries in Mayin, for example, there may be as many
as thirty invited monks present representing monasteries from
fifteen to twenty villages. The Mayin monks named sixteen villages
to which they travel regularly. In addition to these outside activities, some village monks go to Pegu for meetings which occur at
the district headquarters of their particular order, and there are
occasional trips to Rangoon and Mandalay.

Role Interaction and Relationships

In the structure of institutionalized Buddhism in Burma, the
monk can rarely if ever escape the strictly defined normative expectations of his role. The monk is usually under observation in
a manner that laymen are not, even in the monastery. Despite the
relatively public lives led by the Burmese, the ordinary villager is
not bound by a rigid code of conduct as is the monk, and there is
flexibility in the less rigorously defined role norms of laymen
which is lacking in the role norms of the monk. The conduct of
the monk is constantly open to exposure, or, in Merton's terms,
the role activities of the monk are only slightly insulated from observation by members of his role-set. Interaction with the laity
tends to be intermittent, but interaction with other monks and novices is very nearly continuous. It must be recalled that the turn-
over in the population of novices is fairly high so that in a sense
the monks are always before the public.

Despite the many norms which serve as mechanisms to prevent members of the Sangha and the laity from coming into intimate
or close association, there are no physical barriers to the kyaung
compound, which is always open to anyone who desires entry. For

example, access to wells or ponds located in the monastic compound are often through the compound itself.

The role-set of the monk is a local one, consisting primarily of other monks and novices and of villagers in their roles as laymen. The role of monk does not intersect with villagers in their economic, political, or kinship roles except insofar as the norms of laymen are transferred to these roles. The relations of the headman with the monk are those of a layman, never those of a government official. Generally the interaction between monks and laymen requires formal, stylized behavior on the part of both. In addition, the monk usually meets with laymen in groups and only on specific occasions during which the behavior of both is exposed to public view.

The villagers who meet together at the pongyi kyaung on Buddhist sabbaths tend to be above the village average in age. It is not only the elderly that observe these duty days, but it is true that the young unmarried men are not as well represented as the rest of the population.

The role norms of the monk severely restrict his relations with women. The monk may not be alone with a woman and women may not perform various services for monks, such as serving food. Thus, the role interactions of the monks are largely with villagers in their roles as laymen, more with older adults than with youths, and less with women than with men.

The location of role interaction between the clergy and laity is also highly restricted, with most interaction taking place in the monastery. On certain specified occasions, such as a funeral, the monk may go to the home of a layman, but the duration of such visits is usually short and tends to be limited to the specified purpose of the visit. After the monks have been fed, have chanted the law, and have been presented with alms, they return to their quarters. Rarely does a monk visit the home of a layman alone, the case of Thudhamma monks taking medicine to the sick being an exception.

The most characteristic feature of the relationship between monks and laity is the special content of their interactions. Members of the Burmese Sangha and villagers meet only in the related roles of monk and layman. The communication between them is culturally prescribed, consisting mostly of the transmission of religious lore from monk to layman. The relationship has many of the characteristics of the teacher-pupil relationship with the monk in the role of teacher, as indeed he is on many occasions.

Regardless of any verbal communication that may take place, the cultural content of the interaction between monks and laymen always involves the making of merit. The high status of the monks reflects their more meritorious life and functionally the role provides a mechanism through which the layman is able to improve his own karma by honoring the monk. The vast majority of situations that bring monk and layman together are situations in which merit is being made by one or both.

The relationship between the monk and layman is characterized by its formality and the ritual distance imposed by the norms of the society. These norms reflect the higher social status of the monk in Burmese society, making the relationship one-sided in its patterns of deference and respect. The language used by the monks among themselves in the monastery and when speaking with members of the laity clearly reflects the status hierarchy in the kyaung and in Burmese society. The terms of address and reference are more than linguistic forms reflecting perfunctory politeness, for the behavior of monks and laymen show this status difference in many other ways. Since it is more polite to address a person by title than by name, for example, an inferior addresses a superior by title and is addressed by name. This is the form used between clergy and laity. Laymen address monks as "reverend teacher" and refer to themselves as "your eminence's pupil" or avoid self-reference altogether. Honorific terminology as employed in the terms of address is found also in reference to certain actions which are performed by monks but dignified by the use of different verbs. Ordinary men "eat rice," "smoke cheroots," or "drink tea"; monks performing the same actions are said to "honor" or "glorify" the alms-food, "honor" the cheroot, etc. Men are said to "walk" and to "sleep" but monks "proceed" and "remain dormant" or in a "state of repose." These and other linguistic usages showing the high status of monks are never under any circumstances applied to laymen.

Other ways in which monks are shown respect are found in positions of posture and the location and height of the laymen relative to the monk when seating arrangements are made. When entering or leaving the presence of monks, the layman makes an obeisance known as the shikko in which he kneels with knees and feet on the floor, raises the hands with palms together, then bends forward to place the palms on the floor with the thumbs on the forehead. This is repeated three times and is a gesture reserved for paying respect to superiors. Children shikko parents, pupils shikko teachers, wives shikko husbands, and laymen shikko monks. The knees and thighs of a man are often exposed when sitting cross-legged on the floor or ground, but because this is impolite in the presence of monks the legs and feet are carefully tucked beneath the body and well covered in such situations. Feet are never to be pointed in the direction of another, but special caution is observed in the case of monks. Superiors are always seated in the southern or eastern portion of the guest room, the more auspicious directions, and this is always where monks are placed when they enter a house. They are also given finely woven mats on which to sit, which not only assures them a clean spot but raises their height relative to that of the laymen present. In like fashion, laymen walk about in a stooped position when monks are seated nearby so that their heads will be no higher than those of the monks. When food is prepared, monks are always fed first with the choicest curries. Laymen do not initiate conversation with monks and are careful to direct conversation among themselves to appropriate subjects when monks are in their presence.

These are only a selection of the many ways in which the Burmese show their respect for the pongyis, whose role is the only one in the society which demands and always receives this pattern of deference.

Values and Norms

More than any other role in Burmese society, the role of monk is associated with cognitive, moral, and transcendental values. These values in Burmese culture are derived from Buddhism and in part are realized through the Sangha. Members of the Burmese brotherhood of monks epitomize a life dedicated to personal salvation or enlightenment through adherence to a monastic code and a rejection of personal or material attachment in the world of the laity. Monks are pledged to lives of poverty, humility, continence, austerity, and self-denial. (To understand something of the values associated with the role of monk, one need only recall the ten well-known major virtues or understandings, Parami, incumbent upon those who aspire to Buddhahood: charity, morality, renunciation, wisdom, strenuousness, patience, truthfulness, resolution, loving kindness, and resignation or aloofness.) As Brohm (1952: 43) has put it, "The Sangha, philosophically speaking, is the means by which the individual can follow the Dhamma and achieve Buddhahood himself. In theory at least, only one who has renounced the world and its mundane goals can achieve Buddhistic enlightenment, and the Sangha is the refuge of just those persons who have made this renunciation. "

The decision to abandon the world for the monkhood is a decision to spend a life in the accumulation of religious merit through the study of Pali texts and the practice of Buddhist virtues. The Burmese recognize the karma of the monks as so vastly superior to that of laymen that the very presence of monks has a ritual sanc-

tity about it. The greater the number of years spent as a monk,
the greater the karma and the greater the reverence for such a
monk. Without this appreciation of the relationship between karma,
merit, and the role values of the monk, an understanding of this
role in Burmese society is incomplete. Whatever deviations may
eixst from ideal behavior on the part of the monks, it is this general framework which provides the basis for their role values and
norms and against which their conduct is assessed.

Although the role values of the monk stress withdrawal from
the world, it would be mistaken to think that they are entirely unconcerned with the village society in which they live. Burmese
monks have always had a concern with enlightening laymen regarding the teaching of the Buddha. As repositories of learning, monks
have traditionally been teachers and for many centuries had a monopoly on the education of the young. The high status of monks is in
part attributable to their command over the sacred literature of the
Pali canon, and their teaching is based on the Burmese belief that
there is wisdom in knowledge and learning. Reading was, and still
is, taught in the monasteries so that students can become acquainted
with Buddhist texts. An education in the monastery has been religious and moral in nature -- designed to equip the student with the
moral values of Buddhism for his return to village life or as a first
step in his preparation for a life of the yellow robe if he is so in-
clined.

The role of the monk in education remains a potent one in
rural society for it is one of the most significant roles in the transmission of cultural values. In the Mingalathok or Discourse on the
Thirty-Eight Blessings, for example, we find laymen urged to cher-
ish wisdom, respectfulness, regard for parents, etc. There is no
doubt that the establishment of secular schools has lessened the influence of the monk among segments of the population who find no
"market value" in the type of education taught by the monks. In
rural Burma, however, the vitality of Buddhism must be attributed
partly to a continuing educational influence of the monks and the belief on the part of the villagers that an entirely secular education
is only half an education.

Monks and villagers alike are committed to a society based
on the religious values of Buddhism. Members of both the Sangha
and the laity commented on the incompatibility of Buddhism and
Communism, for example. The idea of Burma adopting a Commu-
nist ideology is not seriously entertained in the village for no one
believes that the Burmese could ever support a regime avowedly
antireligious or atheistic, as Communism is believed to be.

The role norms of the monk operate not only to limit his free-

dom of action but also nearly to obliterate his personal individual-
ity. As Bishop Bigandet wrote many years ago (1911: 296) of the
monks, "Every individual is bound to lay aside his own self and
unconditionally follow the impulse of his guiding influence." All
expression of emotion is kept at a minimum; clothes are to be regarded as not decorative but merely a concession to modesty and
a means for making extremes of temperature bearable. Food is
eaten not for enjoyment but to maintain bodily strength, etc. Monks
are expected to eat only in the presence of other monks and should
avoid frivolous or amusing topics of conversation.

The strict limit to the amount of interference by monks in
personal or community affairs is one of the marked departures
from past practice. The accounts regarding the role of the monk
in Upper Burma in the early days of the British residency are not
descriptive of the role of the monk in Lower Burma today, since
state and local officials have assumed many of the secular functions
monks performed in the days of the Burmese monarchy.

The monks of Mayin do not, for the most part, take an active
role in secular affairs and, increasingly, do not even attempt to
influence villagers on specific issues with religious or moral consequences, being content to recite the relevant portions of the
Dhamma and allow laymen to decide on its interpretation or appli-
cation. For example, although monks take the position that taking
any form of life is sinful, they do not advise laymen to refrain from
using rat poison or DDT; they do not state preferences for particular candidates in local or national elections; nor do they interfere
in the execution of the responsibilities of local government on the
part of elected or appointed officials. Various areas of social life
in which monks formerly exercised authority and control over the
actions of laymen are now viewed as the province of the headman or
the village council. This is one of the major changes in the role of
the monk during the past few decades and is part of a progressive
secularization of Burmese society.

The only non-Buddhist religious specialist in the village was
what might be described as a temporary spirit medium, the natkadaw.
On a single occasion during the period of field research this individual, whose role as a natkadaw was unknown to some villagers, exhibited behavior said to indicate possession by a spirit or nat. This
occurred on the evening prior to the annual almsgiving ceremony at
one of the monasteries. Before the only village spirit house an
offering of coconuts, bananas, tobacco, and betel had been placed
along with three candles. The woman apparently possessed by the
spirit was kneeling about twenty to thirty feet from the spirit house
swaying back and forth with clasped hands, speaking with a high
quavering voice said to be the voice of the village spirit Bobogyi.

The incident is worthy of mention since some of the witnesses to
this event were openly mocking the natkadaw by addressing rude
questions to her and snickering at her performance. Some said
later they did not think she was actually possessed at all.

Conclusions

The student of Burmese religion frequently encounters statements in the literature to the effect that within the blend of Buddhism
and animism in Burma the basic element is animism. Typical of
these statements is the following: "In Burma Buddhism has certainly
not succeeded in destroying the Animism of the people, for all observers agree that the Burman, despite his now ancient official
adoption, after a long fight, of the purest form of Buddhism, is at
heart an Animist, his professed faith being little more than a 'thin
veneer of philosophy laid over the main structure of Animistic belief.' In local parlance, the Animist of Burma is a Worshipper of
the nats" (Temple 1906: 1). It is asserted that, because Theravada
Buddhism cannot possibly appeal to the masses (Conze 1951: 72),
the Buddhism of rural society is a veneer covering a basic core of
spirit worship and that the philosophic structure of the belief system rests on a foundation of belief in good and evil spirits which
are propitiated daily while Buddhist ceremonies are restricted to
less frequent and ceremonial occasions.

It may be artificial in some cases to try and distinguish between Buddhist and animistic elements in the Burmese religion,
but my observations nevertheless lead me to conclusions opposite
to those just reviewed. In my opinion the dominant element in the
religion of Lower Burma is clearly Buddhist, not animist. (One of
the few writers clearly recognizing this fact is Slater in his work
Paradox and Nirvana). The Buddhism of rural Burma is not only
that of the Pali canon, but a living social reality of patterned religious activity which has enormous popular appeal. By almost any
standard or index one can apply, this point is clear. The institutionalization of religious roles, the number filling these roles, the
elaboration of rituals, and the symbols and intensity of emotional
involvement all point to the dominance of Buddhism in Burmese
religion.

In comparing the religious roles associated with Buddhism
and those associated with the nats or spirits, we find that rural
Burmese villagers in Mayin support numerous monks and novices
in two monasteries. The village nat is confined to a small and generally unkempt shrine within the north monastic compound and there
is not a single permanent religious specialist role associated with
the spirits or their propitiation. We have described the high status
of the monks as well as the patterns of respect and deference shown

to them on all occasions. On the single occasion when a spirit medium claimed possession by a spirit, she was openly mocked by some
witnesses. It would be unthinkable for a villager to mock a monk.

It is the village monks who are at the center of most religious
ceremonies, and these Buddhist ceremonies occur far more frequently than rituals concerned with spirits. The same can be said
of private or family observances. There is no nat-propitiation
ceremony which ever involves more than a handful of people, but
Buddhist-oriented ceremonies may involve the entire village. These
occasions involve the expenditure of enormous time, effort, and
money on the part of many people who willingly volunteer their services for a chance to share in the merit and companionship. Only
a fraction of this effort goes into any nat-propitiation ceremony.
Daily offerings are never made to the spirits, yet many if not most
families make a daily offering to the Buddhist monks and to an image of the Buddha in their homes. The only equivalent in the nat
world is that of keeping a fresh coconut for the house nat. The belief system clearly indicates that the indigenous local nats have
been absorbed into a Hindu-Buddhist pantheon of beings, all of
which are subject to the laws of karma. Spiritual power is derived
from the accumulated store of karma, making monks spiritually
superior to the lower nats and theoretically safe from their evil
influence. An even more telling indication of the superior spiritual
purity and strength of the monks is in the fact that they can be called
upon to disperse the evil nats by a recitation of Buddhist scriptures.
The texts of Buddhism are at the very base of the monastic school
system in village Burma and cannot be compared with the vaguely
known origin stories of the nats.

Other expressions of the dominance of Buddhism are to be
found in the association of village leadership with the monastic
schools, which village leaders are particularly active in supporting. Status in the village is in part related to Buddhist-oriented
activities and their sponsorship. It cannot be said that anyone
gains stature in the social hierarchy through association with nats.
And, finally, Buddhists make frequent pilgrimages to Buddhist
shrines but rarely go out of their way specifically to visit a nat
shrine or attend a nat festival. Mayin villagers in huge numbers
attend the annual pagoda festival in Pegu, where one of the principal activities is the offering of alms to one thousand district monks,
but it is rare to hear of one who has gone to the annual nat festival
in the same city.

The Buddha is loved and respected. His teaching forms the
basis of Burmese values and of the moral code taught to the young.
The most highly respected individuals in society are religious
specialists following the way of the Buddha. The attitude toward

many of the lower nats is one of fear, and the propitiatory offerings
to them are designed more to keep them at a distance than to invite
their intercession. The element of animism in Burmese religion
cannot be denied, but it is a subordinate element when compared
with Buddhism, which in rural Burma is a main cultural focus.

The increasing secularization of Burmese society and the
progressive restriction of the activities of the monks in secular
affairs has caused some changes in the role of the monk and in his
influence. However, it is just as important to note that although
religious institutions in Lower Burma have experienced severe
shocks in their comparatively short history, they have manifested
enormous resiliency. There was the rapid economic growth and
unsettled agrarian conditions following the British annexation, the
nationalism of the 1930s, the invasion and destruction of World War
II, and the civil rebellion after Burmese independence. It is certainly not difficult to find changes in the role of the monk which
have their origins in this stormy history, but there has also been
a remarkable vitality and stability in Burmese Buddhism during
these years. In part this accounts for the fact that despite the political turmoil of the past decade, rural Burmese society does not
appear to be characterized by the upheaval of values experienced
in many nations during this period. The importance of the Buddhist
monk as the living embodiment and symbolic focus of Burmese
values continues. The popular ceremonial and ritual activities
with the monk as their focus continue to provide the laity with a
means of religious expression while at the same time providing
the mechanism for the fulfillment of other social needs -- an important one being the sense of social integration in the villages in
spite of the political struggles which sometimes surround them.

REFERENCES CITED

Bigandet, Rt. Rev. P.

1911   The Life or Legend of Gautama: The Buddha of the
            Burmese, Trubner's Oriental Series, 4th ed.
            London, Kegan, Paul, Trench, Trubner.

Brohm, John F.

1952   "The Function of Basic Religious Roles in Burmese
            Culture, " unpublished master's thesis, Cornell
            University.

Conze, Edward

1951   Buddhism, New York, Philosophical Library.

Scott, Sir James George (Shway Yoe)

   1910   The Burman: His Life and Notions, London, Macmillan.

Slater, Robert Lawson

   1951   Paradox and Nirvana, Chicago, University of Chicago Press.

Temple, Sir R. C.

   1906   The Thirty-Seven Nats, London, W. Griggs.

RITUAL AND CEREMONIAL CYCLE IN UPPER BURMA*

Manning Nash

University of Chicago

A ritual and ceremonial cycle is the temporal enactment of the
meaning and impact of the religious sphere in the lives of members
of a society. Ritual complexes have, like other cultural subsys-
tems, their own inner structure and coherence. The patterning of
ritual activity is not well understood in contemporary social anthropology, and exploratory research and rather bold conceptualization
is the order of the day. It is my contention that ritual and ceremonial activity is structured along three axes. These axes are
chosen because they order the material I have collected in Upper
Burma, but beyond that they appear to reflect the actual dimensions
of choice as people seek to strike a balance between the demands of
everyday life and the imperatives implicit in their religious system.
It is obvious that the decision to use these axes as the grid for ordering ritual and ceremonial activity is somewhat arbitrary, but I
attempt to transcend the level of "content analysis." My aim is to
provide a way toward a series of generalizations to account for the
formal properties of a ritual cycle. My point of departure is that
ritual activity is always oriented to some point along the following
three continua:

1. communal versus individual or familial ritual
2. remote and ultimate benefits versus immediate crisis
   handling
3. laity versus specialist as ritual custodian or performer.

Next I assume that societies will vary as to the point of balance
along the continua and that this variation is the fact of ritual activity which is worthy -- and susceptible -- of generalized explanation.
Finally, I would derive the explanation of the structure of the ritual
cycle from three other aspects of organized social life:

1. the ecological and economic setting
2. the concrete units of social organization
3. the authority pattern in the family and political spheres.

Let me be explicit as to what I am about. I mean to order the
ritual cycle along three axes which I take to be the inherent lines
of structure. These axes are inherent because society and culture

---

* I am indebted to the National Science Foundation for supporting
the field work in 1960-61 on which this paper is based.

are differentiated systems and because a balance of some sort
must be struck among the whole realm of activity patterns. The
placement of each society along the continua is determined by its
ecological and economic organization, the actual constitution of
human groups in the society, and the distribution of authority in
the family and political system. The analytic yield from this perspective is to present a method of systematic comparison among
ritual cycles, to categorize the cycles into nonoverlapping types,
and to assess concomitant variation between kinds of ritual cycles
and the aspects of social and cultural systems outlined above.
This venture is ambitious and beyond the abilities of a single investigator, but a start can be made.

II

        The ritual and ceremonial cycle here presented comes from
two communities in the Sagaing district in Upper Burma: Yadaw,
a predominantly irrigated rice growing village about seven miles
south of Mandalay, and Nondwin, a mixed dry crop village about
forty miles southwest of Mandalay. These two communities are
representative of the major ecological and economic types in the
Upper Burma area. There are other kinds of villages, like the
artisan community of Thabeiktan, or the keba villages near Mandalay, or the areca nut and fruit growing communities near
Myingyan, but these villages are atypical and their particular
specializations often appear explicable on historical grounds, e. g.
the begging bowl village of Thabeiktan is a result of a royal order
grouping all makers of begging bowls into a single community and
the keba villages derive from the hereditary status of the outcaste
mein. In any case the existence of other type villages does not
materially affect the analysis here offered, nor does it modify the
status of Nondwin and Yadaw as typical of the major ecological and
economic adjustments from the 40" isohyet to the hills north of
Katha.

        My description of the ritual and ceremonial cycle is not differ-
entiated by village unless noted (see ritual "wheel" for a graphic
comparison). The basic pattern is similar, and the slight variations in performance or in occurrence will be pointed out. I shall
begin with the first month of the Burmese year, Tagu. Burmese
months only roughly correspond with those in the Western calendar
since the Burmese month is lunar, made up of approximately
thirty days. Tagu falls sometime in the months of April and May
but does not begin on the same day each year. I start with the
calendrical rituals, i. e. those that are spaced out through the
solar year, to give a framework of the basic ritual rhythm, and
then I shall give a summary of the rituals that are tied not to the

RITUAL CYCLE OF TWO VILLAGES IN UPPER BURMA

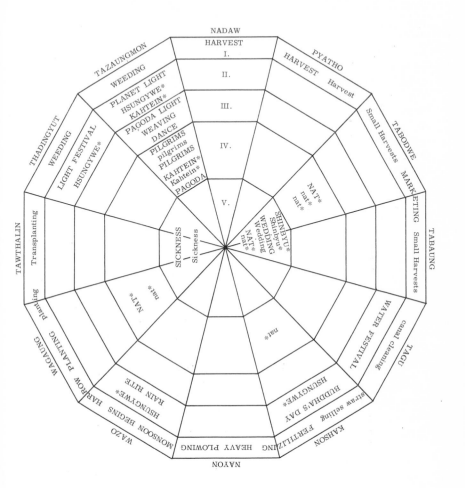

LEGEND:

RING I. AGRICULTURAL CYCLE (HARVEST = BOTH
VILLAGES, Harvest = Nondwin, harvest =
Yadaw)

RING II. COMMUNAL FESTIVAL IN BOTH VILLAGES

RING III. COMMUNAL RITE (HSUNGYWE = NONDWIN,
Hsungywe = Yadaw)

RING IV. INDIVIDUAL, CALENDRICAL (UPPER CASE
= NONDWIN, lower case = Yadaw)

RING V. INDIVIDUAL, CRISIS (UPPER CASE = NONDWIN,
lower case = Yadaw)

* Specialist involved.

calendar but to personal or communal events, and finally I shall
try to say how and in what ways these two rhythms are related.

Thingyan starts off the Burmese year. This is the water festival and extends over a three-day period during which what little
work might normally be done at this time of year is suspended. It
is a villagewide festival, but individuals and families celebrate it.
No religious specialists are involved, and the religious ends sought
are vague. For a villager, Thingyan has two meanings. It is, first,
the closing of the old year, symbolized by such acts as washing
one's hair to get last year's dust out, changing to fresh clothing,
sweeping out the house, and cleaning the grounds -- in other words,
a general cleaning up of the dirt of last year so that one may enter
the new year "fresh." The second meaning relates to the aged and
is expressed by the bringing of scented water to elders. This is
an act of kindness and a reinforcement of the general principle of
age respect. Especially are grandparents to be offered cool water
to drink and sprinkled with cool scented water. Age respect is
observed in the usual shikko (a bowing, sometimes with forehead
to the earth, which younger people perform before respected seniors just as laymen do before monks). Among young age mates,
Thingyan is a frolic of water splashing unencumbered by the double
meaning for older villagers of washing away last year's dirt and
paying respect to the aged.

Following New Year's is the main day of the Buddhist year.
Kahson labyi (the full moon of Kahson) is the day commemorating
the major events in the life of the Buddha: birth, enlightenment,
first sermon, death, ascension into the upper world, and revela-
tions on the way to nirvana. This is the Buddha's day, celebrated
in the village by watering the base of a banyan tree, the Burmese
version of the Bo tree under which Buddha reached perfect understanding of the meaning of evil and how to overcome it. People
drift out individually to the banyan tree at the edge of the village
(both these villages in fact have the banyan tree planted near their
entrances) and with pots of water pour some water at the base of
the tree. Nothing is said, nothing invoked, the gesture is informal,
the setting relaxed and unstructured. No monks are needed, though
monks from the village kyaung (temple school) may come by and
also water the banyan tree. This is an early morning rite. Later
in the day the monks will be fed. The village, as a whole, will prepare a meal for the monks from several nearby kyaungs. The
monks invited will come and eat in a prominent man's compound
(in Nondwin) or in the space near the dhammayone (in Yadaw).
This hsungywè (the giving of foods to monks) is communal. Most
of the villagers will come and drink tea and eat sweets, pickled
tea, fried beans or the other usual Burmese delicacies. The
meaning of monk feeding is certainly clear: the earning of merit

(kutho). Everybody in the village earns merit by contributing to
the feeding of the monks. Kutho is earned chiefly by giving, although the keeping of the precepts and the taking of extra precepts
on duty days also means merit. Merit is accumulated to better an
individual's kan, the nucleus of whatever it is that goes from existence to existence. A person has good or strong kan or bad and
weak kan. The goodness or badness of a person's kan is the resultant of all the merit and demerit he has accumulated in the countless existences through which he has passed. The state of one's
kan, his moral balance in terms of accumulated kutho and akutho
(demerit), determines the condition and place of the next corporeal
embodiment. The strength or weakness of the person's kan determines (along with the notions of intelligence and industry) what he
is able to accomplish in this particular existence.

Feeding a monk is a ceremony that gives a substantial increment of kutho, for in the hierarchy of kutho or merit making activities feeding a monk ranks just after giving a bell to a pagoda and
is much more meritorious than feeding a beggar, a nun, a stranger,
a friend, or a relative. Giving, and especially to monks and monasteries or pagodas, is the major means of making merit. So the
ceremony on the Buddha's day is a communal rite requiring the
presence of monks and is oriented toward the ultimate end of inch-
ing one's way toward a favorable rebirth and eventually to freedom
from the wheel of never ceasing birth and death. The themes of
the Buddha's day -- giving, food, water, age respect, kutho, and
building kan -- are the recurrent elements in all communal rituals
requiring the presence or participation of members of the monkhood.

There are seven obligatory times to give hsungywe, i. e. to
feed the monks by invitation: the full moon of Kahson, the beginning of Wa (full moon of Wazo which starts the season of special
religious performance analogous to "lent"), the ending of the Wa
season in Thadingyut, the lighting feast of Tazaungmon, during
Thingyan, seven days after a death, and on the anniversary day of
a death. In addition to the obligatory times for giving food to
monks, many villagers will invite monks for a morning meal before embarking on a long journey, on birthdays, or as a commem-
oration of any other event considered important.

Three days before Kahson labyi, in Yadaw, the village nat
ceremony was celebrated. At the south end of the village is a
simple wooden and bamboo structure within which are some flowers in a chipped vase. This is the nat shrine. It goes unattended
and unnoticed throughout the year though the flowers are changed
from time to time by the natkadaw (lit. nat's wife, a woman who
has been at one time possessed by the spirit and is now married

to him in a mystical union which permits the nat to enter her body
and speak through her). The ceremony of the village nat takes
place just outside the fence of Yadaw. It is organized by the natkadaws, who in this region have an informal organization. The
two women of Yadaw who are natkadaws (though not of the village
nat) get in touch with some other natkadaws they know, for they
have danced as nat wives at other nat rites, and these women tell
some of their friends. All told, twelve natkadaws from six villages and the city of Mandalay were involved. A Mandalay orchestra, invited to provide the music, is paid by the onlookers for playing certain tunes and so earns whatever the crowd offers. In addition to the nat women dancers there are two men from the village
who act as nat "guardians." The nat wives, the guardians, and
any of the onlookers (both from the village and from other communities) may, if so moved, dance to the music of the band. The band
plays the 37 stock nat tunes, one for each of the 37 "official" nats
recognized during the Pagan dynasty.

The dancing is performed in front of a series of nat images.
All of the natkadaws bring at least one nat image, a small wooden
carved figure of their particular nat. The images are lined up in
a small bamboo and wood structure built for the performance.
From time to time some of the images are addressed. The language is always the honorific special language used in addressing
pongyis (monks). The nats are offered food, bits of cooked rice,
and curry, just like the cooked food offered to monks (but not to
nuns or beggars, or to the strange poor, who must get uncooked
rice, a lower category of offering). The nat of the day was offered
a silk turban by the natkadaw from Yadaw. The whole ceremony is
marked by one of respect for the nat (manifested by the language
and the food and turban offering) and a spirit of "warding off" evil.
This nat, like others, can do no positive good but remains a potential source of trouble and calamity. The respect and food eases
the touchy pride and spite out of which nats maliciously interfere
in human affairs. The dancing and music, the devotion of the natkadaw, and the contributions of the bystanders serve to placate the
nat, who after this ceremony contracts to abstain from harming
those who have paid their respects. In this particular ceremony
two things that I have seen happen at other nat ceremonies did not
occur. At some nat ceremonies the natkadaws get possessed by
the nat and begin to predict the future for those of the crowd who
ask them. For this they are paid, and those who regularly follow
the regional round of nat festivals sometimes make a fairly good
income. Another occurrence is that a dancer who is just paying
respects may be chosen by the nat to be a natkadaw. These women
are seized but become dizzy and virtually faint, for unlike the natkadaw they are not prepared to receive, nor do they know how to
handle, the nat force when it enters them. The description of a

natpwe (nat ritual), truncated as it is here, serves as a model for all that I have seen or have had described to me. The essential features are clear, however much more they are elaborated in the huge natpwes for Taungbyon brothers and other important nats. The natpwe is a relation between individuals and a powerful spirit, a spirit with a capacity for evildoing and mischief. Respect and food offering indicate the relative power between mortals and nats. Dance, music, and women placate a capricious spirit. The ends sought are avoidance of whatever evil the particular nat is able to inflict. The ends are then immediate avoidance of crisis, and the specialists -- natkadaws - serve as a media to localize and focus the attention of the nat so that he may see and note who it is that pays him homage and is mindful of his wrath. In a village like Yadaw only about half the population pay much attention to the village nat, but that is deceptive for in every household at least one member gives at least five pyas for one of the nat tunes. It is a small hedge against malevolent fate and even the scoffers (there are some) say it is a small thing to give the nat a little honor.

The next month, Nayon (roughly June-July), is not marked by any calendrical ritual. It usually is the month of heavy plowing and there is a plausible fit between the demands of breaking new ground and the work in the fields and the absence of a calendrically fixed ritual obligation. The next month, Wazo, marks the beginning of the special religious time of year, called Wa, tied to a period of the Buddha's life. Wa is a three-month period of suspension of sensual and secular appetites. No marriage, no pwes, no shinbyus, no races, and no ordinations are countenanced during the Wa period. Wa, in Upper Burma, coincides with the rainy season, and the general suspension corresponds with a time of reduced ability to travel and some small but continual agricultural tasks like weeding, harrowing, planting, and irrigation canal cleaning.

If the monsoon does not break by the beginning of Wa, there is a special rain-inducing rite. This is a nat ceremony for nats of the upper category. These are the devas in the nat country of the hierarchy of the levels of existence, sometimes referred to as the "Buddha's nats" to distinguish them from the lower nats, most of whom were historic personages who met unfortunate ends through struggles over power and honor. The nat in charge of rain is called, simply enough, Mo Nattha (mou nat tha, the rain nat). The themes of food, sex, deference, and placation, however, mark the rite for this upper nat just as strongly as they do for the so-called lower nats. With a late breaking rain, the men of the village gather on one side and the women on the other for a tug of war. The two sides pull on a rope until one side is dragged off its feet. It is an earnest pull, and both sides try. The opposition between the sexes is to remind the nat that water is needed for

earth fertility and that human fertility is dependent on earth. I
leave the appropriateness of the tug of war, the notion of sexual
conquest, the relation of water to fertility, and the linking of earth
and human fecundity as symbols to the Freudians and only remark
that these linkages are at the manifest level of Burmese conversation. This rite is communal, immediate, and without the utilization of specialists. Although a gadawbwè (the ritual offering of
banana and coconut arranged in a tree form) is given to the nat,
and some cooked rice is offered, monks are not necessary to this
rite.

During the remaining two months of Wa there is only one calendrically fixed ritual, and that does not belong to either village but
is regional and almost national -- the festival of Taungbyon nats.
As this is elsewhere well described, I will note merely that individuals and families from the villages make the pilgrimage to the
site of the Taungbyon images and nat shrines, which are permanent elaborate stone and wood shrines and monuments. The whole
affair is a magnified attempt to placate and revere an especially
powerful pair of potential evildoers, who have a sort of nat suzerainty over Upper Burma.

Wa itself is introduced by a hsungywè. A communal feeding
of the monks is undertaken with the usual structure of monk feed-
ings: cooked food, honorific language, ultimate ends of kutho,
giving, and the presence of specialists to make the giving carry
weight in the building of kan. This hsungywè is important, for the
monks will stay close to their kyaungs during the rest of the Wa
season, precluding another formal hsungywè.

Wa ends as it began, with a feeding of the monks, again communitywide. Monks throughout the region receive invitations from
villages and must choose where they will dine. With the end of Wa,
the months of Thadingyut and Tazaungmon (October and November,
roughly) are the most crowded ritual months, both as to calendrical and noncalendrical ritual. Thadingyut is the festival of the
lights; it marks the end of the Wa period and commemorates the
ascension of the Buddha to the level of the nat world, where his
mother awaits him. The Buddha ascends to a small pagoda, Hsule
Mani Hpaya, in the nat world. In the villages, paper lanterns with
lighted candles are freed to soar into space to light the Buddha's
way. Individuals may invite monks. The lightheartedness of the
light festival may be judged by the frequency with which villagers
told me that the lanterns they were sending heavenward were
"Burmese sputniks." But, in a more serious vein, they do not
think that they are actually lighting the Buddha's way, for he is
remote; it is merely commemorative and re-evokes gratitude for
the great gift of the Buddha's teaching.

In early October most Nondwin people, and a few from Yadaw, take pilgrimages. Leading in popularity is the pilgrimage to the famed Thanbotte pagoda. At Thanbotte there is a large fair, a kind of donnybrook with sellers lining the entrances and grounds of the pagoda, with the usual array of begging lepers clogging the approaches, and with that mixture of noise, gaiety, children, and dust that attends a pagoda celebration. The purpose of the trip is to pay respects at a pagoda which is famous. It is individual, for otherworldly ends, and monks are like laymen here: both come to perform their own particular devotions. At the pagoda a villager will stop at any of the special places and recite whatever devotions he wishes. The atmosphere is extremely informal. When some are engaged in meditation or devotion, others talk, chew betel, smoke, spit, or walk around. Each devotee is able to abstract himself from the immediate context and arrange himself for devotion, apart from whatever others are doing or not doing. Another pilgrimage is to a place in a crest of hills about four miles from Nondwin, where there is supposed to be a footprint of the Buddha. There is indeed a depression in stone about eight feet long and one foot wide which, with the proper imagination, can be seen as the imprint of a giant human-like foot. Villagers individually come, look, eat, and return. It is a picnic.

The last days of October are the time for the Kahtein, the ceremony in which the monk is presented with his eight necessities. In both villages there is a communal Kahtein, and many of the richer households have, in addition, individual Kahtein. In the communal Kahtein many monks are fed at the invitation of the village and the arrangements involve a great display. All of the things that will be given to the monks are fixed up in various forms -- spread out on bamboo mats, pinned to wooden trees, tied to bamboo poles, or heaped on flowerpots. The point is to make a splendid display of all the things in a single place. More than the eight monastic requirements are always given -- blankets, towels, tumblers are included, and the money tree is omnipresent. To make a money tree the villagers stand a stick in a flowerpot, tie fans or other sticks to the "trunk" as branches, and then pin on kyat notes. The Kahtein goods are sometimes displayed for as long as a week before the monks actually receive them. The Kahtein thus has a feature common to all villagewide ceremonies -- display. In many ways the ceremonial aspects of village culture are oriented toward the making of facade. It is the front, the immediate impact, which counts for the villager. The ends are remote but the rewards are a display of gilt, a heaping of food, an assembly of people, a fleeting sense of dominance and abundance, and great hope for kutho building.

At the beginning of Tazaungmon there is another lighting festi-

val. In both villages, individuals come and place lights on a local
pagoda and devotional groups come to the pagodas to recite the
standard formulary -- awgatha, Triple Jewel, one or two thok,
and the taking of the five precepts. This is individual, ultimate,
and nonspecialist ritual. In Nondwin, whose social structure is
more integrated and of longer duration than Yadaw's and where the
political and power situation is cleanly and neatly defined, there
are also two Buddhist organizations. One is a young men's Buddhist group which, under the aegis of a rich, retired storekeeper-
farmer-cotton broker, acts as the alms collecting group for the
Kahtein and which sometimes sends dancers to other pagoda festivals. The other is a Buddhist devotional group, chiefly of young
and unmarried girls, who meet nightly for recitations. In Yadaw,
by contrast, there is only an informal organization of older persons, one of whom, acting as the Neikban pointer, leads frequent
nightly devotions in the village dhammayone. In Nondwin the two
devotional groups turn up at the pagoda and light candles before a
Buddha image; Yadaw has no equivalent.

One of the richer families in Nondwin decided to put 50 kyats'
worth of candles on the pagoda for the light festival of Tazaungmon.
The family was assisted by members of their kindred and by the
two youth devotional groups. This was then an individual ritual,
modified by calling on some corporate elements. Specialists were
not employed.

On the day of Tazaungmon, many people from the region go to
the hills near Sagaing to visit the cluster of famous and revered
pagodas which overlook the Irrawaddy near the Ava bridge span.
I do not know whether distance or devotion accounts for the fact
that there are always more people from Nondwin than from Yadaw.

In Nondwin, on the night of the full moon in Tazaungmon, the
matho yetchin, or matho thingan, ceremony is held. This night
when the lights of candles are put on local pagodas is an astrologically important one, being in popular belief the time that all the
planets form a straight line across the heavens, an auspicious
occurrence that calls for lighting up. No connection (at least none
that I could discover) was made between the lighting done for the
Buddha and the lighting done for the planets. Buddha lighting gives
a small increment of kutho; planet lighting helps in a very slight
way to assure favorable astrological dispositions.

But the main effort of Nondwin is the matho yetchin ceremony
to make a monk's robe in one day, i.e. before the dawn of the next
day, which accounts for the term matho, the "early" robe. A
mock planting, harrowing, tree growing, cotton plucking, and gin-
ning of cotton is done in the afternoon. That evening cotton is

brought to a large compound and about thirty girls work on spinning wheels and a large loom. Firelight and a pressure lantern
provide illumination as the girls take turns spinning and running
the loom. Every household with an unmarried girl sends at least
one representative. These girls may range in age between thirteen
and twenty, though at the ceremony I watched most were fourteen
or fifteen. The elders of the community participate by watching,
by providing pickled tea for the weavers and spinners (this is supposed to keep one awake), and by tea drinking. A few boys attend
the amplifier which blares music from old records. Everybody
involved earns some kutho, and this kutho has a "territorial" aspect. Even though kutho is, in the last analysis, something that
accrues to an individual, there is the belief that those who share
in kutho-getting activities may be reunited in the next incarnation.
Families, neighbors, villagers, and friends come together as kutho
groups in events like this, and the more often they earn kutho together the likelier it is that they will be on the same level of existence in their next rebirth and even in close spatial proximity.
But this territorial kutho and the notion of a kutho group is ritually
and in belief a minor theme compared to the individual getting
kutho for his passage along the chain of existence.

In both villages a communal monk feeding was carried out.
Nondwin also had several private Kahtein; Yadaw had only one.
Two days after the early-robe ceremony, the villagers of Nondwin
sent a dance team to a nearby (Legyi) pagoda dedication. The hti
(umbrella) was hoisted on the Legyi pagoda and costumed dancers
from nearby villages came to celebrate. Yadaw does not have an
organization of dancers and is not accustomed to sending delega-
tions to such celebrations.

Nondwin's local pagoda ceremony fell just after the middle of
Tazaungmon. The pagoda festival entails the feeding of monks and
the presentation of gadawbwes before the pagoda. One family, the
lineal descendant of the builder of the pagoda, has the special privilege, if it so wishes, of making all the food and gadawbwe contributions. The present family members, the fourth and fifth generation from the founder of the pagoda, in 1960 elected to apportion
the contributions to the local pagoda festival among the whole village. It is always a communal affair since the descendants are
the custodians of the pagoda, not the owners of the ritual, which
is a communal hsungywè. The burdens of the food and other offerings were apportioned by ability to pay, i.e. the four classes of
food gifts, varying in expense, were assigned along a rough division representing four levels of wealth. Every household was included, the burden being apportioned by household -- the concrete
co-resident group with a single domestic economy -- not by family. So far as I have data, the family is never an organizational

unit, whatever it may be as a sentimental or socialization entity.
The strict inclusion of every household in communal food giving is
a striking feature of all village rites and ceremonies. No one is
ever excluded; communal efforts require and get the participation
of everyone. Communal efforts tend to be toward the ultimate
goal of individual kutho, with a minor component of what I have
earlier called territorial kutho, and to require the presence of religious specialists.

The intensified rhythm of rite and ceremony after Thadingyut
plays itself out in two months. In both villages there is a great
slackening during December and January when heavy harvest work
keeps men and women in the fields most of the time. It is a period
of labor shortage in the village, or more accurately intensive labor
use, and extensive rituals organizing more than a couple of households is virtually ruled out by the sheer physical demands of the
agricultural pattern. Only private, individual crisis rites are
carried out. (I reserve description of the major crisis rites until
the calendrical or annual cycle is completed.)

After the height of the harvest season in December and January, the postponed weddings and shinbyus take place. February
and March are also the months in which most of the activity of
placating the inherited mizaing and hpazaing nats occurs. The only
harvest festival is a minor one propitiating the tract nat at the desire of the individual cultivator. In Yadaw this takes the form of
a first-fruit offering and in Nondwin offerings may be made in the
field. This rite is payment to the tract nat, spiritual protector of
the land, for the suspension of troubles which could have interfered
with the harvest. Yadaw, the rice community, has a rite found
only in communities growing significant amounts of paddy: propitiation of the Bomagyi or Bonagyi nat. When rice is placed in the
godown (storeroom), a food offering is made to Bomagyi so that
the stored rice will not diminish in the godown. The offering is
sweet rice cakes, or fried rice cakes, sometimes supplemented
with thanahka, a comb, or a mirror. A natkadaw is often hired
to do this placing of the offering in the godown in the early morning
of Bomagyi's day. Many cultivators, even in Yadaw, even those
with rice in the godown, do not perform this ritual, so it must be
considered individual rather than universal. Another rite connected
with the rice harvest and common to both villages is the passing
out of sticky rice cakes to neighbors. This is a first-fruit rite,
done because one wishes his neighbors to share in the good fortune.

A wedding is a simple enough rite, joining man and woman
under the eyes of the villagers, who are fed at least tea and cakes,
and with the consent of the village elders, whose presence ratifies
the union. The chief aim is publicity, an announcement of the

formation of a new bond.

Here I sketch very briefly the sequence of events in a shinbyu
observed in Yadaw, one which was similar to other shinbyus I
have seen. This ceremony for making a novice is by far to be
preferred over the simple, undramatic, less publicized way in
which a boy is just taken to a kyaung, chanted over, shaved, robed,
and accepted as a temporary member of the monastic community.
The shinbyu takes place in a specially rigged temporary shelter, a
mandat, with cardboard gilt exterior and an interior to simulate a
palace. The whole shinbyu, "the making of a lord, " is of course
based on the renunciation episode in the Buddha's life, and the
young boys are treated as though they were in fact royalty. The
mandat has been built, like all Upper Burmese structures temporary or not, by first placing a special nat pole adorned with flowers
and leaving that for several days before the rest of the structure
is put up. The day for putting up the nat pole is set astrologically
according to the birthday of the sponsor of the shinbyu. A monk is
usually consulted for this astrological data though the pongyi is but
one of a number of astrological specialists. Food is a prominent
feature, and all guests entering the mandat for tea and cakes are
greeted at the entrance by girls handing out cigars and the flower
of prosperity. These girls dress for the occasion by adding a
hairpiece, which is worn in a style reserved for shinbyus and weddings (other than their own). The shinbyu is conducted by a special
sort of master of ceremonies, beiktheik hsaya, who places the anti-
witchcraft string around the necks of the shinlaungs, makes food
offerings to the upper nats (and to the mizaing-hpazaing nats in the
Patheingyi region according to June Nash, see below) of rice, fried
fish, red and white cakes, and the gadawbwe. The Buddha is
praised, then the shins and their sponsors. There follows a re-
partee with the orchestra which gives a traditional sort of Burmese
history. Next a conch shell and water are used to play the tune of
Asoka, the manifest meaning being blessing and fertility. The village and the people attending are compared to the mythical past
times of better mortals, greater prosperity, and sounder morality.
The Buddha is called on to be a witness. The master of ceremonies
sprinkles water over the boys, and the girls who will have their
ears bored by the beiktheik hsaya. Then the company and the upper
nats, the village guardian nat, the tract nat, and the inherited
mizaing and hpazaing are invited to eat. The monks eat, seated
on a dais, with the laity eating below them. The monks then shave
the heads of the koyings, and there is the water-blessing ceremony.
Next a verse is read by the monks to drive away evil spirits and to
call on upper nats and lower nats to take heed. The gaily decked
shins ride to the monastery on noble steeds, the band plays, the
villagers and guests line the roads. After circling the monastery
three times, the boys enter and become members of the order.

Next day they will receive their order names and begin the round
of monastic life.

So far I have stuck to the calendrical ritual, giving little
attention to the diurnal and weekly rites. Daily rituals are presentation of food to the monks on their begging round, the taking
of the precepts before a Buddha altar (which may or may not have
an image), providing food for the birds and crawling creatures,
and the offering of food on the altar or special spot. Weekly ritual
is confined to the pre-duty and duty days. (These fall on the four
phases of the moon. Duty days are the eighth and fifteenth day in
the Burmese lunar month, whose days are numbered in two cycles
of fifteen. Pre-duty days are the days preceding the moon phase.)
On pre-duty day the nuns come for their uncooked food. On duty
day some people go to the kyaung to take the eight precepts. As a
rule it is only the older people who regularly take the eight precepts; my censuses in the two villages show that four times a year
for adults in the twenty to fifty age group is modal. Part of the
ritual each villager does is the counting of the beads to the repeti-
tion of aneiksa dokhka anatta (change, suffering, noself) at least
once in the morning and once in the evening. Two minor nat celebrations complete the time-tied ritual for these two villages.

Many crisis rituals center about events in the life cycle. Birth
requires the separation of the pregnant woman from the household.
A separate temporary structure is built for her in the west or south
part of the house or compound. (Direction is important in almost
all Burmese ritual: north and east are auspicious (mingala), south
and west inauspicious. Hence unclean, defiling, or unsettling activities have their locus in the inauspicious directions -- birth,
death, sex relations, and cooking are oriented south and west;
Buddha altars, nat shrines, shinbyus, honored guests, monk seating are north and east.) She is "roasted" after birth over hot
stones and the afterbirth buried to the south of the house. An
astrologer is called in to cast the horoscope of the newborn, whose
exact minute of arrival has been noted. There is a naming ceremony, with token food distribution to elders and neighbors. This
occurs any time after the first month but usually within three
months after birth. There is a first-time-in-the-cradle ceremony,
again with token food for neighbors and relatives. Other life cycle
events are touched on later in this paper.

The most compelling crisis rite is that of death. When a Burmese dies, the whole village is implicated. Death is an unclean
event, putting the whole community in a delicate state. If a villager dies outside his village, he cannot be brought in for burial,
for that would contaminate the entire village. But if he dies in the
village (and is not a monk, for monks are cremated), the body is

washed and prepared for burial. It is put in a coffin with 15 pyas
to pay the ferry fare across the river that divides the world of the
living from the dead. The body is carried to a cemetery outside
the village and put in a hole where other remains are moved
around to make room for it. No stone or other marker is erected.
The cemetery is a patch of unkept ground, a place to avoid, to forget about, not to keep up or make attractive. Returning from the
cemetery, the burial party stops at a zayat outside the village to
hear a sermon by the monks, who expound the transitory nature of
life, the whirl of birth and rebirth, and the rightness of the middle
way. At the edge of the village the burial party and other mourners
close a path so that the soul of the departed will not come back into
the village. For seven days somebody must be awake at all times
in the house of the deceased, both to keep the departed's soul from
reentering and to keep the relatives of the dead person from being
alone and hence mournful. Food, tea, and condiments are available at all times during the seven days, and each household in the
village sends at least one member to sit with the bereaved. To
pass the nights, men sit and gamble at cards or the Burmese version of dominoes. The soul that must make the transfer is the
leikpya (butterfly) soul, which comes out with the breath and is a
sort of animating spirit. How it fits with what is reborn is a problem the villager does not feel called on to solve. The soul of the
dead person is in peril for a seven-day period during which the
community effort guides it toward where it should go. After seven
days the village returns to normal.

What I have called crisis ritual is tied to sickness, to special
venture, to fear of bewitchment, to protection against malevolent
influences, to death, to birth, and to exposure to the perils of
travel. The incidence of these rites is widely varied and tied in
many ways to the local household group, but this needs microanaly-
sis which is not germane here. The ingredients of crisis ritual
are these: planetary power, Buddhist power embodied in the monk
or in the scripture, and the inherent power of objects like mercury
balls, tattoos, amulets, and medicines. The important thing about
crisis ritual is the technological feel of it. All powers that affect
daily life can be overcome or at least placated by other sets of
powers in the proper combination, and it is a technological skill:
find the expert who knows how and the crisis is solved. This expert may be a monk, a hse hsaya, an astrologer, a witch expert,
a natkadaw, or a knowledgeable layman. It is strictly a client-
patron relationship, but sometimes it requires a change of state of
the actor or a bringing forth of the strong parts of his kan. Meditation is also a device for overcoming evil and placating spirits.
It is a bit aphoristic but basically true to say that in crisis the
Upper Burman tries everything until he gets cured or leaves the
world. Description is here stinted, only to note that monks are

necessary in death ritual but are not necessarily the ones who call
the leikpya or butterfly soul. The magical elements built into
ordinary Buddhism -- like stone lifting, or instant kan by setting
animals free, or certain verses to banish minor spirits from green
deaths -- are all taken to be part of the whole Buddhist complex
and not separated out in the hands of specialists as are other parts
of the technology of the sacred.

III

How does the description of the ceremonial cycle of two villages in Upper Burma bear on my earlier assertions? First the
essentials of the ritual cycle must be sketched in broad strokes.
The two communities have in common a basic opposition in the
ritual sphere -- a dichotomy between communal rites in the hands
of specialists oriented toward ultimate ends and individual rites in
the hands of nonspecialists for immediate ends. The dichotomy is
analytical; it is my thematic separation. In empirical fact, however, the two sorts of rituals rarely overlap in time, space, or
personnel. They come together, sometimes, as stages of a ritual.
The shinbyu exemplifies this. The shinbyu is a ritual oriented
chiefly toward the ultimate end of favorable rebirth (both for the
novice entering the monkhood and the donors who get kutho). A
monk or many monks are necessary, and although it is a family or
household affair the whole village gets involved, as well as those
invited from the village network of intervillage relations. As a
rite, it belongs squarely on the communal-specialists-ultimate
ends side of the category division. Yet, before the rite can take
place, the nat pole must be put up and the nats propitiated, just as
the master of ceremonies offers food to the nats before the monks
come so that the nats will suspend any evil they might inflict. So,
in daily life, the immediate and the ultimate, the individual and
the communal, the specialist and nonspecialist rite, are in constant
interplay. Nonetheless, the category division is an important principle of ritual organization, and it can be, and is, sometimes,
articulated by villagers themselves.

Another striking dimension of characterization is the relation
of obligatory ritual to social structure. None of the obligatory,
calendrical rituals can be organized at the household level. All of
them require at least villagewide participation, and they frequently
draw on special organizations in the village (like the lubyo and
aphyo groups) and on persons and resources beyond the village
level of organization. Being a Buddhist, participating in the ritual
cycle, and getting along with one's neighbors are but different
modes of expressing membership in a local society. The diagram
of the ritual cycle indicates that it is the communal, ultimate,

Buddhist-specialist ceremonies which are obligatory and which transcend local organization. These rites make a religious community out of the villages of Upper Burma; nat rites regionalize this community (in one dimension), make it village-structured, and finally personalize it.

The dichotomy in ritual is another way of saying that Upper Burma is a Buddhist community, but Buddhism does not deal with the local, the regional, and the personal in any effective, immediate manner. So, woven into Buddhism is a technology of the sacred -- nat worship. And it is between these two religious elements (I leave out other nonreligious predictive and divinatory systems like astrology, alchemy, and magical tattooing) that the dialectic of this world and the other world is played out. In a way, Upper Burma is an example of Durkheim's opposition between religion and magic, between a church and a collection of clients, but that kind of interpretation would overlook the more remarkable fact that it is the interplay of these oppositions that makes up the religious system rather than their opposition. Further, it is not the sharing of belief that makes the religious community but the other way around: the sharing of social relations is putative evidence of common beliefs. The concrete organization for all communal ritual includes everyone in the village through the mechanism of drawing at least one member from each household. The point need not be labored. The equation is: obligatory = communal. The expansion of that equation is: communal = Buddhist, Buddhist = member of society, member of society = social relations, and social relations = interaction. Hence, a villager may reason: it is those with whom I interact that I have continual social relations, and they will be members of my society; as members of my society they are Buddhist, and as Buddhists they will participate in the same rituals I do; so we have the same ritual obligations, and we may be reunited in the next incarnation. The opposite set of equations, or equivalances could be, of course, set out for nat practices.

What has been characterized is the general ritual framework of Upper Burma, but what of the differences between the villages? Nondwin (the mixed drycrop farming village) is, compared to Yadaw (the irrigated wet rice village), much heavier on communal rituals, has more individual and calendrical rites, and employs more specialists, both pongyis and natkadaws. These differences stem from the differences in political integration between the villages and from disparities in wealth levels. Nondwin is not broken into competing political factions but rather is united under the aegis of a powerful man -- a man of pon, charismatic power on the local level. Yadaw is bitterly divided into two political factions which compete for adherents. There is no man of pon, only claimants and pretenders. It is this fact of on-the-ground political organization (for in formal features the villages are identical, under a headman, a council, ten household heads, and the other function- aries to be found listed in the Village Organization Manual) which accounts for the fact that communal rites which are not obligatory, and could be organized as individual events, become villagewide in scope in Nondwin but are either absent or at the household level in Yadaw.

The greater use of specialists (who are costly, e. g. monks must be fed) is tied to the differences between the wealth of the two communities. Yadaw is poorer than Nondwin, essentially be- cause rice growers tend to carry heavier debt burdens than do farmers of mixed drycrop areas. To grow rice one needs hired labor, at least for transplanting which involves narrow time con- straints. Every rice farmer borrows money against his harvest and pays it back in harvested paddy. Chronic debt is the lot of these rice farmers, who cannot even benefit from market swings since the State Agricultural Board fixes the price of rice. In Nondwin, where crop diversity means there is usually some cash coming in from peanuts, cotton, sesamum, beans, or pulses, debt is less widespread and not so crushing (though at least half the households borrow money from time to time). Also there are richer men in Nondwin, who tend to use specialists where there is an option to do so.

The temporal spacing of ritual in the two communities is re- markably similar. Harvest time sees no communal rituals, since all the hands available are needed for the heavy agricultural tasks. But the incidence of heavy labor demand and the absence of com- munal ritual is not perfect. The smaller harvests in Nondwin can be interrupted for a nat festival, and canal cleaning falls at the time of the water festival in Yadaw. There is, outside of the in- tense period of transplanting, enough give in the use of labor and time to allow the rituals to fall almost anywhere in the agricultural year. That rituals are heaviest in October and November is of course due to Buddhist canon. This is the end of the Wa season, and the contained pressures stemming from the prohibitions of the sacred season are released. But the release comes at a time when people are lowest in their assets, i. e. in their stock of money and food, so that the costliest rituals -- the shinbyus and the weddings -- come after the major harvests. This is not because time is re- leased, but because income goes up. These rites tend to cluster in the two months after harvest and then gradually peter out.

In the overall temporal spacing there is almost an oscillation pattern between the Buddhist and nat festivals, and between the in- dividual and communal rites. However, it appears that individual and nat rituals are not fixed in any apparent pattern, nor do the villages differ significantly in this aspect.

The axes presented here do lead to a simple, straightforward classification of some formal properties of ritual cycles (as would many another set of axes). Their utility, beyond purposes of classification, is that they can be closely related to economic, ecological, political, and familial patterns in the society. It is the interaction of these classes of variables against a given religious tradition that accounts for the pacing, clustering, and participation of people in a ceremonial cycle.

LIVING WITH NATS: AN ANALYSIS OF ANIMISM IN BURMAN
VILLAGE SOCIAL RELATIONS

June C. Nash

Yale University

In Burma a system of beliefs in animistic spirits coexists within
the framework of Buddhist religion, and in the villages of Upper
Burma in which I studied[1] belief in spirits, or nats, is in fact a
complementary part of Buddhist belief, integrated in the daily and
seasonal religious ritual. The origin of the nats and the historical
situations giving rise to their belief has been the subject of inquiry
and speculation for several scholars of Burma. [2] In these analyses
the historical origins of the nats have been explored but no one has
raised the question of the persistence of the cult and its significance in the social structure of the village and region.

Here I shall examine the role of the nats, not as a distinct
category of experience, but as it affects everyday social relations.
This approach follows that of Simmel (1959: 11), who saw the immanent sources of religion in the relations of men to the world of
man, and of Firth (1959: 131), who defines religion as "a concern
of man in society with basic human ends and standards of value,
seen in relation to non-human entities or powers. " Through this
approach I hope to show (1) how the nat cult is perpetuated through
obligations inherited at the structural level of the family, village,
and region, (2) how the relationships between the nats and their
spirit relatives and spirit mediators link villages in a subsystem
of ritual and spiritual identification, and (3) how the adjustment of
these Burman villagers to the subsociety of nat spirits living among
them parallels the adjustments they make in ordinary human relationships and in interpreting catastrophic events. Finally I shall
show how, in the villages today, concern with soul crises is resolved in Buddhist ritual rather than in the development of new nat
cults.

Origins of the Nat Cult

There is no single definition of nats since the designation
covers a wide variety of distinct categories. The major division
that the villagers recognize is between the ahtet nats and the auk
nats, i. e. the upper and lower nats. The ahtet nats, who are big
nats awaiting Buddha in the sky, have no personalities or legends
associated with them in the Burmese villages. The ahtet nats
correspond to the dewas who figure in Hindu myth as the kings and
virtuous people who are rewarded with happiness in the six seats
of heaven (Scott 1927: 232). These spirits appear in the cosmology
of all Buddhist countries. The king of these nats is Thagya Min,

and the Burmese count their New Year from the day he descends
to earth, celebrating the occasion with their annual water festival.

The auk nats belong to a different order entirely, and the villagers never confuse the two. It is with this group only that this
paper is concerned. The auk nats include both named and unnamed
spirits drawn from indigenous pre-Buddhist cosmology as well as
from Hindu or other outside sources. The core of the nat cult is
the Thirty-Seven Lords, or Thirty-Seven Nats.

The leading figure in the cult of the Thirty-Seven Nats is Min-
Maha-Giri, or Einzaung Nat. This nat was officially recognized
by King Kyaungtha in an attempt to give symbolic unity to the Pagan
kingdom (Scott 1900: 20). The pantheon of Thirty-Seven Nats was
first officially recognized during King Anawrahta's reign about the
beginning of the eleventh century. In an attempt to establish Buddhism as the religion of his kingdom, King Anawrahta first tried
to suppress the cult but, failing that, took the images of thirty-six
nats worshiped in the Pagan kingdom and placed them in the compound of the Shwezigon pagoda. In order to regularize the cult,
Anawrahta established as the overlord Thagya Min, the Buddha nat.

Since that time the list has varied: some old nats have been
displaced by new and the personalities of later nats have become
merged with earlier. But the number of nats associated with the
cult of the Thirty-Seven Nats has not been changed (Htin 1956: 81).
Villagers differ in their account of what nats are to be included in
this list, and even specialists concerned with propitiating the nats
are not consistent. Most of the nats were legendary figures either
of royal blood, or associated with royalty, who died sudden and
tragic deaths (Htin 1956: 99). Their deaths were, in many instances, ordered by a king jealously guarding his throne against
real or imagined rivals. Major nat figures have associated with
them a cluster of relatives who died of sorrow or sacrificed themselves on the nat's death. Some of the nats were granted overlordship of certain regions by the reigning king and towns in these regions became the center of annual celebrations.

The landscape surrounding the village and cultivated fields is
alive with nats. Among these are the Earth Guardian, Bonmazo,
the paddy land owner, Ashingyi, and a host of spirits inhabiting
woods, mountains, streams, and rivers. Every large tree is occupied by the tree nat, Yokhkazo, and most of the village Burmans
show respect to Yokhkazo by removing their slippers when they
approach a large tree. The villagers honor the Rain Nat, Mogaung
Kyawzwè, during times of drought with a tug-of-war ritual. Mer-
chants offer flowers on their weighing scales to the nats concerned
with commerce (unnamed) before beginning the day's business.

When a Burman makes a trip beyond his own locality, he almost
always takes the precaution of placing a bunch of thabye leaves on
his cart, boat, or even his truck as offering to the nats who may
occupy the regions through which he travels.

Nat propitiation enters into every significant phase of the villagers' life. I shall explore below the occasions for these ceremonials and the different structural responsibilities involved in
the propitiation of the various categories of nats.

Household, Village, and Regional Nats

The responsibility for propitiating the nats is transmitted at
three distinct structural levels: the household, the village, and the
region. The household nats are selected from among the Thirty-
Seven Nats; those of the village may be one of the Thirty-Seven or
a local nat or even a "village nat" without name or personality;
the regional nats include any of the Thirty-Seven Nats who have
attained some eminence as well as those omnipresent nats of the
field or trees who are recognized throughout a wide area.

The Household Nat. In the crowded disorder of the Burmese
village house will be found, almost universally, a coconut slung
from the southeast pole of the house, in the upper level if it is two-
storied. This offering to the houseowner nat, or Min-Maha-Giri,
gives a sense of security to the houseowner, who looks upon him
as a guardian against thieves or unwanted spirits. Members of the
household are constantly aware of the presence of Min-Maha-Giri
in their house. When the house is being built, as soon as the
udaing or southeast corner pole is raised, [3] an offering of bananas
is made to Min-Maha-Giri, and 1.25 kyats (about 25 cents) is sometimes placed in the post hole by the carpenter in the name of the
owner. Min-Maha-Giri dislikes the presence of birth or death in
the house. Therefore, when a baby is born, the coconut which represents his presence is taken out of the house, disposed of, and
replaced with a new one after the New Year celebration of Thingyan.
Similarly, when a member of the household dies, the coconut is removed, sometimes hung in a tree in the compound, and replaced
after the seven-day period during which the house is thought to be
unclean. Even during a serious illness of a member of the family,
the coconut is removed in order not to offend the sensibilities of
the houseowner nat. Min-Maha-Giri is also offended by sexual
intercourse, and the houseowner usually will keep his bed far from
this pole if he is sexually active. Since Min-Maha-Giri was burned
to death while tied to a tree, he dislikes the sight of fire. If the
householder does not have a separate kitchen, he tries to locate
the hearth as far from the sight of the coconut as possible, and
some say that Min-Maha-Giri does not like the offering of cooked

food because of the association with fire.

Along with Min-Maha-Giri, every household offers to one or
more nats known as the mizaing-hpazaing. Mizaing refers to the
nat spirit inherited through the mother's matri-line, hpazaing to
the nat spirit inherited through the father's patri-line. The two
nouns used collectively refer to the Thirty-Seven Nats as a group,
from which personalities become the inherited responsibility of
the female lines of descent and of male lines of descent.

How the responsibility for nats originally became assigned to
certain families is unknown and no historical research has been
done in this area.[4] The mechanism for passing on the responsibility was, however, ascertained in the villages under study by
interviews and census.[5] Some say that women receive their nat
obligations from their mother, men from their father. Others say
that they received their nats from both parents. If this latter statement were true, there would be an accumulation of many nats for
each household. However, there are conditions which counteract
this tendency. In the first place, men and women from the same
village frequently have the same nat and each child would receive
just one. If the parents' nats differ, the woman's nat is the one
likely to be inherited. Women are more concerned than men about
the propitiation of the nats and are the ones who give all the food
offerings on all domestic occasions for all nats. Men are more
frequently serious Buddhist meditators, attending the pongyi
kyaungs or monasteries and maintaining the five precepts. This
activity sometimes gives them confidence that they can overcome
the power of the nats or leads them to cease believing in the nats'
power. The woman's nat is, in consequence, the one most attended
in the family, and the one most likely to be perpetuated.

Women make large ceremonial offerings to their own and to
their husband's nats once a year. Sometimes the offerings are
given simultaneously, sometimes the family may give a contribution to an elder female relative who knows better how to give the
offering. This contribution ranges from 25 pyas to one kyat (4
cents to 21 cents) and the elder relative calls the names of all who
have contributed as she makes the offering. It is the gift and not
the giver which is of importance to the nat. "The nat," said one
informant, "is interested only in the offering, not in the person
giving it." The amount of the offering is set by custom and the
nat may become insulted and cause trouble if the offering is short
of the traditional sum.[6] Women assume the responsibility for this
offering when their mother, on her deathbed, pleads with them to
carry on the propitiation or beware of the wrath of the nat.

At almost every life crisis, offerings are made to the mizaing-

hpazaing. Seven days after birth, a naming ceremony, called
kinbun tattè, is held. At this time a food offering is made for all
Thirty-Seven Nats of the mizaing-hpazaing, along with the nat or
nats which are the special responsibility of the house. Thus thirty-seven small fish are fried and offered along with, for example,
betel nut which the Taungbyon brothers favor if they are the
mizaing-hpazaing, or duck egg which Ma Nègale, the niece of
Min-Maha-Giri, likes if she is one of the mizaing-hpazaing, as
well as the red food and white food, monni and monbyu, which all
nats like. Relatives of the father and mother of the child are invited and actually consume the food first offered to the nats.

Before a wedding ceremony, the couple offer bananas and
pineapple to the mizaing-hpazaing at the bride's and the groom's
houses. This offering is similar to that made to the elders of both
the boy and the girl during the ceremony. The nat offering is essential, even if there is no other ceremony attending the marriage
of a couple. [7]

The household nat is not forgotten even at the shinbyu, the
initiation of boys into the Buddhist monastic order. For the shinbyu, which is a reenactment of the Buddha's own renunciation of
the material pleasures of life in taking on the robe of the mendi-
cant monk, the boy is dressed in rented silken clothing recalling
the elaborate robes of a royal prince of the past century and, to
complete the likeness, is rouged and powdered and decked out with
golden ornaments. Along with his male siblings or cousins, he
sits on velvet cushions before his parents, relatives, elders of
the village, and most of his own and neighboring villagers. Because of the elaborateness of the ceremony and the fact that the
children are the center of attention, parents fear the wrath of the
nats whose envy is so easily aroused. One woman commented,
"At the shinbyu, the mizaing-hpazaing will harm the children if
they are not offered something." Throughout the ceremony, three
large platters of bananas and coconuts remain in place before the
initiates -- one for the parents, one for the Buddha, and one for
the nats. The beiktheik hsaya, master of ceremonies hired for the
occasion, ties a white thread in the children's hair, asking that
the nats protect them. After making the offering of fruit to the
Buddha and to the elders, the beiktheik hsaya offers the red and
white food to the Thirty-Seven Nats. This is done so that they will
become guardians of the ceremony.

The offering to the nats at the very time that a child is introduced into the Buddhist order indicates the thorough penetration
of animism in Upper Burma village life. Some monks claim to
have raised objection to nat offerings at a shinbyu only to have the
village elders refuse to eliminate this part of the ceremony because

the parents would fear for their children.

When sickness strikes a member of the family, the villagers
suspect that they have aroused the anger of the household nats.
Certain ailments are typically caused by nats -- skin diseases,
sudden falls, madness. The housewife may confirm her suspicions
by going to one of the nat shrines and lifting the pwe shidè, the
fortune-telling stone placed before the nat: if the stone appears
heavy when lifted, the trouble is felt to be caused by the nat. She
may check the diagnosis by going to the hse hsaya (curer). In all
his consultations, the first question the hse hsaya asks is whether
the patient has kept up the offerings to the household nats. The
first course of treatment then is an offering to the houseowner nat
and the mizaing-hpazaing.

In talking to the villagers about the nats with whom they live,
one discerns that these nats are petty and irascible tyrants, quick
to take offense or to feel jealousy if any member of the household
or the other household nats receive special attention. Nats require
constant attention -- some housewives even fan them during the hot
season as well as keep their water offering and flowers fresh. In
return they give nothing but appeasement of their wrath and the
sense that their presence keeps strange nats away. The house nats
do not control decisions, but their wishes are taken into account
whenever the household acts. Their presence is made known only
through disaster, not through success.

The Village Nats. The villagers say that the nat looks after
the village as a grandfather looks after his family, i.e. he is concerned with their general welfare rather than, as a father would
be, their daily maintenance. By his presence he guards the village
against strange nats and even human invaders, just as the house
nat, like a sentry box, serves as a warning to anyone who wishes
to do harm to members of the household.

In a survey of seventeen of the villages in Patheingyi township,
the following nats were identified:

Nat	Character	Number of villages
I. Bobogyi	No legends	5
II. Myinbyu Shin	White horse owner	4
III. Personalized nats	Lived and died in immediate area of village	8

None of the village nats were found as household nats in the three villages in which a survey of the latter was made. This suggests that different categories of nats may be associated with the village and with the household, but the negative instances are too few for generalization. About a third of the villages did not personalize the nat, simply calling him Bobogyi. The personalized nats (III) were identified immediately with geographical features of the landscape such as a hill or stream where they had lived or met an untimely death. Only one of the eight -- the Lord of Aungpinlè -- was identifiable in Temple's list of Thirty-Seven Nats. Except for the third category, the characteristics of the nat did not give a clue as to the basis for selection by the village.

In those villages with personalized nats, greater attention was paid to them. Sometimes the nat houses in these villages were elaborate shrines with large figures of the nat and associated figures in the legend, such as Ingyin village's series of shrines for Mè U, the beloved of the Taungbyon brothers who was killed by them for having refused their love. In the village of Hsèdawgale is enshrined the nat Aserotakima, the queen who committed suicide in order to become guardian nat of the dam her husband was constructing on the river running past the village. So sacred is this shrine and the area surrounding it that until eleven years ago the people residing in this village never wore slippers, carried umbrellas, or rode horses. Since she was pregnant at the time of her suicide, pregnant women are particularly fearful of disturbing her and carefully avoid the waters in which she killed herself. However, eleven years ago the natkadaw (nat wife) charged with care of the nat at a village pwè (celebration) for Aserotakima divined by certain signs that she would be less demanding of these observances if she were given a three-day pwè instead of the usual two. And so it is said that from that year on the people have worn slippers and carried umbrellas, but they still dare not launch a boat on the waters near the dam.

In addition to the annual pwès, not always observed by all villages, offering to the village nat is made whenever disaster strikes or threatens to strike a village. This may be combined with the efforts of the monks to exorcise evil spirits through the special prayer session called the payeit yuttè. After a fire in Zigyogon, which demolished only one house but threatened the entire village, the village natkadaw and four other women made an offering of water, fruits, and betel nut to the village nat, at which time they asked for his protection against fire in the future.

When the village must change its locale, as happens frequently to the island villages of the Irrawaddy river, the monks are called upon to rid the place of any resident devils or spirits with the payeit yuttè, a natsin is erected on the east side of the village, and a special offering is made to the village nat. Only then is the village thought ready for occupancy.

An offering is made to the village nat preceding the celebration of the shinbyu. The day before the celebration, the shinlaung, the Buddhist initiate, goes in a cart drawn by white bullocks to make offerings of fruit to the village nat as well as to older people of prestige in the village. As in the case of the offering to the mizaing-hpazaing during the shinbyu, this offering is made from fear of the nat, whose envy would be aroused by the attention and interest the village folk focus on the initiate.

The village nat has been cast in the role of the lord protector of the village. When people migrate from their village, they frequently use the annual natpwè as an occasion for visiting their relatives. If they are unable to return, they send a contribution to one of their relatives living in the village to make an offering to the nat. In this sense, animistic faith ties the Burman more strongly to his village than does the village pongyi kyaung since, on moving, he becomes identified with the kyaung in his new neighborhood, whereas he retains the obligation to propitiate his hometown nat.

The Regional Nats. Three types of nats will be considered in this category: (1) nats whose personality is so strong that they are honored throughout an area encompassing several towns, (2) nats with special functions to perform who are honored throughout a region on special occasions when their services or powers are called into play, and (3) generalized spirits of the paddy land, of the stored rice, etc., who have no locality or village but are recognized as powers throughout a wide region.

A geography of nats, tying them to particular villages or regions, would clarify questions concerning the spread and persistence of the animistic cult. This work remains to be done for Burma. However, the limited survey which I did suggests some aspects of village-regional nat relations. The regional nats include both village and household nats. Certain villages in the Mandalay district have become centers of regional nat cults. In Aungpinlè, there is a large nat shrine with images of the nats most frequently honored throughout the area. Taungbyon is another center for the celebration of the nats.

The Taungbyon brothers, Shwebyingyi and Shwebyinngè, are the two most popular nats of Upper Burma (Temple 1906: 25-26). The legend associated with them does not in itself explain their popularity:

King Anawrahta, accompanied by the brothers, who were
the offspring of an Indian adviser to the court and an ogress
of Popa, went to China to secure a tooth of Gotama Buddha.
The Chinese emperor treated the Burmese king with contempt,
and so the two brothers, who could become invisible, entered
his chamber and wrote on the wall asking the emperor to meet
the Burmese king. The emperor did, and apparently handed
over the tooth. But on the return trip, the tooth disappeared.
Later the brothers were asked to superintend the building of
a pagoda which now can be seen in Taungbyon. During the
construction, the brothers got drunk on toddy palm juice, and
two bricks were missing from the entrance arch. The king
had them executed for their failure to carry through the job.
The king tried to return to his palace, but encountered many
difficulties on the boat trip. His ministers advised him that
his troubles were caused by the spirits of the brothers who
felt that their execution was unjust, particularly after they
had served the king loyally in the attempt to get the tooth.
Therefore the king ordered that regular offerings were to be
made to the nat spirits of the two brothers.

In one of the songs commemorating the brothers, the final verse
says: "Now all ye pretty maidens, love ye us, as ye were wont to
do while yet we were alive. " Apparently this plea was taken seriously, and the nats have a coterie of nat wives (natkadaws) attached
to them. The younger brother is the most favored and has the
greatest number of wives. It is a standing joke in the villages to
suggest that he shares his wives with his older brother.

The widespread popularity of the Taungbyon brothers can probably be explained by the devotion of their natkadaws. The natkadaws go from town to town, offering dances and prayers to their
images. They are frequently, but not always, the daughters of
natkadaws. Two of those interviewed said that their mothers had
asked them on their deathbed to undertake the responsibility of
dancing for the nat and making offerings to him. When they ignored
this request, they became seriously ill. They were advised by nat
wives to join their ranks, and they were then cured.

The natkadaws attached to a particularly favored nat, such as
one of the Taungbyon brothers, have an internal hierarchy through
which they are related to the nat. The most important natkadaws
are called natmayagyi, big nat wife. Others who do not devote full
time to the cult are known as hnama aya, sister of the nat. The
lesser wives give offerings to the big wives in thanks for the in-
structions given by the latter on how to please the nat. There is
some rivalry between the natkadaws in attracting the attention of
the nat, who visits them in dreams or reveals his presence by a

kind of bodily seizure which may cause them to shake when they
offer him food.

The natkadaws gather in the centers for the nat festivals.
Some travel in professional troupes along with their own musician
and images, which they set up in villages which have called upon
their services for the annual pwè. With their battered images and
contorted dances, they perpetuate the legend of their nat's powers,
and the nat who commands the largest number of natkadaws has the
largest reputation and following.

Some of the nats in the Mandalay district are remembered
only during special events requiring their appeasement. Among
such nats is Anauk Mèdaw (Lady of the West) who is said to be
"owner" of the mother and child at birth. She is served by Ameg-
yan, a rough-speaking nat who can cause harm to either mother or
child. To prevent this, an offering of 1.25 kyats is made at birth.
Those who are unable to give the money make a special request
for credit extension until after the harvest. The money is actually
collected by the midwife. Before the war, Anauk Mèdaw was given
only 25 pyas but the offering has since increased to five times that
amount because, as the people explain, the price of rice has increased by that amount.

The nats of the paddy field and the stored rice are directly
concerned with the basic crop. Even men who are serious meditators and who scoff at the idea of nats see to it that the paddy field
owner nat is propitiated. This nat, sometimes called the lè nat
(paddy or rice field nat), or Ashingyi, or even the frequently encountered term Bobogyi, must receive an offering at the time of
transplanting the rice and at the harvest, the first of these offerings
to ask that a good crop result and the second to give thanks for the
harvest. The offering is made on the east side of the field by the
work gang leader, usually the eldest of the women who do the work
of transplanting and harvesting. A female nat, Bomagyi, is guardian of the stored rice bins. She was a spinster who, while working
for a rich landowner, was killed by a co-worker. After the harvest, when the rice is threshed and in storage, an offering of
sticky rice is made to her, along with thanahka, a skin cosmetic,
mirror, and comb (since she was a spinster she was concerned
with beautifying herself and had the leisure time to do it). Because
of the circumstances of her death, i.e. while winnowing the harvested rice, people say she does not like the sound of threshing
and they endeavor to be quiet when giving her an offering.

Beyond the village and paddy field limits, the woods and fields
are thought to be inhabited by a host of named and unnamed spirits.
Those who venture daily into these regions as woodcutters or fruit

gatherers always offer some of their lunch first to these nats. [8] If
a village is established on new territory, an offering is made to
the earth owner, Bonmazo (given as "Bumaso" in Temple).

These nats are the lords of all that is important to the village
Burman, and it is by their sufferance that he is permitted to use
the fields, or enter the forest, or even to store the grain he has
harvested in safety. In making offerings to these nats, he gains
some sense of security, and nobody with whom I spoke, even the
most devoted meditator, was so foolhardy as to risk the anger of
a nat concerned with the basic needs of himself and his family.

The world of the nats is, then, tied to the structurally significant units of the society through responsibilities inherited in
familial, village, and regional contexts. In assessing the strength
of the three levels of animistic belief, the word of the informant
strengthens the conclusion based on structural analysis. One village Burman said that he may ignore all the nats except those he
acquired as his mizaing-hpazaing. The fact that the obligation to
propitiate the mizaing-hpazaing nat is acquired through the strongest kinship bonds, that of mother to daughter and secondarily that
of father to son, assures that these nats will be perpetuated. A
housewife's failure to carry out this responsibility is a source of
gossip and criticism. Negligent as the average village woman is
about her housekeeping duties, the only thing I have ever heard
neighbors criticize is failure to propitiate the nats. At the level
of the village, the responsibility of the elders to the village nat is
evoked less frequently and there are fewer incidents to indicate
failure in fulfilling this responsibility. Nat worship at this level
might easily succumb if it were opposed. Regional nat cults will
probably survive as long as the natkadaws are convinced that they
have been called upon for this mission in life and as long as they
receive sufficient profit to pay the musicians who inspire them.

Nats as a Subsociety in Burman Villages

The village Burman is from his earliest years introduced to
the world of nats. While the nats do not control decisions or im-
pose patterns of action, all the exigencies of daily living and the
crises in the life cycle are interpreted in terms of them. Marriage
alliances are not determined by the mizaing-hpazaing preferences
of the families involved, but if the marriage violates other customary preferences it is feared that the nats will be displeased. Their
presence is honored at those ceremonial occasions attending naming
ceremonies, Buddhist initiation, and marriage; their representa-
tions are removed at birth, sickness, and death, conditions which
make the house "unclean."

This constant awareness of the nats and the interpretation of misfortune in terms of their known likes and dislikes is illustrated by the response of the people of Patheingyi to the fact that the headman became insane. All agreed that his insanity was caused by the nats but accounts differed as to which nats were ultimately responsible and as to how he had failed in his responsibility. One account went as follows:

> U Chan, the headman of Patheingyi center, was ordered by the township officer to chop down some large trees in order to line the streets of the village. He called forth from the village a voluntary work group and set to cutting down the trees. This angered Yokhkazo, the nat who lives in the big trees. He in turn roused the anger of the village nat against the headman. Within a short time, the headman became insane, wandering about the village and talking wildly.

According to another account, told to me by a village elder:

> Even though U Chan was just carrying out the orders of the township officer, it was his own responsibility to advise the nat of this before cutting the trees. The village men who were ordered to do the work along with him went with an offering to the tree nat before they set to work. They said to the nat that it was the headman who ordered them to cut the trees and they were just doing as they were told. It was the headman's own fault that he had not shifted the blame to a higher authority. U Chan was always a hasty and aggressive man who often failed to confer with the elders before going ahead and doing things. His failure to explain to the nats that he was cutting the tree only because he had been ordered to do it caused them to turn against him.

The headman's nephew made a different claim of responsibility:

> About three years ago, the headman bought some pigs which he intended to raise and breed. Now Htibyuzaung is the mizaing-hpazaing of the headman, and this nat does not like the presence of pork even when not slaughtered for human food. Of course he caused the headman to go mad in his anger that his tastes should be ignored. The headman lost a lot of money on the pigs, many of which died because he could not take care of them properly. It was evident from the start, then, that the mizaing-hpazaing nat objected to having the pigs.

U Chan was himself responsible for his sickness because he failed in his role of headman to placate the village nats when under-

taking a project which would displease them; he neglected, as a
subordinate of the higher government authority invested in the township officer, to explain that he was not responsible to the tree nat;
and, even before this, he had incurred the displeasure of his
mizaing-hpazaing nat by harboring pigs, which are detested by this
nat.

Thus any misfortune in the lives of the villagers evokes this
kind of interpretation which, in turn, re-evaluates and redefines
the responsibility to the nats in terms of the role in which one is
acting. Since each individual fills more than one role, and in enacting these roles is required to make offerings to different nats,
his misfortunes are interpreted in a variety of accounts.

The villagers' relation to the nats has parallels in other social
relations. Wives show the same consideration to their husbands;
one woman said that having a husband is like having a nat in the
house -- he must be cared for, deferred to, and any impingement
on his hpon, or male power, must be avoided. Most adults tend to
treat children under the age of understanding as they do the nats:
they cater to every wish of the child, constantly appeasing him and
attempting not to frustrate him. [9] The avoidance of conflict and the
consideration for the sentiments and interests of others evident in
the treatment of nats is a characteristic of all social interaction,
expressed in the term a nadè. [10]

Spirits and Nat Cults

In the villages today, the concern with spirits persists, but it
is no longer the basis for nat cults. As we have seen in the legends,
nats originated in spirits of the dead who died a violent and unnatur-
al death and whose souls failed to become incorporated in a new
life. Because of the annoyance these spirits caused to people of a
region, they were granted overlordship of an area by the kings and
were thus appeased by annual and intermittent offerings and celebrations. Since the kings were overthrown, no new cults have been
established. The problem of laying to rest the restless souls of
those who died a green death -- aseinthe -- is now resolved through
Buddhist ritual offerings for the dead so that the spirit will enter a
new life. This resolution indicates the thorough integration of animistic and Buddhist tradition, as I shall illustrate in the following
case:

> The headman of Kangyi, Patheingyi township, was killed by
> Communist insurgents along with his brother. The headman
> had been giving tribute of rice and supplies to the insurgents
> in order to gain security from their raids for the villagers.
> Government authorities forced the headman to reveal the

names of the insurgent leaders and to forewarn the military
police the next time they were to come for tribute, threatening
to beat the headman if he failed to do this. The headman com-
plied, and the leaders were caught. Shortly afterward, the
headman and his brother were killed in an ambush by the in-
surgents, one of whom was the headman's brother-in-law.
The mutilated bodies were taken to Mandalay and buried
without village ceremony. The knot of hair from each of his
surviving children was cut and put in the coffin, along with a
length of string measuring each child's height. This was a
substitute for the child so that the soul of the dead man would
not be tempted to take his children with him.

In the weeks following the headman's death, some of the
people of the village had dreams in which the headman and
his younger brother appeared. The younger brother's wife
was pregnant, and his restless spirit indicated in the dreams
that he was worried about her. The younger brother said to
one dreamer (not a relative) that the headman was leading
the life of a devil.

The widow, concerned for the life of her children and for her
dead husband's spirit, consulted the elders of the village who
advised her to hold a shinbyu for the children with the money
she would receive from the government as widow's compensation. The shinbyu would be held in the name of the dead
man so that, with the final offering, the kutho or merit would
add to whatever merit he had acquired in his lifetime of offerings and ensure him a new life.

The shinbyu was held at the pongyi kyaung to avoid the expense of a mandat. The day before the shinbyu, the headman's wife made her offering to the village nat at the natsin
and to her own and her husband's mizaing-hpazaing nat in
her house. She offered a pot of water to the spirit of the
hill, asking him to come to the shinbyu. Just the night before the shinbyu, a villager dreamed that the headman appeared in a tree outside the town wall; the dreamer asked
the headman why he appeared in his dream, and the latter
replied that he had come to see his son's shinbyu.

Throughout the shinbyu the widow wore at her neck her husband's scarf. As she offered the gift of robe, matches, rice,
and fans with money to the monks, she held the scarf at her
cheek and gave these items in her husband's name. The
eldest of the monks who officiated prayed, saying that the
widow made these offerings for her husband so that he could
continue on the path to Neikban (Nirvana). While he prayed,

the widow poured water, catching it in a plate (this ritual, the yeizet chadè, is symbolic of the Buddha's custom of pouring water on the ground when making an offering so that the ground should be witness to the good deed). The widow then said:

> I am offering the monks food and clothing. I am making my two sons koyin [monks]. That which I am now doing will cause the five enemies of man to disappear. For this life and for the afterlife we assemble here to get rid of bad luck and worries.

The headman's clothing lay folded on the mat before the monks on which his widow sat: his sleeping rug, longyis, and eingyis. The longyis were later made into curtains for the kyaung windows and the shirts cut into table doilies.

On the day following the shinbyu, the mother went with the children in their koyin robes to the fort where her husband's spirit had appeared in the dream. She took his clothing along and called upon his soul, telling him what she had succeeded in doing. About 300 villagers, friends and relatives, attended her, along with one monk who did a payeit yuttè -- recital of prayers to rid the site of devils. He said to the dead man's spirit: 'It is not your duty to remain here any longer. Your spirit is free to go (ameint pyandè).' He then gave the people present the five precepts.

The ceremony was successful -- nobody had dreams in which the spirits of the dead men appeared in the two-month period that followed the shinbyu, according to my last inquiry.

Even natural death is attended by a danger period of seven days in which the spirit of the deceased hovers near his home. The wake carried on at this time is a period in which villagers, friends, neighbors, and relatives guard the body and keep off evil spirits, as they while away the time with gambling, eating, and drinking. During this period the entire village is unclean and all offerings to the nats are postponed until after the final ceremony in which the priests offer the five precepts. The offering of food to participants in the wake, and the offering of rice, candles, etc. to the monks who give the five precepts at the burial, is the deceased's last chance to gain merit.

On the seventh day after the death, in the late afternoon, a spirit caller, usually a young male relative of the deceased who is not afraid of spirits, calls the spirit at the grave while holding a piece of the deceased's clothing in a ceremony called the leitpya

kwèdè. If the deceased has young children, particularly in the
case of a mother of young children, there is some danger that the
soul of the children will accompany the parent to the grave. In
these cases, a string measuring the height of the child or a knot of
the child's hair will be put in the coffin as in the case of the mur-
dered headman. As a further precaution, two bananas are taken,
one ripe one which is given to the child to eat in the house and the
other, an unripe one, which is thrown to the west of the village in
the direction of the graveyard. The final act is for the monks to
gather on the morning after the soul-calling to give the five precepts to all those who participated in the wake and burial.

The concern for the soul contradicts the Buddhist doctrine of
denial of anatta or the ego-identified soul substance. However,
the one solution of the soul crisis now lies in the Buddhist doctrine
of reincarnation. If passage to the next life is interrupted because
of the circumstances surrounding the death or appearance of the
restless soul in dreams, the traditional Buddhist ceremonial is
resorted to as a means of acquiring merit for the deceased which
will make the transition possible.

Conclusion

Animism, since it was first defined by Tylor, has been a
grab-bag category of all forms of spirit worship. In Upper Burma,
however, the animistic spirit cult has a specific content with distinctions in the kinds of spirits worshiped which are related to the
structural units of the society through which this worship is carried
on. The nat cult is tied to the family, the village, and the region,
and these different ties affect the strength and persistence of the
cult. The mizaing-hpazaing nat, which is transmitted directly
from parent to child, is the most consistently honored and the last
to be given up. The village nat, though he is of less importance
to the individual than the household nat and has no direct transmission of responsibility for his maintenance, is, nevertheless,
an important link with the home village and must be propitiated
even if one moves away. The regional nats are those of the household and village nats which have attained fame in a wide locale and
whose popularity depends upon the natkadaws and other specialists
associated with the cult. Misfortune resulting from failure to meet
the responsibilities to the nats which the villager inherits and acquires by virtue of being a member of a family and living in a village meets with little sympathy from his fellow men, for this is
felt to be a basic obligation.

The nats are an extension of the human society in the villages,
and propitiation of them affects one's fortune in this life. In the
words of one informant, "When we do something for Buddha, we

do it for the next life, and when we do something for the nats, we do it to help us in this life. " As a subgroup in the society, their presence is feared and honored in almost every house and in special shrines. Crises and misfortunes are interpreted in terms of the nats' likes and dislikes. Serious Buddhist meditators ignore nat offerings, but they too admit their presence in saying that their taking the five precepts daily gives them power over the nats.

Nats, when analyzed in the social context of belief, emerge as integrated figures of the society, existing in an order that never competes with Buddhist ideology. They have survived the monarchs who established their domain and continued to receive their tribute during the rule of the British. They have persisted in the period of independence, their survival due in part to the chaos which followed the war (personal disaster still being attributed to their power). The social aspect of religion, negated in the Buddhist ideal of the monastic life (Durkheim 1915: 67), survives in the nat cults, and the relations with the nats reflect the conventions of social interaction. No new nat cults have emerged, but the soul crises of transmigration which gave rise to belief in them persist. The resolution now lies within Buddhist rites of gaining merit through giving.

NOTES

1. Research for this study was carried out in three neighboring villages in the township of Patheingyi, Mandalay district: Patheingyi center, Nyaungbintha, and Zigyogon. Surveys were made in 20 of the 65 villages of the township. I am indebted to the National Institute of Mental Health for money in support of the research.

2. See especially, Langham-Carter 1933; Brown 1915; Htin 1955 and 1956; Scott 1900 and 1927; Temple 1906.

3. Compass points are significant orienting points for the Burmans in all their activities, and particularly in reference to the nats. The significance is based on the reckoning of Indian astrologers who formerly were advisors to the kings. East is the direction of good fortune, west of misfortune. In the east of the village, therefore, the natsin is located, offerings are made, and the coconut is hung in the east of the house; in the west is found the cemetery, refuse from the village, and in the west of the house is located the birthroom.

4. In fact, in the studies cited, no mention was made of the mizaing-hpazaing in discussing the Thirty-Seven Nats. It is

not, however, an obscure feature of the communities, and I
was made aware of it in the first week of my study.

5. The majority of the people have the same nat in any one vil-
    lage, or a nat favored in the neighboring towns, as the results
    of a census taken in Nyaungbintha show: 26 of the 59 house-
    holds were questioned about their mizaing-hpazaing; 16 of
    these, or 61 per cent had the relatives of Min-Maha-Giri; 3
    had Htibyuzaung, the white-umbrella owner; 5 had the two
    Taungbyon brothers; 1 had Badone; 1 had Bodawgyi, the Man-
    dalay district nat; 1, whose grandparents were from Lower
    Burma, brought one of these Lower Burma nats with him; and
    another family, from Shimbogale, had the komyoyin eindwin,
    the nine-village nat. Five of these families had another of
    these same nats along with the nat counted above, and in the
    remaining cases, spouse's nat was the same or the nat was
    not mentioned. The census, though inadequate in that ques-
    tioning about second nats was not pressed, shows that the
    mizaing-hpazaing nat is linked to a locality.

6. One woman tried to give a smaller contribution than usual to
    her mizaing-hpazaing nat because of her poverty. She was
    seized by a violent illness during which she seemed to be
    bound by invisible ropes, with water and froth coming from
    her mouth. In order to cure her, her family offered rice and
    lahpet (pickled tea leaves) to Htibyuzaung, the slighted nat,
    and she recovered. She subsequently took the responsibility
    for nat offering when her mother died.

7. The family of one girl who was marrying a man separated from
    his first wife had neither the money nor the inclination to have
    a large ceremony (because of shame in the face of the deserted
    first wife and her children). However, they made an offering
    to the mizaing-hpazaing nats in their house so that misfortune
    would not result from the wedding.

8. One man who gave some of his pork curry to the nats when he
    was in the mountains returned to find his cow missing. He
    realized immediately that the Taungbyon brothers, who are his
    own mizaing-hpazaing, were insulted by the offering because
    their father is a Muslim.

9. Leach (1954: 173) saw in the relation of the Kachins to the
    nats an extension of the human class hierarchy to a higher
    level. The way in which people deal with the nats parallels
    the way in which they deal with human superiors.

10.   Mrs. Conrad Becker is currently doing research on the
      social implications of this concept.

REFERENCES CITED

Brown, R. Grant
   1915   "The Taungbyon Festival, " Journal of the Royal
             Anthropological Institute, 45.

Durkheim, Emile
   1915   Elementary Forms of the Religious Life, Paris,
             Alcan.

Firth, Raymond
   1959   "Problem and Assumption in an Anthropological Study
             of Religion, " Journal of the Royal Anthropological
             Institute, 89, 129-48.

Htin Aung
   1955   "The Lord of the Great Mountain, " Journal of the
             Burma Research Society, 38, 75-82.

   1956   "The Thirty-seven Lords, " Journal of the Burma
             Research Society, 39, 81-100.

Langham-Carter, R. R.
   1933   "Lower Chindwin Nats: (1) Bodawgyi, (2) Amye Yeyin,"
             Journal of the Burma Research Society, 23.

Leach, E. R.
   1954   Political Systems of Highland Burma, London, Butler
             and Tanner.

Scott, J. George
   1900   Gazetteer of Upper Burma and the Shan States, 1,
             pt. 1.

   1911   Burma: A Handbook of Practical Information, London,
             Alexander Moring.

   1927   The Burman: His Life and Notions, 2nd ed. London,
             Macmillan.

Simmel, Georg

    1959   Sociology of Religion, New York, Philosophical
            Library.

Temple, R. C.

    1906   The Thirty-Seven Nats, London, W. Griggs.

Vogt, E. Z., and W. Lessa

    1958   Reader in Comparative Religion, Evanston, Illinois,
            Row-Peterson.

BAN PING'S TEMPLE: THE CENTER OF A "LOOSELY STRUCTURED" SOCIETY

Michael Moerman

University of California, Los Angeles

It has been said that Thai Buddhists "passively accept the superstitions of their forefathers without ever enquiring or even caring whether they are . . . true" (Young 1907: 272-73). This accusation is better directed at us who study Thai Buddhists and passively accept the two great principles that village society is loosely structured (Embree 1950) and that the temple is at its center (Landon 1939: 190; Blanchard 1958: 111, 400). Since I believe with perfect faith that the two principles are true, the present paper's only break with tradition lies in attempting to understand what they mean.

By a "loosely structured society, " Embree meant one which tolerates "variation from the rule" (1949: 496) and sanctions "considerable variation of individual behavior" (1950: 182; cf. Firth 1961: 3). Since Embree found it "a basic cultural difference between Laos, Cambodia, and Siam on the one hand and Vietnam, China, and Japan on the other" (1949: 496), such looseness is probably not irrelevant to the practice of Theravada Buddhism, to its value of noninvolvement (ubekha), and to its injunction, "Work out your own salvation with diligence (Maha-Parinibbana-Sutta). " Embree (1950) characterized the manifestations of loose structure in Thailand as essentially negative, e. g. lack of uniformity in dress and artistic expression, of regularity, discipline, regimentation, neatness, willingness to cooperate, and an industrial time sense, and of clear reciprocal rights and duties. These insights into Thai individualism have probably stimulated valuable research on the personality structure which encourages it (Phillips 1965), the ecology which permits it (Wilson 1962: 47), and the calculus of movements which gives it social pattern (Mosel 1957: 311 ff.; Hanks 1962: 1249, 1252-53). They have also, I think, had the unfortuante consequence of discouraging students of Thai village life from looking for the kinds of structural regularities which the present paper describes. Because of this and despite the existence of rather numerous studies of Thai communities, [1] I quite frankly do not know whether and to what extent the ways in which I will show Ban Ping's temple to be central to its social structure are typical of Thailand, of isolated Northern Thai villages, of the Lue, or merely of Ban Ping. [2] Furthermore, I do not know whether the positive manifestations of "loose structure " which I will describe in Ban Ping are typical of Thailand, although I am fairly confident that they are elsewhere so prevalent as to diminish the label's descriptive value.

I will first discuss the individual in relation to the temple, and
then the temple in relation to the village. For these discussions
to be useful for those interested in Thailand, it is first necessary
to point out some of the relevant ways in which Ban Ping may differ
from other Thai villages.

Ban Ping's Peculiarities

The fieldworker in Central Thailand is commonly faced with
the problem of establishing the boundaries of the effective village.
Administrative jurisdictions, topographic borders, local names,
and school zones often fail to coincide and the investigator finds
that only the Buddhist temple defines and unites the local community (Textor 1958). Aside from the temple, there appears to be
little social integration between the levels of household and of
nation. In much of North Thailand, however, this is not the case.
The village of Ban Ping is a physically and administratively demarcated named community of kinsmen whose children attend the same
school and who share a common history and a common, peculiar,
ethnic identification (Moerman 1965). Although Ban Ping also has
a Buddhist temple, even in the realm of religion and ritual that
temple is not the village's sole source of unity. The Lue, like the
Siamese (Central Thai), respect the spirits (phii) as well as the
Buddha. Unlike the Siamese, Lue personal and household spirits
are of minor importance, for the village spirit claims far more
attention. Once a year, [3] each member of the community contributes to a ceremony for the village spirit at which Ban Ping is
closed off to outsiders.

In Central Thailand, "[major] events in a person's life (birth,
coming of age, birthdays, marriage, death . . . the erection of a
new house) . . . are marked by a tham bun or 'merit working'
ceremony" which features participation by the Buddhist clergy
(Rajadhon 1961: 84). In Ban Ping, funerals and, within the last
five years, housewarmings are the only home-centered rites which
involve the clergy. The calendar of temple-centered ceremonies
is similarly sparse. Only during the three months of Phansaa do
villagers attend holy day (wan sin) services in the temple. In
Chiengkham district, temples are less wealthy than in Central
Thailand: 102 temples own but a single acre of productive land.
The temple in Ban Ping also has few obvious extrareligious functions. In Bangkhuad the temple serves as community center,
counseling agency, hospital, school, community chest, hotel,
news agency, charitable employer, bank, clock, sports center,
morgue, poorhouse, landlord, home for the aged, reservoir, insane asylum, music school, and refuge for criminals (Kaufman
1960: 113-15). Although Ban Ping's temple has rarely performed
any of these services, it is still central to an understanding of

community life. Ban Ping thus provides an intriguing instance of
the importance of Buddhist organization even to a community which
makes comparatively little use of it. [4]

   In Ban Ping, the temple's most striking disability is the low
secular prestige of its clergy. Approximately 30 per cent of men
over fifteen have been ordained and there have always been priests
and novices in its temple, [5] but no village cleric has ever led the
community or offered counsel to its laymen; none have been curers
or diviners. Although during ceremonies the clergy receives the
same signs of respect given to their Central Thai colleagues, in
other situations -- even when ceremonies are being planned -- the
clergy defers to the laity. The immediate cause of this anomaly
is clear. The village has never had a priest older than thirty; the
present "abbot" is twenty-two; of the ten living villagers who have
been priests, none served beyond the age of twenty-four. In Ban
Ping, the prestige of age and the prestige of the yellow robe do not
coincide.

   Child clergy with low secular prestige are not unique to Ban
Ping. Of Chiengkham's 183 priests, only about 25 are more than
forty years old. The youth of the district's clergy reflects a major
difference in clerical careers between Central Thailand and Chiengkham. In respect to this difference, Chiengkham seems to represent an old (Curtis 1903: 211) pattern typical of North Thailand
(de Young 1958: 117, 127-28) and perhaps of the entire region
(North Thailand, North Laos, Thai Yunnan) which Dodd (1923:
345), on the basis of its temple alphabet, calls the "Yûn [Yuan]
cult area. "

   In Central Thailand, there are three main avenues to the
priesthood. A great number of young adults temporarily forsake
the secular life to become priests for a single Phansaa. In addition,
many priests enter the sangha upon retiring from their responsibilities as farmers, husbands, and parents. It also happens that
some novices remain in the order beyond their twentieth birthday
in order to become priests. In Chiengkham, only this third path
is used; all priests begin as novices. [6] Some time after ten years
of age boys don the yellow robe. Most leave after a few years,
but a few remain in the sangha to become priests for a year or
two before returning to the secular world to find wives and begin
a family. A bare handful stay in the temple to make it their life.
This clerical career is reflected in the fact that in Ban Ping and
in Chiengkham novices outnumber priests. The ratio of novice to
priest in North Thailand indicates that Chiengkham's normal clerical career -- with its implication of low secular status for the
clergy -- may characterize the entire region. In Central Thailand
there are about five priests to every novice. For all of North

Thailand, as for Chiengkham, there are about three novices to
each priest (see Table 1).

Table 1. Clergy in North and Central Thailand, 1960

	Priests	Novices	Ratio of priests to novices	Total
North	7,591	20,935	1:3	28,526
Central	85,955	19,010	5:1	104,965
National	159,701	95,838		255,539
Chiengkham	183	608	1:3	791

Source: All figures except those for Chiengkham are from a personal communication, Department of Religion, Bangkok.

The Buddhist Career

Laymen. The villager's main goal as a Buddhist layman is to
earn merit (daj bun), negatively by avoiding wrong actions (baab)
and positively by attending the temple and by making offerings to
it and to its clergy. The goal is a "loose" one, however, in that
members of different social categories are neither subject to identical temptations nor have the same obligations for positively earning merit. In addition, it is expected (and the belief in karma presumably requires) that individuals of the same social category will
behave differently because they do not have the same capacity for
earning merit.

Since the ideology and economics of village Buddhism are beyond the scope of this paper, I shall concentrate on participation
in temple ceremonies, an important part of the layman's role but
one which has received little analytic attention.

In formal status, indicated by such things as pronoun used,
order of being served, and bowing -- but not always in power and
influence -- men outrank women and seniors outrank juniors. This
formal ranking is reflected in seating at and participation in temple affairs. The arrangement, however, is "loosely structured"
in that alternative rules sometimes take precedence and individual
variation is permitted. Consider, for example, the morning service seating plan presented in Figure 1. Men sit closer to the

Figure 1. SEATING PATTERN IN VIHARA
DURING MORNING SERVICE

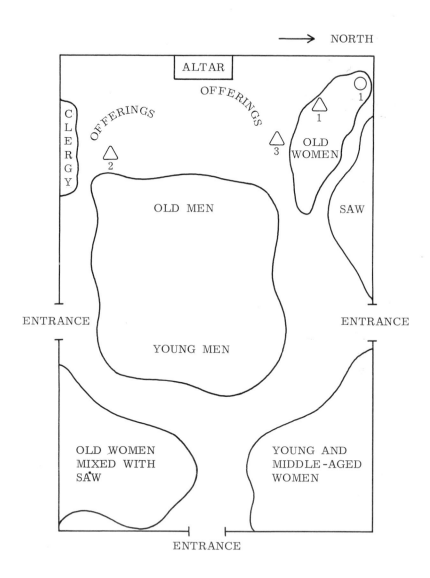

Triangles represent men, circles women. Numbers designate
individuals described in text. Drawing is approximate and not to
scale.

altar and to the clergy than women do, seniors sit closer than juniors. Yet woman 1, although the most senior and the only woman
to spend holy day (wan sin) eve in the temple, sits quite far from
the clergy so that she can lean against the wall and perhaps also
because, by an alternative rule, North is the honorable direction
outside the temple. Man 1, who also sleeps in the vihara on holy
day eve, sits with the women so that he can be near his sister.
The saʼw (unmarried girls) who crowd the old women and sit "above,"
and thus more honorably than, their elders at the rear, remain
near the door they entered, too "shy" to cross to where the young
women and other saʼw are seated. Man 2, seated so prominently,
is the lay leader (acan) of the congregation who requests the precepts on its behalf and chants the names of those who have sponsored the service. These sponsors, led by man 3, the very prominence of whose seat places him closer to the women than to the
high ranking men, are a major feature of Ban Ping's temple organization, an instance of the importance of the temple to village social structure, and an example of Ban Ping's high degree of organization relative to Central Thailand.

As in many Northern villages (de Young 1958: 115-16), the
clergy of Ban Ping do not beg for their food. Rather, the village
is divided into residential sections (mot). Every week the households of a different section send daily food to the temple. There
are as many sections as there are holy days in Phansaa and the section whose week it is sponsors the holy day services through offerings of special sweetmeats, plants decorated with money, and such
goods as soap, condensed milk, cushions, and banners (cf. Moerman 1964: 34-35). The section is ritually represented and its
offerings collected by its oldest active member, whose responsibility extends to beating the small gong which signals the time for
daily offerings of cooked food and to passing the gong along to the
next section's leader when the week is over. Although their origin
and main task is to provide offerings to the temple, the mot are
often used as the administrative unit for communal labor, school
contributions, and other secular affairs. Thus the organization of
merit-earning -- like merit-earning itself, since it is always a
public act -- integrates Ban Ping and occupies a central place in
its society.

Aside from special occasions like the New Year, temple services occur only on holy days during Phansaa. There is a morning
(6:00 to 7:30 a.m.) service of which the core is offering food to
the clergy and receiving the precepts (sin) from them and an afternoon service (noon to 5:00 p.m.) at which the clergy read from
the scriptures (tham). On the eve of holy day there is a short service for those who take the eight vows[7] and spend the night in the
vihara.

Buddhism, which focuses on the next life, is in many ways the religion of the old. Participation in its services is expected to increase with age and actual attendance does, in fact, reflect age and sex. Only a few ancient villagers who have retired from secular affairs spend the eve of holy day in the temple where, in the words of one of them, they "listen to the scriptures and wait for death." Along with other old persons and the middle-aged, they attend the afternoon services as well. The old and middle-aged also attend the morning services at which many young persons are present. Each household is expected to be represented at morning services and it is usually the oldest member or couple who attend. Households headed by young parents are frequently unrepresented; young parents who reside in their parental households hardly ever attend. [8]

Young children accompany their parents or grandparents[9] to these services and so learn the simpler Buddhist rituals at an early age. The headman's five-year-old daughter and her friends, for example, liked to sit in our house and pretend to make holy water in our bright plastic teacups. Her two-year-old brother would hold his hands in a respectful waj and attempt to repeat the namotatsa after her, although he could barely talk. Older children, unless they become clerics, rarely attend the ceremonies. Girls older than eight are occupied with younger siblings. Boys of six to twelve form a horde which runs and screams outside the temple during services or tries to raid the sweetmeats placed on Indra's altar. Occasionally their elders have to disrupt the service and go order the boys to leave. On reaching the age of courting, young people once again participate in temple affairs. Girls (saw) devote a great deal of energy to weaving and embroidering offerings of pillows and banners, their relative skill being a source of widespread interest and comment. Boys of courting age (baw) dance and form an orchestra for temple processions. At major ceremonies the baw and saw together make elaborate paper and bamboo floats covered with offerings of money and utensils which are presented to the temple in the name of all baw and saw. Young people, especially girls, put on their finery to attend morning services[10] but are not permitted to attend the afternoon scripture readings. The young, even after marriage, are said to have their minds on earthly and earthy things which would prevent them from understanding the texts and so interfere with their elders' concentration and enjoyment. As they mature, women and, still later in life, men come to temple more regularly. At the afternoon scripture readings, unlike the morning services where women predominate (sometimes by as much as 2:1), the sexes are equally represented.

The layman's career is summarized in Figure 2, which indicates that it is possible to describe the age and sex categories of

Figure 2.   LAY PARTICIPATION IN TEMPLE SERVICES,
BY AGE AND SEX

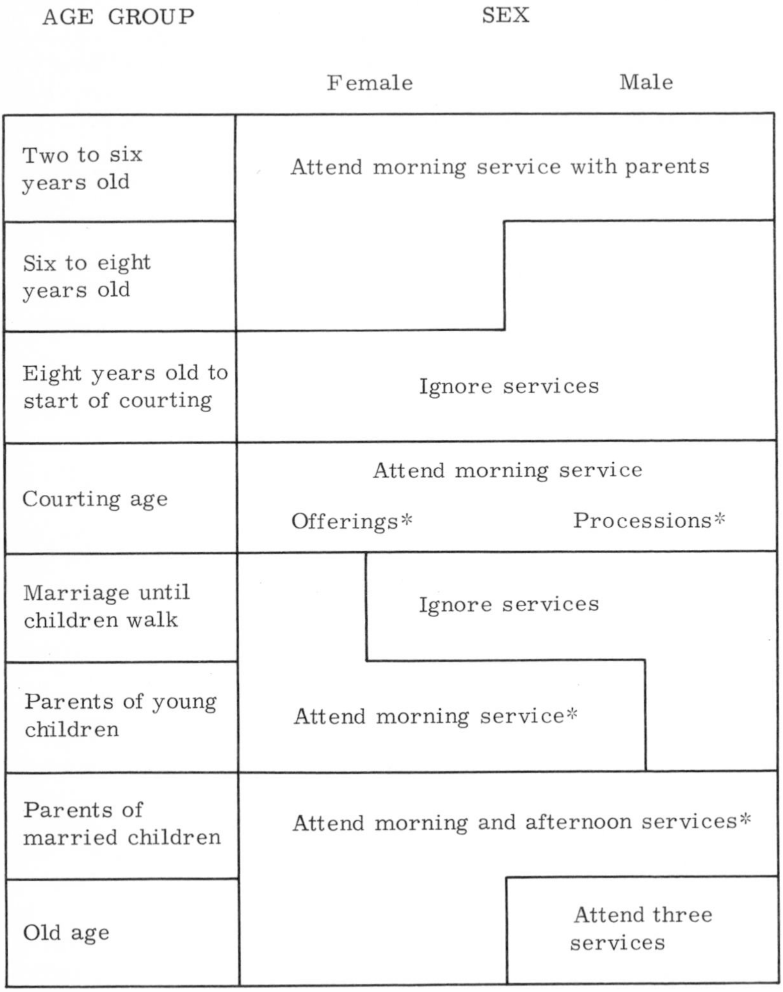

AGE GROUP	SEX	
	Female	Male
Two to six years old	Attend morning service with parents	
Six to eight years old		
Eight years old to start of courting	Ignore services	
Courting age	Attend morning service	
	Offerings*	Processions*
Marriage until children walk	Ignore services	
Parents of young children	Attend morning service*	
Parents of married children	Attend morning and afternoon services*	
Old age		Attend three services

Absence of a vertical line indicates equal participation by sex.
Asymmetrical lines indicate unequal participation.
Asterisks indicate normative rules, e.g. elders should listen to
the reading of scripture.

Ban Ping in terms of participation in Buddhist services. Although some of the regularities are merely numerical norms, others are normative. If adolescents fail to make an offering and participate in processions, or middle-aged persons are absent from morning services, or elders are absent in the afternoon, it is legitimate to request an explanation. Consistent failure is a subject for gossip which becomes more severe with the age or the moral pretensions of the offender. In addition, the weaving and embroidering of the sa'w, the processions of the baw, and the afternoon attendance of the old (thaw) are so often mentioned by villagers and are of such concern to their actors that they can be said to signal and validate the participant's membership in his social category.

The differentiation of the layman's task by sex and age is clearly less pervasive, formalized, and sanctioned in Ban Ping than it is among the Mangshih Thai (T'ien 1949) but it is nevertheless a means of village integration and a source of symbols for expressing and publicizing the differences of seniority so important to Thai-Lue social structure. Ban Ping's regular associations between stage of life and temple activity are "loosely structured," however, in that few of them are explicit, individual violations of most of them are common and go unnoticed, violation of explicit rules is permitted in many circumstances, and unexcused violations of explicit rules are punished only by gossip.

Clergy. Ban Ping has three successive clerical statuses: trainee (xajom), novice (pha), and priest (tu). The xajom, young boys who frequent the temple and aspire to membership in it, differ from the temple boys of Central Thailand since the youth of the Ban Ping priests precludes their being the boys' patrons as priests often are in Bangkok temples. In the villages of Central Thailand temple boys are casual groups of youngsters who make themselves useful to the clergy; in Ban Ping xajom are on the first step of a clerical career. All xajom become novices within a year; all novices were xajom; all priests were novices.

Recruitment of xajom is a simple process. A priest or novice visits the home of a young boy and invites him to become a xajom. Having accepted, the boy tries to influence his closest friends to join too. Yet clerics report that it is often difficult to convince boys and their parents to accept the invitation to become xajom. Since Ban Ping lacks a professional clergy and the prestige of its temporary priests and novices is relatively low, it is appropriate to ask what motivates boys there to join the temple.

Purely religious considerations are undoubtedly of great importance. Like "wealth" or "adjustment" in our own society, religious merit (bun) is a transcendant value: it explains one's human

condition, is good in itself, and translates into other goods in this
and future lives. Moreover, the popular understanding of the
course of merit both sanctions parents and children to accept the
invitation and shows us a further aspect of the temple's position
in village society. Parents share the merit their sons make by
being clergy. Specifically, a novice's merit goes to his mother,
a priest's to his father. This belief presumably compensates the
parents for the loss of a son who by his very absence continues to
benefit his family.

Another reward for becoming a cleric is the drama of the
ordination ceremony itself. Dressed in a glorious imitation of
Prince Siddartha, the previously undistinguished village lad is
now a "precious child" (luk kaew) -- a subject of great attention
and the focus of an impressive ceremony. "If you're good, perhaps you can be 'precious children,'" an old man told the wide-
eyed youngsters who surrounded a xajom about to don the yellow
robe. The temple rituals, and the sight of honored elders bowing
before novices who yesterday had been junior and therefore, like
themselves, subordinate to all, must also appeal to the young.

To those invited to become xajom, the clergy enlarge upon the
pleasures of temple life: secret snacks, practical jokes, and other
boarding-school thrills. Adults have fond memories of their time
in temple. The headman, for example, once entertained a solemn
meeting with an elaborate tale of how he and other novices tricked
the priest who should have been supervising them.

Some of the rewards of temple life are material. Most village
households try to prepare especially tasty dishes when it is their
turn to send food to the temple. Of more importance, one-third of
all cash offered to the temple becomes the personal property of the
clergy who may spend, save, or, quite commonly, loan or give it
to their parents and siblings.

Table 2. Temple Tenure of Living Former Priests

Number of years a priest	Frequency
1	3
2	3
3	1
4	2
5	1
Over 5	0

To the xajom and young novice, the pleasures, prestige, and

profit of life in the temple are greater than those available outside.
As the cleric grows older, however, this becomes progressively
less true. Of the forty-seven living laymen who were ever ordained, only ten remained in the temple long enough to become
priests and only one, an orphan, remained a priest for longer than
four years (see Table 2).

Not every village boy is invited to become a xajom. The qualification of which villagers speak most often is "having enough
merit, " but this is an explanation in retrospect. "Inadequate
merit" is how the "unripe" man explains never having been ordained, how the ex-novice explains not having become a priest,
how the former priest explains the brevity of his tenure. There
are also secular qualifications which reflect the vulnerability to
external forces and the primacy of economic considerations that
often characterize peasant communities.

Villagers complain that government regulation has delayed the
age at which boys become novices, for Thai law requires that boys
first pass the fourth grade of elementary school. In Ban Ping,
where the trainee must be taught the Northern Thai script before
he becomes a novice, this restriction applies to xajom. Because
children usually enter school at the age of eight, only the brightest
boys will have completed the fourth grade by age twelve; many take
longer. As Figure 3 records, attendance at the government school
has advanced the average age of ordination as a novice from thirteen (12.6) to fifteen (14.6) and the modal age from twelve to fifteen. Since most clerics have always left the temple at or before
the age at which they can become priests, this delay curtails temple careers and thereby also lowers the total number of clergy
concurrently in the temple.

The second major qualification is economic and thus beyond
the scope of the present paper. But since it has received such
scant attention in the literature, [11] it should at least be mentioned
here. From Figure 4 it can be calculated that the average tenure
in the temple after ordination as a novice is over five (5.3) years.
We can therefore presume that a boy becomes a xajom only if his
household can afford to dispense with his labor, i.e. recruitment
to the clergy may depend on surplus labor and, conversely, a
clerical career may provide highly valued temporary employment
for surplus household members.

After their selection, the trainees eat, sleep, and spend most
of their time in the temple. Sweeping, drawing water, carrying
offerings, they become accustomed to the routine of temple life,
learn to cooperate and to identify with the priests and novices who
casually instruct them in the Northern Thai alphabet, and learn to

Figure 3.   AGE OF NOVICES AT ORDINATION

Age before villagers began to attend school

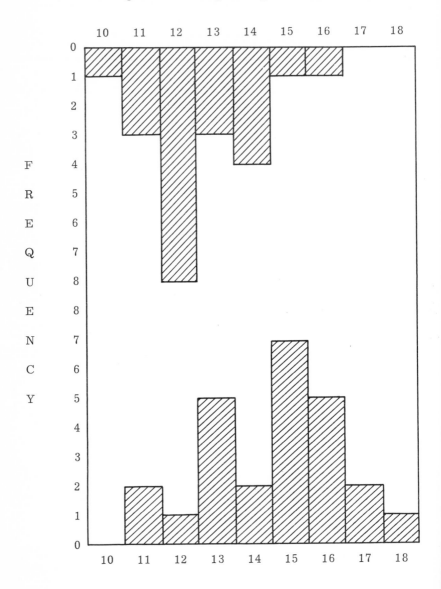

Age after villagers began to attend school

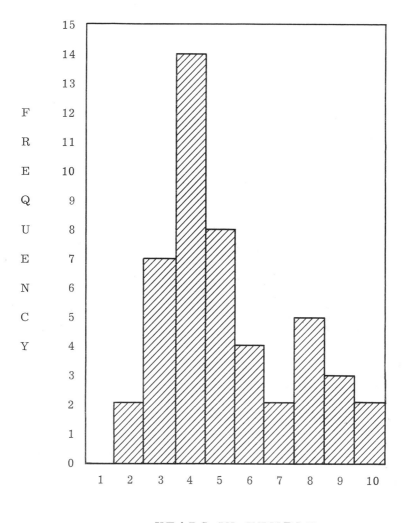

Figure 4.   TEMPLE TENURE OF FORMER CLERGY

FREQUENCY

YEARS IN TEMPLE

respect the teachings of the lay leader of temple services, a former priest, who helps to coach them in the proper responses for
the ordination ritual. A few weeks before Phansaa trainees are
ready to become novices, and novices are ready to become priests.
This annual ordination is one of the most important village ceremonies.

In Central Thailand, a candidate's family usually pays for both
the ceremony and the still more expensive hospitality which accom-
panies it. In Ban Ping these costs are met in ways which maintain
and illustrate village homogeneity. The chairman of the temple
committee summons a meeting of all males and announces the
amount that the committee has decided each villager must contribute. In 1960 every villager of courting age and above was told to
contribute four baht, about the village price of a small chicken or
of 10 liters of unmilled rice. This money pays for the robes, umbrellas, and other ceremonial paraphernalia the candidates need.
Any surplus will be divided equally among the individual candidates
to help their sponsors pay for other ceremonial requisites and for
the food and liquor consumed by their guests. The strength of the
household in Ban Ping is illustrated by the fact that the contribution, although levied against individuals, is usually paid by its
head.

The people of Ban Ping are no less concerned with gaining
merit than other Thai villagers, and aiding an ordination is among
the most meritorious acts. Nevertheless, not all contributed their
four baht. Those who plead poverty are readily excused, but the
most grudging contributors are the close kinsmen of the candidate
and of his sponsor who will help to meet the costs of secular hospitality. This help is considered merit-making and those who offer
it think it unjust and demeaning to have to pay the smaller villagewide levy in addition. In "loosely structured" Ban Ping there is no
way to make them pay if they are unwilling to.

The people of Ban Ping consider it improper for a candidate's
parents to bear the entire cost of his ordination. Such support
would give the parents an unfair monopoly of the religious merit
above that which accrues automatically from having a son in the
clergy. In 1960 three trainees became novices and one novice became a priest in two days of ceremony on the 18th and 19th of
June, but as late as the fifth no one was sure who the sponsors
would be. The candidate's parents were busily visiting potential
sponsors to make veiled requests and the most exciting topic of
village gossip remained, "Who are the sponsors going to be?"
The sponsor holds an important position. By his financial support,
he shares in the merit made by the ordination and establishes a
tie with the candidate which lasts throughout their lives. He is the

por ork   "the father of leaving" the secular life. The candidate
becomes his luk kaew, or "precious child." The luk kaew visits
his sponsor nearly every day throughout his years in the temple
and, on returning to secular life, may call upon his "parents of
leaving" to perform any of the duties normally expected of real
parents. Por ork -luk kaew may be used as a set of kin terms
and sometimes replaces terms based on genealogical connection. [12]   Because parents are not permitted to be the sole support of their son's ordination, a bond of ritual parenthood is con-
tracted which reinforces one kin tie out of many that are otherwise
equivalent. So, for example, when Maj N (Figure 5b) refused to
accept payment for building the house of Nan U, he and the other
villagers explained it by saying that when Maj N became a novice
thirty-eight years ago Nan U's grandfather had been his sponsor.
(Maj is the secular title of a former novice, nan of a former
priest.) No one mentioned the close genealogical kinship between
Maj N and his benefactor. [13]

        The sponsor makes merit, validates his status as a devout
and substantial elder, enjoys the fun and celebrity of the festivities, and fulfills his obligations to kinsmen. The candidate refines
his universe of bilateral kinsmen by establishing a meaningful connection with an elder of some substance. Ban Ping is a fairly
small, predominantly endogamous community of bilaterally related kinsmen. Almost all of its 639 inhabitants have the same
surname and can be traced back to fourteen ancestral couples.
This means that every individual has more kinsmen than he can
use. One simply cannot be especially intimate, especially sup-
portive, especially helpful to all of one's many relatives. In Ban
Ping, and probably throughout Thailand, extragenealogical considerations are extremely important for determining whom one calls
and behaves toward as "kinsman. "[14]

        The candidates and their sponsors shown in Figure 5 are close
kinsmen. But families are large, so the candidate has many relatives as close as his sponsor; the sponsor has even more young
kinsmen as close as the candidate. Like proximate age, common
experience, close residence, and short-term mutual self-interest,
sponsoring a Buddhist ordination singles out some kinsmen for
greater intimacy than it is possible to accord others of the same
genealogical position. Their volitional basis and their need for
continual maintenance make extrahousehold kinship ties "loosely
structured" in Ban Ping.

        Religious merit, the costs of making it, and effective ties of
kinship are all spread more widely by discouraging parents from
being sponsors. In 1960, a son of Maj M, the village's wealthiest
man, was ordained as a novice. As shown in Figure 5a, he was

Figure 5. KINSHIP BETWEEN VARIOUS CANDIDATES
AND THEIR SPONSORS

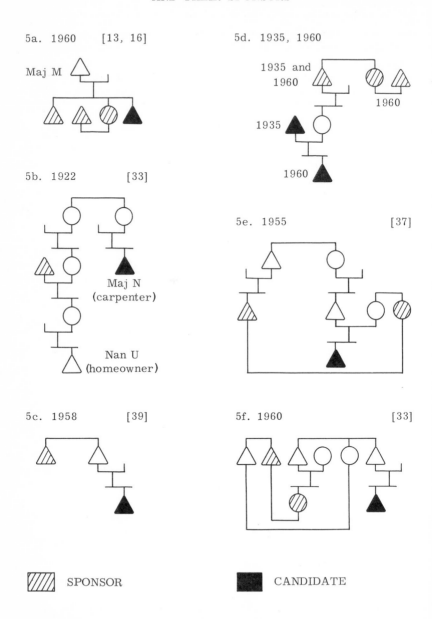

5a. 1960   [13, 16]

Maj M

5d. 1935, 1960

1935 and
1960

1960

1935

1960

5b. 1922   [33]

Maj N
(carpenter)

Nan U
(homeowner)

5e. 1955   [37]

5c. 1958   [39]

5f. 1960   [33]

SPONSOR   CANDIDATE

In Lue kinship, generation is less important than age.
Candidates are junior to their sponsors by the number of years
enclosed in brackets.

sponsored by his brother and brother-in-law, both rather young.
Many villagers criticized Maj M for using his dependents to mask
his own sponsorship of his son's ordination. Although this innovation involved Maj M in great expenditures, the other villagers
called him "stingy" or "selfish." Religiously, they were criticiz-
ing his unwillingness to share the merit. Socially, they were re-
acting to his failure to make use of sponsorship as it functions to
define the bonds of kinship and expand them beyond the sibling
group and household. In "loosely structured" Ban Ping, neither
basis of criticism permitted them to do more than gossip.

The costs of the reception and ceremonies, along with the continuing obligations to his luk kaew, preclude a poor man from being
asked to become a sponsor. The belief in sharing the merit thus
results in sharing the wealth, a consequence comparable to that
produced by the politicoreligious offices found in villages of Middle
America (Carrasco 1961: 483 f.). A further egalitarian consequence is to permit poor boys to have ceremonies and receptions
as elaborate as those of the wealthy. Villagers feel that a rich
man should spend his money. Ceremony and hospitality -- the two
are inseparable -- are approved ways of his doing so. But one can
be criticized for spending too lavishly and conspicuously even on
merit-making ends.

The secular reception and non-Buddhist ceremonies that accompany ordination used to take place in private homes, but a few
years ago communities in and near the market town began to hold
them in the temple. In 1958 the father of a Ban Ping novice insisted
that his son's ordination as a priest and all attendant hospitality occur in the temple. His reasons were frankly economic: At a home
ordination many people come not to make merit but only to eat and
drink; people contribute only a baht or two and then eat two or three
times; two people finish off a bottle of liquor, go elsewhere to
drink, and then come back for more; therefore it's better to hold
the affair in the temple [where liquor cannot be served]."

By 1960 the innovation had taken hold. The guests at three of
the village's four ordinations were entertained in the temple. Only
Maj M, the wealthiest villager, entertained at home. In public,
sponsors justified their choice in the vocabulary of Buddhism:
"Ordination is a religious matter, so no one should drink liquor, "
said those who served their liquor at home. "The scriptures forbid eating in the vihara, " said Maj M, although he had supported
serving food there at a ceremony earlier in the year. Privately,
the sponsors made their choice for economic reasons. One group
computed the prices of condensed sweet milk and of liquor and
chose the temple because it would be cheaper. Maj M boasted of
how much he would spend. It would be a mistake, I think, to call

either camp hypocritical. [15] One of the tasks of Buddhism, and perhaps of all religions, is to permit private interests to be phrased
in transcendent terms. One of the features of Ban Ping, and an
aspect of its "looseness," is that individuals are often expected to
give primacy to their divergent private interests and are never
publicly accused of inconsistency or hypocrisy for the rhetoric
which conceals their selfishness.

I have already indicated that the rewards of the clerical career, relative to its alternatives, progressively diminish. About
80 per cent of the boys who become novices do not stay on to become priests: many of them leave the temple just before becoming
eligible for the priesthood; the few who do become priests do not
remain priests for long. This reluctance does not result from the
severity of priests' rules (Winai). All villagers know that a priest
should observe more rules than a novice, but no one knows the
individual rules or even their major categories. Except on holy
days, the life of village priests differs little from that of novices.
Priests and novices both eat meat; priests and novices both eat a
secret evening meal. In "loosely structured" Ban Ping, there is
neither an authority who requires conformity nor an expectation
that conformity is appropriate. As the village sage explains:

> Earning merit is like working. The more one does, the more
> one gets. Some people have the endurance to work hard [just
> as] only some clergy have the endurance to fast after noon.
> Those who do, get more merit. It's up to the individual.

The difficulty of being a priest comes not from the rigors of
temple life but from the blandishments of the secular life outside.
Boys who have been in the temple for any length of time complain
about "boredom" and "loneliness." They fret that they cannot join
their lay peers in farming, courting, and earning money. The
longer they have been in the temple, the duller life seems there.
The older they get, the more urgent becomes the appeal of the
courting and the saving that lead to marriage. Older novices complain that they have less fun and earn less money than the bachelors outside. They are often kidded by their lay age-mates -- as
when a teen-age girl shouts after a group of young priests whose
heads have just been shaved, "Are you off to Chiengban [a neighboring village] to get a permanent?"

Village elders have tried to forbid young bachelors from visiting the temple to regale its clergy with tales of profitable trade
ventures, entertaining festivities, and exploits of courtship. But
the visits continue and as the cleric grows older he becomes more
and more oppressed by the disabilities of the yellow robe. Within
the temple, the boy has little status, less fun, and no prospects.

As he matures, the value of his potential labor both to his family
and to himself increases. Often just before he is old enough to become a priest, the boy has had his fill and quits.

For the temple to function, "for the elders to earn merit, "
novices are not enough. The priest, as if in compensation for the
greater sacrifice he makes and the greater ritual responsibility he
incurs, receives more than the novice. Not only is his status
higher, his material rewards are greater. A priest's share of
cash offerings to the temple is regularly at least twice that of a
novice. The ordination ceremony is itself quite profitable since
all of the offerings brought by guests become the candidate's property. In 1960 each candidate received about 500 baht as his personal share of the offerings. To convince his novice son to become
a priest, one father argued that by just one more year in the temple he would make about 600 baht from the ordination alone and
then earn more than twice as much as he had while a novice. Such
an argument, while it may gain a priest, cannot keep him long.
Since the more priests there are, the easier it is for any one of
them, the incumbent priest may try to convince a senior novice to
join him by promising not to leave the temple as soon as the other
becomes a priest. Nevertheless, soon after the ordination of a
new priest, the former priest usually resigns. To do so, he must
have the formal permission of the villagers.

Assemblies at the temple are rather common but, except for
the one at which the priest announces his decision to resign, they
are summoned and led by the lay temple committee. When the
priest announces that he wants to return to secular life, the village
elders try to convince him to change his mind. They remind him
that it is "correct, " and good for Ban Ping's reputation, and pleas-
ing to the old men for there to be more than one priest. The temple committee may threaten to resign if the priest leaves the order.
Respected elders "beg him to stick it out for just one more Phansaa."
But the decision is his and, although he may have to call meeting
after meeting, the elders always give their permission. The priest
then offers his formal resignation to the head abbot of the district
and returns to the secular life and to his parental family which,
even while in the temple, he had continued to visit daily. In
"loosely structured" Ban Ping, the child who won't take his medicine or the bride who won't sleep with her husband, like the priest
who won't serve any longer, can rarely be made to do what he is
unwilling to do.

Former clergy. In Ban Ping, honor and even power are the
rewards less of being a cleric than of having been one. For the
rest of his life, the former novice will always be addressed as
maj, the former priest will always be addressed as nan. Only his

wife and child (and, sometimes, members of his wife's natal family if co-resident with him) may omit the title when speaking or
referring to him; only government officials will fail to include the
title in his name. Actually these titles have become more than
honorific for almost without exception the political leaders and
moral counselors of the village have served in the temple, i. e. a
maj or a nan is almost invariably a village leader. Although villagers do not explicitly recognize it as a prerequisite, almost all
who have held the office of headman have been ordained (see Table
3). At village meetings, those who have been ordained monopolize

Table 3. Temple Experience of Headmen and Other Male
Villagers of Like Age Compared

	Number ordained	Number not ordained	Percent ordained
Headmen (1900-1960)	6	1	85
Male villagers over thirty-six years old who have never been headman	33	47	41

the discussion. The informal village council is composed largely
of the ordained. The committee that controls temple affairs has
only one member who was never ordained. Litigants in trouble
cases are likely to ask their ordained kinsmen to speak on their
behalf. The lay leader of temple services and the aged authority
on the spirits and the Buddha were both once priests. Temple service, then, is a basis of future status as a layman. There are a
number of reasons for the secular prominence of the maj or nan.
One of these is the ideal Buddhist stratification of woman-man-
priest, but these ideal strata are rarely spoken of in Ban Ping
(although I frequently heard of them in the market town where
former clergy are not especially regarded and where women are
more prominent than they are in the village).

Another, perhaps firmer, basis for the secular prominence
of former clerics is that the texts of Ban Ping's temple are in the
Northern Thai script. Clerics must be literate in Northern Thai
and until the government schools came twenty-five years ago there
was no other written language. Only those who were ordained
could read and write. In Ban Ping, there was no "temple school"

of the sort reported elsewhere in Southeast Asia. Instruction was
always limited to those who were to be ordained. Of the sixty-two
villagers literate in Northern Thai, only three were never clerics.
Before Central Thai came to be taught in government schools, any
position requiring literacy was restricted to those who had been
priests or novices.

Now 85 per cent of all men under forty-five are literate in
Central Thai. Although the national language is becoming more
influential, it has yet to eliminate the Northern Thai script or to
deprive former clerics of their monopoly of learning. This is true
because the two alphabets are used in different areas of life. Central Thai is the means by which the national administration, but
not yet the national culture, penetrates into the village. The older
script -- called by the villagers "the temple's alphabet" or "the
letters of the Buddha" -- records traditional culture. In Ban Ping,
the Northern alphabet, the temple that teaches it, and the clerics
who learn it are still quite highly valued. It is becoming increasingly difficult to replace the handwritten Northern Thai scriptures
as they wear out, but even the few printed texts in Central Thai
are read with deliberate phonological and lexical transformation
into the Lue dialect. Pure Central Thai is used almost exclusively
for following the national lottery -- and for reading medicine labels.
Occasionally, young people amuse themselves by reading lyrics or
cheap stories in Central Thai. Of incomparably greater interest
are the young people's courtship letters, which are now written in
Central Thai characters but with most words and phrases in Lue
or Yuan. Those of courting age are all literate in Central Thai
but some are considered more talented than others. Bachelors
often have a friend with a better hand and wittier style write their
letters for them. In every case that I observed, the scribes were
former priests. Young people apparently feel that those who have
been in the temple can express themselves more eloquently and in
a finer hand. Young nans are sought to write courtship letters in
Central Thai characters much as older nans are sought to write
horoscopes and charms in "the Buddha's characters." The higher
prestige accorded to nans than to majs is presumably an incentive
for novices to remain in the temple long enough to become priests.

Northern Thai is also the script for the songs and legends
which are the core of all festivities and the coin of all rhetoric.
Young people value this literature no less than their elders do. It
is characteristic that Ban Ping's only radio is often turned off so
that its owner's twenty-six-year-old son can amuse himself by
reading aloud from the old tales. Although, as will be discussed
below, the temple links the village to the nation, it is also a focus
of community loyalty and a support for some of the peculiarities
of dialect and tradition which are the symbols of Lue ethnic identi-

fication. (Moerman 1965).

This description of the careers of laymen, clergy, and former clergy has, I hope, both documented the central importance of the Buddhist temple to the society of Ban Ping and explicated some meanings of "loose social structure." A further meaning of loose structure should be apparent from the ways in which the data were presented and analyzed. Many of the major patterns of life in Ban Ping are regularities which can be observed but which villagers do not and often cannot express as formal rules.

Temple and Village

The temple and reciprocity. The society of Ban Ping operates in terms of something got for every something given. This is not merely an analytic device which permits a predictive, if crass, view of any human society. It is the way in which villagers explain and evaluate their own behavior. Favor for favor, visit for visit, meal for meal, one should return what he receives. "We help our kinsmen because they help us. If a kinsman, however close, didn't help me, I wouldn't help him." "We care for our children when they are young; they will care for us when we are old." Actions which Westerners might justify in terms of compassion, generosity, public spirit, patriotism, or pride in a job well done the Lue villager speaks of in terms of reciprocal short-term self-interests.

Buddhist ritual reinforces this principle by dramatizing reciprocity at every ceremony. An offering is always made to the clergy who accepts by touching it while the donor still has it in hand. At a major ceremony the donors form a human chain, each man's hand on his neighbor's shoulder, which connects all of them to their offering. When the clergy accepts it, the donors all grunt or sigh audibly. "The merit flows one way, the gift flows the other," the village sage explains. The acceptance of an offering is·always immediately followed by a blessing. The most solemn rite at a major service is the lay leader's long high-pitched chant which lists all the principal donors and details the blessings of health, prosperity, and longevity they have earned. The clergy confirms this with a blessing to which all respond "satho" (amen).

In return for economic support, the clergy enables the villagers to make the religious merit that provides prosperity and contentment in this and future lives. The fruits of merit, as villagers describe them, are largely material. Villagers are also quite explicit about the reciprocity involved. In former years, each cleric began every meal by blessing his sponsor over the first ball of rice. Were he not to repay his debt in this manner, he might be reborn as the water buffalo of those who furnished his

food. Merit-making is understood in terms of reciprocation. In
Ban Ping there is a wise and gentle former priest who is acknowledged, even in other villages, as a great religious authority. Novices, priests, lay leaders, and diviners all defer to Thamacaj's
judgment and await his explanations of the rituals all share but few
understand. Thamacaj's articulate description of the clergy's function is thus of some interest.

We make offerings in order to gain merit to get things in the
next life. It's not as some people think that for each 50 cents
offered one gets 50 cents in return. It's like planting the seed-
bed; one gets far more than one gives. We make offerings because we desire happiness in the future and not merely to support priests who sit about doing nothing. We wouldn't make
offerings to just anyone who gives up wife and child in order
to sit about and do nothing. The priests give us the precepts,
so we make them offerings. We make them offerings in order
to be born in heaven and have happiness in the future. If one
did not get back far more than one gives, very few people
would offer anything at all.

The temple as a corporate group. We have seen how kinship
and marriage present each villager with a plethora of relatives.
The standards by which some are drawn closer than others are
often unrelated to genealogy. Among these standards are close
residence, proximate age, and common experience. These, of
course, are shared by those who have been in the temple together.
Even though the villagers do not speak of it, we should expect co-
tenure in the temple to be reflected in the composition of groups of
friends and intimates.

In Ban Ping there is one group of friends that is proverbial.
Three men in their fifties, who are not especially close kinsmen,
act as siblings at each other's ceremonies. In trade, when one
goes, all go. Whenever I visited one of them, at least one other
was always there. When the temple treasury was embezzled, the
three formed a united core of leaders to express village resent-
ment. The three were ordained together thirty-eight years ago.

A looser, more complex, but probably more characteristic
group of associates is clustered about the village headman. Though
not popular, he has a rather clearly defined group of seven friends
and associates. [16] Figure 6 presents a highly edited genealogy of
the headman, who is represented by a hatched triangle. His
friends, indicated by solid triangles, are also his kinsmen, as is
most everyone else. The significant fact is not that most of the
headman's friends are close relatives but rather that so few of
his close relatives are his friends. A vertical arrow indicates

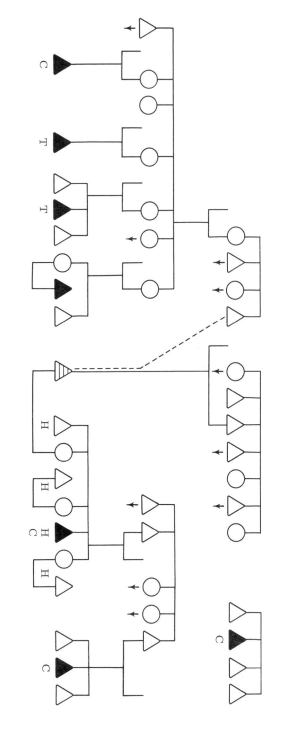

Figure 6. GENEALOGY OF HEADMAN'S ASSOCIATES

HEADMAN

--- ADOPTION

↤ MALE PROGENY OF SUITABLE AGE FOR
CLOSE ASSOCIATION WITH HEADMAN

HEADMAN'S FRIENDS
AND ASSOCIATES

T   FORMER FELLOW TEACHERS

H   FORMER CO-RESIDENTS

C   FORMER CO-CLERGY

persons whose offspring are of the age and sex suitable for friendship with the headman. From this large universe of kinsmen, the
headman has chosen few for friendship. The letter "T" indicates
two of the three villagers who, by an historical accident, were
school teachers at the same time as the headman was. The letter
"H" indicates those who have lived in the same household as the
headman when both were adults. The letter "C" marks four of the
seven villagers who served in the temple during the four years that
the headman was a novice. In the headman's case, and in others,
it is fairly clear that co-tenure in the temple provides one of the
many principles which help define and structure the small proportion of one's bilateral kinsmen with whom close relations are possible.

Figure 6 is rather complicated. Ban Ping's "loose structure"
means that neither co-tenure in the temple nor any other single
principle provides the "key" to village social organization. Co-
tenure is but one of many extragenealogical ties that bring people
together and so help them define their effective kindred. Extragenealogical kinship ties are probably important in all relatively
endogamous, bilateral communities where everyone is simultaneously related to everyone else in a number of ways (cf. Foster
1961; Kaut 1961: 267). In Ban Ping, where all are farmers, few
are drafted, and no one goes away to high school, co-tenure in the
temple is the only such tie which is based on an enduring organization. The organization, of course, is the Buddhist temple, which
is also corporate in that it stands for the community, can store its
property, and helps train its leaders.

Some of the ways in which the temple stands for Ban Ping will
be discussed below. Its ability to store community property can
be described briefly since there is so little property to store. The
mats, buckets, dishes, plates, and other housewares offered to the
temple are stored there to be borrowed by any villager who needs
them. The temple's money, like its precious objects, is in the
custody of the temple committee who may use or loan it before it
is spent on temple business. There is no institution other than the
temple which can hold communal property. When the district office
ordered villages to provide themselves with buckets and a hook for
fighting fires, the elders of Ban Ping complained that such property
stored at the headman's house would become his personal possession. They decided instead to store the equipment in the temple so
that all would have access to it in an emergency. In "loosely structured" Ban Ping even this decision could be effected only because
the temple committee which accepted it is composed of the active
elders who made it.

The Ban Ping temple helps to train community leaders. We

Figure 7. THE LEADERS OF BAN PING

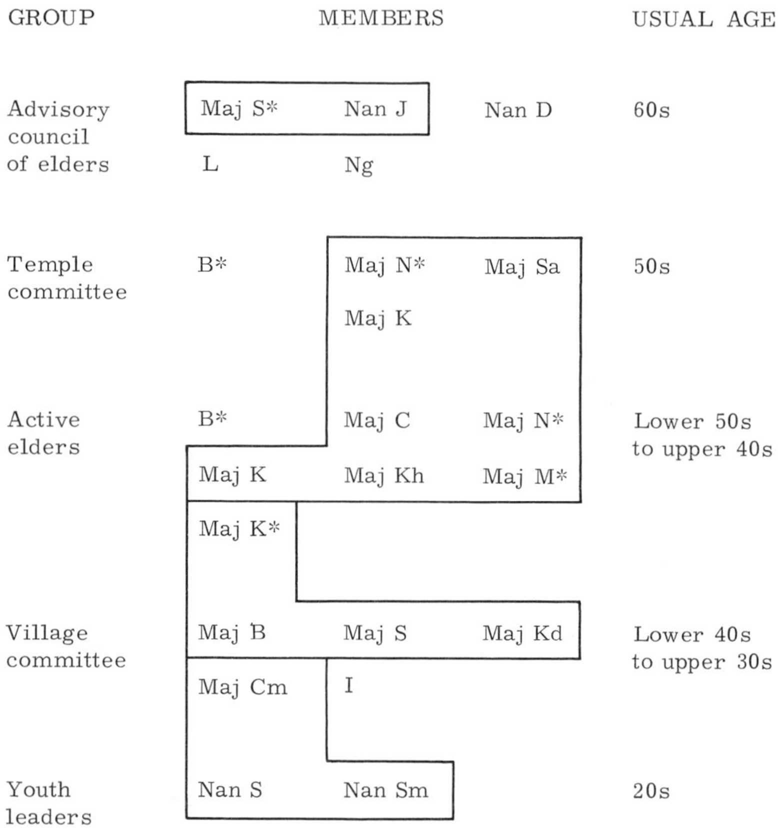

GROUP	MEMBERS			USUAL AGE
Advisory council of elders	Maj S* Nan J	Nan D		60s
	L Ng			
Temple committee	B*	Maj N* Maj Sa		50s
		Maj K		
Active elders	B*	Maj C	Maj N*	Lower 50s to upper 40s
	Maj K	Maj Kh	Maj M*	
	Maj K*			
Village committee	Maj B Maj S Maj Kd			Lower 40s to upper 30s
	Maj Cm I			
Youth leaders	Nan S Nan Sm			20s

Lines enclose those who served together in the temple.
Asterisks designate former headmen.

have already seen that secular leadership is largely restricted to
former clerics. Further, we have seen how friendships formed
in temple may persist as the former clerics mature toward prominence. Since village leadership is rather clearly stratified by
age, it is possible for us to speak, although the villagers do not,
of a hierarchy of temple-educated age-grades. Like classmates
at a military academy, those who were contemporaries in the temple work together to organize secular life.

To the groups I have called the advisory council, the temple
committee, and the active elders (see Figure 7) the villagers often
give the collective designation of "the group of elders" (mu thaw)
or "the group of prominent men" (mu samkhansamkhan). The
advisory council, whom villagers sometimes refer to as "the group
of old men" (mu thaw mu kae), are consulted by the other elders
and by the headman and also help to adjudicate trouble cases which
involve the entire village or in which old people are disputants.
They are, however, much less active than the active elders and,
also unlike them, do not meet as a group. The active elders advise the headman on policy toward government directives, are used
by him to influence village opinion, and help to adjudicate trouble
cases even when they do not involve their immediate kinsmen. The
temple committee (kamakan wat), although its members are all
active elders, meets and is termed separately. The village committee (kamakan ban), whose members have been delegated by the
headman to perform specific tasks assigned to the village by
government officials, also meets as a group. The youth leaders,
for which there is no Lue term, organize temple processions and
speak at trouble cases which involve all baw and såw. They also
write courtship letters and are considered by the headman to be
responsible for the behavior of baw at processions.

It would be a distortion to equate Ban Ping's vague temple-
based age groups with the ladder of offices -- each with specific
occupants and explicit prerequisites, tasks, and rank -- of Meso-
American civil-religious hierarchies (Cámara 1952; Carrasco
1957: 19-20; 1961). In Ban Ping only the village and temple committees are formal organizations with specific functions and clearly designated members. An additional aspect of the village's
"loose structure" is that no single principle determines leadership.
Wealth, age, eloquence, and experience can all -- like temple
training -- help to make a man a leader. Nevertheless, in the
temple a boy learns to cooperate with a larger group of peers than
he ever encountered in secular life. Some of these peers will work
together once more when they become old enough for secular responsibilities. The loyalty and social training which successive
sets of village leaders owe the temple help to provide Ban Ping
with an enduring corporate group despite its "loosely structured"

bilateral organization.

   The temple and other communities.   In Chiengkham, individuals often go to other villages in order to trade or to visit relatives
but temples are the only sources of voluntary intervillage contacts
on a community level. When Ban Ping ended construction on its
new vihara, notices were sent to thirty-two other villages. Each
village sent a representative and an offering to the festival. When
other villages invite Ban Ping to a ceremony, the temple committee decides how large an offering is appropriate, who should build
it, and who should go. An effort is made to choose as representative someone who has friends in the recipient village, but the offering and the delegation are understood to come from the community
of Ban Ping to the community of the recipients.

   Its temple represents Ban Ping in another, and more important, sense as well. The honor of the village and the self-respect
of its inhabitants are implicated in the reputation of the clergy.
When police observed some clergy gambling, the entire village
"lost face, lost name. " In intricate maneuvers of concealment,
compensation, and bribery, appeals to Ban Ping's reputation often
overcame substantial self-interests. The clergy was encouraged
to lie to ecclesiastical superiors about the number and rank --
whether priest or novice -- of those who were guilty and thus com-
pelled to leave the temple. The headman, temple committee, and
elders signed an agreement (of dubious enforceability) that any layman who incited the clergy to gamble or acts as their dealer would
have to pay the entire cost of ordaining a new set of clergy. Despite the unity with which Ban Ping weathered this crisis, it must
be emphasized that throughout eleven days of meetings and nego-
tiations, agreements were reached by means of the elaborate dove-
tailing of individual interests and that any principal could, and
sometimes did, by his obduracy threaten to destroy the village's
good name by "breaking its temple and forcing its old men to make
merit elsewhere. "

   Ban Ping's most important relations with other communities
are its ties to the nation. As has been shown, part of the prestige
of those who have been ordained comes from their literacy in
Northern Thai. Despite the advent of the national language, mas-
tery of the old script is still quite highly regarded, but its societal
function has changed. The "alphabet of the temple" no longer links
the village with the great traditions of Buddhism and Northern Thai
legend. Instead, it helps to decrease Ban Ping's participation in
the new national culture and to provide standards of intellectual
accomplishment independent of certification by government schools

   Classes for the clergy are held daily in Chiengkham town.

They are established by national law and supervised by the govern-
ment-appointed head abbot of the district. Newly ordained clergy
are required to attend the lowest grade of religious instruction.
After the third degree naktham examination, they may pursue their
studies for the second and first degrees. Those who pass the lowest degree are exempt from military service while in the temple.
Those who pass the highest degree may substitute it for the secondary school training required for becoming a civil servant. Some
conservative villagers blame the innovation of naktham instruction
for the ancient unwillingness of Ban Ping's priests to remain in
office. Their opinion, however incorrect historically, is of sociological interest as an example of the tension between the temple as
an agent of village solidarity and the temple as an agent of the
national state. These conservatives point out that young clerics
from the market town pass examinations their village seniors fail.
Ban Ping priests, embarrassed by their ignorance, quit the temple.

In many of Chiengkham's villages, clerics have achieved the
second and first degrees, but no one in Ban Ping has ever gone
beyond the lowest degree and very few get that far. Of 1960's
eight clerics, only two had passed the lowest degree. The present
priest has failed the examination a number of times. Few villagers
are disturbed by this for, to them, the clergy functions to enable
its parishioners to make merit. A priest's prestige depends on
his personal attributes of age, rectitude, and spiritual power --
not on his position in the official hierarchy. To the villager, young
or old, significant religious knowledge has nothing to do with what
is taught in the government's naktham classes. The decreasing
order of significant religious knowledge in Ban Ping is: extrasen-
sory powers, magical charms, knowledge of the spirits and how to
control them, and familiarity with the Northern Thai sacred and
profane literature. But these old things are no longer much studied
in the village temple, nor is the clergy willing to learn the new
knowledge taught in town.

Ban Ping's temple serves the local community which provides
all its support, all its congregation, and all its clergy. But the
village priest is also at the bottom of an ecclesiastical hierarchy
that begins in Bangkok. His knowledge is but a rural version of
lore originating in India and perfected in urban seminaries. His
practices are but a corrupted form of national rites. There is
tension between the national hierarchy and the villagers who ven-
erate only age and mystical accomplishment. There is lack of
sympathy between the urban clerics who strive for naktham degrees
and the villagers who do not. The temple is both the clearest focus
of village identity and the easiest road for national penetration.
The common village remark that "the head abbot of the district is

equivalent to the district administrative officer" shows this am-
bivalence. When the abbot visits, he is given elaborate signs of
respect, but villagers also point out that he is the friend of the
officials and gets a monthly salary. For all of his position, they
say, the abbot is fond of meat and is not as holy as a distant priest
who eats but once a day and can foretell the future.

The district abbot is a fellow Lue and rather well liked as an
individual, but villagers are aware that the standards by which he
was chosen and the hierarchy he represents are alien to traditional
ways. Before Chiengkham came under the direct administration of
Bangkok, there were, in widely scattered temples, a few aged
priests (xu ba) to whom a young cleric might apprentice himself to
learn some special religious skill. There are still such saintly
men whom the villagers revere, but now there are also certified
stages of theological excellence and a national hierarchy of ecclesiastical power. These are the Buddhist aspect of the increasing
centralization of Thailand. As one acute villager describes it:

> In the old days we deferred to age. Now formal learning is
> most important. The old and holy priests must bow before
> the district abbot just as Thamacaj, for all his years, must
> bow before the district administrative officer.

The government attempts to use the ecclesiastical hierarchy
to control the villagers. When Ban Ping was unwilling to help construct a new school building, the district administrative officer
came to the village with the district abbot. The abbot preached a
sermon in which he told the congregation that schools and roads
make as much merit as temples because they bring about progress
and call for cooperation. Just in case the villagers had missed
the point, the district administrative officer summarized the appropriate part of the sermon. Afterward, some villagers admitted
that a road might make merit but their explanation was that without one people could lose their way or be attacked by thieves.
Some admitted that a school might make merit but their explanation was that only after passing the fourth grade can a boy become
ordained. All insisted that nothing makes as much merit as a
temple and since a new vihara was then under construction in Ban
Ping they could not afford to divert any efforts for the benefit of
the school.

The villagers of Ban Ping are suspicious of the national hierarchy and do not understand its social gospel. Nevertheless, the
form and content of the Buddhist church links the village to the
nation. Officials, both clerical and lay, are occasionally said to
have earned their position by means of religious merit. The presence of clergy legitimizes state ceremonies and makes them more

intelligible. Prominent priests are respected and the national
Buddhist vocabulary is universally understood, for Buddhism is
an institution that all Thai, whether Central or Northern or Lue,
whether urban or rural, hold in common. This most general
secular aspect of Buddhism -- as a defining feature of the Thai --
is especially evident in the North where the Thai in the plains are
conscious of their superiority to the tribal peoples of the hills.
The villagers of Ban Ping see a fundamental division of humanity
between "people who have religion, " i.e. Buddhists, and those who
do not. The historical superiority of lowland peoples is expressed
in the superiority of those who have a religion. When the villager
is made to feel that he shares this precious superiority with all
Thais, he identifies himself with the nation.

Summary

        We can now, by way of summary, point out some of the ways
in which a loosely structured society can be said to have a center.
In Ban Ping, and probably elsewhere in North Thailand, the temple performs few social services and its clergy has low prestige.
Nevertheless, social age is expressed and the complementarity of
age groups ritualized by temple attendance. The temple acts to
equalize private wealth, to structure voluntary kinship, and to provide an enduring corporate organization which trains and certifies
village leaders and holds village property. The temple, although
a focus of village loyalty and a repository of Lue traditions, also
binds the local community to the nation. In its ritual and rationale,
the temple dramatizes reciprocity, the basic principle of Ban
Ping's social life.

        Individual behavior is difficult to predict in Ban Ping because
there are few social groups and categories membership in which
enforces uniform behavior, and it is easy to enter and leave those
that do. There are numerous alternative principles which direct
social behavior and an individual is expected to choose the one
which best advances the interests, usually economic, of his household. The regular patterns of social life are, in Leach's terms
(1961: 297), more statistical than jural. Thus, aside from the
mild punishment for deviance which is perhaps related to Buddhist
values, Ban Ping is comfortably within the range we have come to
expect of peasant societies (Fitchen 1961) without unilineal descent
groups. Individual variation, although characteristic, seems to be
less striking than it is in some societies (Friedl 1962: 82) which
are rarely called "loosely structured. " In the course of explicating
the concept's meaning in Ban Ping, I have become less convinced
of its value for depicting Thai society.

NOTES

1. There are book-length community studies of Bangchan (Sharp, et al. 1953) and Bangkhuad (Kaufman 1960) in Central Thailand and of Ku Daeng (Kingshill 1960) in the North. In addition, de-Young's account (1958) is based largely on a village in the district of Mae Rim near the northern city of Chiengmai.

2. The Lue are a Thai people from the Sip Song Panna (100°-101°30'E by 21°30'-22°30'N) in Southwest Yunnan. A general account of their history and culture can be found in Lebar, et al.1964: 206-13. Over 100 years ago, some Lue came to Chiengkham, now a district in Chiengrai province. This report is based upon fourteen months of fieldwork in Ban Ping, one of the villages they founded. Ban Ping is four kilometers from the Chiengkham market and district office which are connected to the provincial capital (Chiengrai) and to Phayao by one of the worst roads in Thailand. I am pleased to be able to thank the Foreign Area Training Fellowship Program of the Ford Foundation for the opportunity to do fieldwork there. I also wish to thank Herbert Phillips and Harvey Sacks for their comments on an earlier draft of this paper.

3. There is also an annual ceremony for the spirit whom the Lue "found" when they came to Ban Ping. It is taken much less seriously and the village is not sealed off for it.

4. Buddhism, although only one component of village religion, is no less important in Ban Ping than in other Chiengkham villages, whether Lue, Lao, or Yuan. LaFont (1957a; 1957b) reports that Buddhism is "still at a missionary stage" among the Lue of Myang Sing in Laos, but my informants denied that this was true of Myang Phong, from which the founders of Ban Ping came.

5. About 15 years ago, Ban Ping was once without a priest for Phansaa and clergy had to be borrowed from neighboring villages.

6. The custom of entering the temple for a single Phansaa began in Chiengkham a few years ago and occurs only in town temples. There were three instances in 1959 and none in 1960.

7. These are the eight vows (Pabhassaro 1957: 4-5) of which all laymen take the first five:
    1) I observe the precept of not killing.
    2) I observe the precept of not stealing.

    3) I observe the precept of living a life of chastity.
    4) I observe the precept of not telling falsehoods.
    5) I observe the precept of not taking intoxicating things
       which are conducive to bewilderment.
    6) I observe the precept of not taking food beyond the
       fixed time [of noon].
    7) I observe the precept of not having anything to do
       with dancing, singing, music, unseemly shows,
       using of garlands, perfumes, and things that tend
       to beautify and adorn.
    8) I observe the precept of not using a high and luxurious
       seat and bed.

8. I observed no normal morning service at which more than 5
percent of Ban Ping's young parents were present. At special
services (e.g. ordination, first and last days of Phansaa, New
Year) attendance is larger and more uniform in terms of age
and sex.

9. Unless context indicates a more restricted meaning, English
kinship terms take account only of the generation and sex of
relatives, not of features significant to the Lue terminological
system. English terms enclosed in quotation marks are
glosses for Lue terms.

10. At morning services at least half of the village's sáw were
usually present, but rarely more than 10 per cent of the baw,
who nevertheless stay near the temple and observe the young
women. In Central Thai, I am told, the expression "a sáw
who is late to temple" means a pretty girl, since an unattrac-
tive one would not call attention to herself through tardiness.

11. deYoung (1958: 118) says: "Village surveys in the north have
shown that about half of village males spend some time in the
wat as a temple boy. Those that do not do so generally come
from families that cannot spare the boys from farmwork."
On the other hand, Kingshill (1960: 101) asserts that: "According to our survey, the kind of homes novices [and temple boys]
come from is not related to economic circumstances of the
household." In Ban Ping, "I did not have enough merit" was
the uniform answer to my question, "Why weren't you ordained?" Only in the household with which we were most intimate did a young man respond, "I would have become ordained, but I had no brothers." When an old Chiengkham
priest mentioned, as though it were self-evident, that only
poor boys made the temple their career, his audience of villagers quickly denied the idea, probably for reasons of politeness.

12. deYoung (1958: 119) mentions the sponsor-luk kaew relationship but does not indicate its incidence or functions.

13. Because only about 15 per cent of all villagers were ordained,
the incidence of sponsorship is far less than that of godparent-
hood in the Catholic world. It further differs from the ritual
co-parenthood of Greece (Campbell 1964: 222), Latin America,
southern Italy, and the Philippines in that the relationship is
essentially one between the boy and his sponsor. Although the
households of both are involved, a close relationship between
the boy's real and ritual fathers is, as it were, accidental and
certainly does not proscribe marriage between their descendants. Nevertheless, there are analogies between sponsorship
in Ban Ping and compadrazgo which make it legitimate to use
an analysis of the Catholic institution to depict the Buddhist
one. In the terms of Mintz and Wolf, sponsorship is "horizon-
tal" in its restriction to members of the same class as the luk
kaew; this is just as one would expect, since Ban Ping is a
"homogenous socio-cultural community with high stability and
low mobility" (1950: 358).

14. "Kinsman," or pi-norng, literally means "senior-junior" and
thus implies a relationship which is both intimate and unequal.
The patron-client bond which is so important to stratified communities and to the articulation of Thai national society is similar to some aspects of kinship in Ban Ping and is often expressed in kinship terms.

15. In a future paper, I hope to consider the possibility that our
social scientific ethnocentrism precludes our discovery of
situations in which facile expressions of material self-interest
could, in some cultures, mask "nobler" motives which the
people believe should not be discussed publicly.

16. My criteria for these seven were: their listing by informants,
their appointment by the headman to assist him, and, from my
own observations, their unusually frequent social visits to the
headman.

REFERENCES CITED

Blanchard, Wendell et al.

    1958   Thailand: Its People, Its Society, Its Culture, New
              Haven, HRAF.

Cámara, Fernando

    1952   "Religious and Political Organization, " in Heritage
            of Conquest, Sol Tax, ed. Glencoe, The Free Press.

Campbell, J. K.

    1964   Honour, Family and Patronage, Oxford, Clarendon
            Press.

Carrasco, Pedro

    1957   "Some Aspects of Peasant Society in Middle America
            and India, " Kroeber Anthropological Society Papers,
            16, 17-27.

    1961   "The Civil-religious Hierarchy in Mesoamerican
            Communities: Pre-Spanish Background and Colonial
            Development, " American Anthropologist, 63,
            483-97.

Curtis, Lillian Johnson

    1903   The Laos of North Siam, Philadelphia, Westminster
            Press.

Dodd, William Clifton

    1923   The Tai Race, Cedar Rapids, Torch Press.

Embree, John F.

    1949   "Review of A Physician at the Court of Siam by
            Malcolm Smith, " American Anthropologist, 51,
            495-96.

    1950   "Thailand: A Loosely Structured Social System, "
            American Anthropologist, 52, 181-93.

Firth, Raymond

    1961   "Suicide and Risk-taking in Tikopia Society, "
            Psychiatry, 24, 1-17.

Fitchen, Janet Mathews

    1961   "Peasantry as a Social Type, " in Proceedings of the
            1961 Annual Spring Meeting of the American Ethno-
            logical Society, pp. 114-19.

Foster, George M.

   1961   "The Dyadic Contract: A Model for the Social Struc-
             ture of a Mexican Peasant Village," American
             Anthropologist, 63, 1173-92.

Friedl, Ernestine

   1962   Vasilika: A Village in Modern Greece, New York,
             Holt, Rinehart, Winston.

Hanks, L. M., Jr.

   1962   "Merit and Power in the Thai Social Order, "
             American Anthropologist, 64, 1247-61.

Kaufman, Howard Keva

   1960   Bangkhuad: A Community Study in Thailand, Locust
             Valley, N. Y., J. J. Augustin.

Kaut, Charles

   1961   "Utang na loob: A System of Contractual Obligation
             among Tagalogs, " Southwestern Journal of Anthro-
             pology, 17, 256-72.

Kingshill, Konrad

   1960   Ku Daeng -- the Red Tomb: A Village Study in
             Northern Thailand, Chiengmai, The Prince Royal's
             College.

LaFont, Pierre-Bernard

   1957a   "Ordination de deux dignitaires bouddhiques tay lu, "
             Bulletin de la Société des Études Indochinoises, 32,
             199-221.

   1957b   "Le that de Muong-Sing, " Bulletin de la Société des
             Études Indochinoises, 32, 39-57.

Landon, Kenneth Perry

   1939   Siam in Transition, Chicago, University of Chicago
             Press.

Leach, Edmund

   1961   Pul Eliya: A Village in Ceylon, Cambridge,
             Cambridge University Press.

THAILAND   173

LeBar, Frank M., Gerald C. Hickey, and John K. Musgrave

1964   Ethnic Groups of Mainland Southeast Asia, New
          Haven, HRAF Press.

Mintz, Sidney W. and Eric R. Wolf

1950   "An Analysis of Ritual Co-parenthood (Compadrazgo),"
          Southwestern Journal of Anthropology, 6, 341-68.

Moerman, Michael

1964   "Western Culture and the Thai Way of Life, " Asia,
          1, 31-50.

1965   "Ethnic Identification in a Complex Civilization: Who
          are the Lue?" American Anthropologist, 67, 1215-30.

Mosel, James N.

1957   "Thai Administrative Behavior, " in Toward the
          Comparative Study of Public Administration, William
          J. Siffin, ed. Bloomington, Department of Govern-
          ment, University of Indiana.

Pabhassaro, Phra Maha Jarai (trans.)

1957   Excerpts from a Book of Recitations for the Order
          of Bikkhus of Thailand, Bangkok, Mahamakuta
          Educational Council, The Buddhist University of
          Thailand.

Phillips, Herbert P.

1965   Thai Peasant Personality, University of California
          Press.

Rajadhon, Phya Anuman

1961   "Popular Buddhism in Thailand, " in Life and Ritual
          in Old Siam, William J. Gedney, ed. New Haven,
          HRAF Press.

Sharp, L., L. Hanks, R. Textor, O. Janlekha et al.

1953   Siamese Rice Village, Bangkok, Cornell Research
          Center.

Textor, Robert B.

1958   Manual for Rural Community Health Workers in
          Thailand, Bangkok, United States Operations Mission
          to Thailand.

T'ien, Ju-k'ang

    1949   "Pai Cults and Social Age in the Tai Tribes of the
            Yunnan-Burma Frontier," American Anthropologist,
            51, 46-57.

Wilson, David A.

    1962   Politics in Thailand, Ithaca, Cornell University
            Press.

Young, Ernest

    1907   The Kingdom of the Yellow Robe, London, Archibald
            Constable.

deYoung, John E.

    1958   Village Life in Modern Thailand, Berkeley and Los
            Angeles, University of California Press.

INTERRELATIONS BETWEEN BUDDHISM AND SOCIAL SYSTEMS
IN CAMBODIAN PEASANT CULTURE

May Ebihara

Theravada Buddhism of the Sinhalese form began to penetrate Cambodia probably during the thirteenth century, carried mainly by the Mons and perhaps to a lesser extent by the encroaching Thai. The historical records are not altogether clear as to the exact processes or chronology involved in the gradual supplanting of Mahayana and Sivaism, but by the mid-fourteenth century Cambodia had been converted to Theravada and was even proselytizing its neighbor Laos.[1] At the present time Theravada is the state religion of Cambodia, practiced by the 85 per cent or more of the population who are the Khmer or Cambodians proper. On the national level, the king is symbolic leader of Buddhists and includes in his advisory Crown Council the heads of the two Buddhist orders. A Secretariat of Religious Affairs (Cults) oversees religious activities and institutions, including a Buddhist Institute and Higher School of Pali. In the mid-1950s there were a reported 2,653 temples and 37,533 monks in this small country (Martini 1955a: 409; 1955b: 417). Not only does the nation's legal code bear influences of the religion but, at the local level, Buddhism offers a normative code that permeates the daily lives and thoughts of the people in numerous ways.

In this paper I should like to discuss some of the relations between Theravada and several aspects of Cambodian peasant culture, rather than concentrate on one particular feature. This presentation has been chosen because Cambodian culture is little known to American anthropological literature, and a more general sort of description may be of some value for comparative purposes. The treatment of Cambodian Buddhism can by no means be exhaustive, but hopefully some preliminary picture will emerge. The data will be based primarily upon field research in a lowland agricultural Cambodian village, to be given the pseudonym Village Kong, with the most intensive investigations concentrated upon one of its hamlets.[2]

The Religious System

The discussion of the interconnections between religious and social systems within the village must begin with a consideration of the religious system itself. Cambodian Buddhism (prea pot sasnaa) is divided into two orders: the Mohanikay ("the great congregation") and the Thommayut ("those who are attached to the doctrine").[3]

The Mohanikay is the older and larger of the two, with over 90
per cent of the total number of permanent monks and 94 per cent of
all temples (Martini 1955b: 416-17). The Thommayut group, which
originated in 1864 with a Cambodian monk who had studied in Thailand, considers .itself more orthodox and stricter than the Mohanikay. While smaller--the number of Thommayut monks is estimated
at less than 1,600 (Martini 1955b: 417) and its temples are located
primarily in Phnom Penh and the provincial capitals--the order is
significant in having been adopted by the king and other high-rank-
ing groups.

It is interesting and somewhat unusual that both of these orders are represented in Village Kong. The village's own temple,
Wat Kong, changed from Mohanikay to Thommayut about seventy
years ago. [4] The Mohanikay temple, Wat Somnang, is located about
one and three-quarters kilometers distant on a road leading to a
nearby town. Both wats have similar temple grounds and similar
personnel. Each compound includes the temple proper (vihià), one
or two open halls (salaa), dormitories for the monks, some tombs,
and a few shrines for animistic spirits. Each wat has its own community consisting of (1) the monks (look sòng) themselves, designated by various terms according to their position in the temple
hierarchy[5]; (2) the temple boys (konsùh look) ranging from about
seven to twelve years of age, who are "given" by their parents to
stay at the temple and assist the monks in various ways; (3) one
or two achaa, a sort of lay priest who does not reside at the temple
but acts as a liaison between the monks and laymen, and who leads
the congregation in prayers and chants at ceremonies; and (4)
several laymen, often elderly persons, who live temporarily at
the temple to earn merit through performance of various tasks for
the monks, through prayer, and through meditation.

There is no real doctrinal difference between Mohanikay and
Thommayut, only some variance as to specific rules of behavior
for monks. According to the villagers themselves, the only distinctions between the two lie in some details of their everyday actions. Thommayut monks carry their alms bowls in their hands,
recite Pali with non-Cambodian pronunciation, will not accept objects directly from the hands of a woman, cannot go anywhere un-
accompanied by another male, do not attend the movies or theater,
and cannot carry money. The Mohanikay, on the other hand, carry
their bowls suspended from the shoulder, recite Pali with Cambodian pronunciation, and presumably can or do perform the other
acts of behavior prohibited to the Thommayut. The villagers usually conclude that "they are really both the same," and a number
of families attend both wats equally often. Yet, as will be discussed later, there are occasions when allegiance to one or the
other wat is distinctly drawn and even becomes the basis for a

factionalism which is rare within the village.

In regard to Buddhist teachings, the intricacies of Theravada doctrine are little known to the average villager (except perhaps to those men who have been monks for extended periods of time). But certain basic precepts are known to all from sermons at the temple, chants or prayers committed to memory, or lessons at school. And the primary concepts of immediate significance to the villager are presented succinctly in a comment made by an eighteen-year-old girl: "I think I will go to three or four Katun festivals this year so that I will be reborn as a rich American." Several critical ideas underlie this remark. An individual goes through a cycle of reincarnations, and the average layman has little hope of achieving supreme Nirvana (nipean). However, one's chances for a better existence in the next rebirth are determined by the number of good deeds accomplished in this lifetime. That is, by living according to the "law" (chbap), abstaining from evil (bap), and earning merit in numerous ways, an individual moves forward on the righteous path. [6] The concept of achieving merit and avoiding evil is the basic principle underlying the influence of religion on behavior, for living by the "law" involves numerous aspects of daily life. Specifically, merit can be earned in the following ways.

(1) Monks are accorded supreme respect as living embodiments and spiritual generators of Buddhism. Not only is there a particular etiquette governing interaction with the monks (speaking to or about them with special linguistic forms, handing them objects in a deferential manner, etc.) but monks are apart from and above the secular world (they live in special quarters, do not vote, cannot be tried in ordinary law courts, etc.). Becoming a monk is the supreme means of earning merit for a man and radiates merit onto his parents as well. Entrance into the monastic state (buah) is an ideal which three-quarters of all males over seventeen years of age in West Hamlet Kong have achieved; they remained in the monastery for an average of two to three years before leaving (suk) to resume secular life.

(2) A second crucial means for the layman to earn merit is to adhere to the Buddhist "precepts": do not lie; do not commit theft; do not have immoral sexual relations; do not drink intoxicating beverages; do not kill living creatures; do not eat after noon; do not indulge in sensual and frivolous activities such as dancing; do not wear cosmetics, jewelry, etc.; do not sleep on a raised bed; do not have sexual intercourse with your spouse on holy days. The first five precepts (sul pram) are the primary guides to evaluation of sinful or meritorious behavior in daily life and ideally should be observed constantly. In reality, they are followed with varying degrees of fidelity. The injunction against killing is the strongest precept; the murder of other human beings is universally regarded

as the greatest sin and horror. For example, after World War II
during a period of internal civil conflict in which a number of the
villagers were involved in rebel activity, one man was said to have
killed some people. He was subsequently ostracized from the village and is still afraid to return. He did not come back even when
specifically invited to his daughter's wedding for fear of being
"beaten up" by his former neighbors. The question of taking animal life will be discussed later. Falsehoods, beyond white lies or
evasiveness for one reason or another (e.g. not registering all of
one's lands to avoid taxes), never came to my attention. Neither
is theft a problem within the village although, if one were to judge
by the villagers' fears and suspicions, barred windows, and locked
doors, thievery in the rest of Cambodia is widespread indeed. The
precept concerning immoral sexual relations is occasionally broken. Weddings of pregnant brides are not unknown, but they invoke
public shame and censurious gossip. A double standard more or
less sanctions adultery for males, though adultery is actually rare
for village men and incurs the wrath of wives. The rule against
consumption of alcoholic drinks is the precept upon which one's
back is most easily turned, especially for men. Weddings and
other private ceremonies include liquor whenever it can be afford-
ed, and it is not uncommon for men to relax with a little beer or
wine when money is available. However, excessive drunkenness
is definitely abhorred and continually cited as characteristic of
ne'er-do-wells. The other five precepts are generally adhered to
only by the most devout individuals or on the holy days.

(3) On the eighth and fifteenth days of the waxing and waning
moons falls tngay sùl, what might be called the holy day. It is
observed nationally by the prohibition of the sale of beef and alcoholic drinks and observed locally in various ways ranging from
complete ignorance that it is a holy day at all to the most rigorous
observance by the devout. Religious persons go to the wat "to ask
respectfully to receive the holy precepts" (som sùl), and some remain the entire day to hear a sermon and recitation of scriptures
by the monks (look tih). Others, such as old Grandfather Pum,
spend most of the day in quiet retreat at home; seclude themselves
to avoid anger, upset, or the possibility of killing insects by walking outside; sip only tea after midday; and meditate and pray.

(4) A final major means of earning merit is through gifts of
food, money, various objects, or labor to the temple and the
monks. The situation that Ingersoll (1961) summarized succinctly
for Thailand is also true for Cambodia: "The monk depends on the
layman for goods; the layman depends on the monk for goodness."
That is, through contributions of material support to religious personnel, activities, and structures, the laity receives spiritual support in return. For the villagers, these gifts are primarily in the

form of food, services, limited amounts of money, and small offerings (e.g. incense and candles), which are contributed on the following occasions. (a) Several times a week some monks come
from Wat Kong to receive rice alms. Actually, however, only a
few houses in the hamlet (families with older persons) give rice
and sometimes a bit of other food. Monks do not come from Wat
Somnang because the distance is considered too far. (b) Every
event or festival at either temple involves the contribution of some
food, money, and/or services by the villagers. For holy days or
other lesser events (e.g. sermons by visiting monks), some food
or very small amounts of money (equivalent to about three to seven
cents) are given. For the important annual Buddhist festivals, the
villagers typically contribute food in the form of special dishes and
delicacies, some money, small offerings such as incense, and perhaps labor services. [7] (They also, of course, accrue additional
merit from saying prayers and from listening to the sermon.) Of
special interest is the Katùn festival, one of the greatest celebrations of the year, which is held after the monks' rainy season retreat (vosaa) and is an occasion for making gifts of clothing, various other useful articles, and large sums of money to the monks
and the temple. [8] Great merit is earned by any individual or group
who organizes a Katùn. The sponsor is usually a wealthy urban
family, business company, or government office rather than the
villagers themselves. Although the villagers do contribute a little
money, their critical role in this festival generally consists rather
of donations of food dishes and services as waiters and waitresses
for the wealthy sponsors and other visitors who come to a Katùn at
their temple. Similar contributions of food and labor occur at the
Bon Pkaa, festivals to raise money for the maintenance or construction of buildings at the temple. (c) Some small gifts (e.g.
cigarettes), money, and perhaps a meal are given to monks whenever they are invited to chant and give blessings at private ceremonies such as weddings, funerals, housewarmings, etc. (d) Finally, sheer physical labor may be contributed to a temple requesting aid in repair or construction work, such pleas often drawing
individuals who are not ordinarily part of the congregation.

As part of this discussion of general religious beliefs and
activities of the villagers, one should note the age and sex differential with regard to religious piety. Children become socialized
into religion at an early age because infants and youngsters usually
accompany their mothers almost everywhere, including the temple.
It was quite instructive to see children of three or four years of
age "playing temple," i.e. sitting with legs folded properly to one
side, hands pressed together, chanting their own version of prayers, just as they sometimes played "house" or "store." They are
also strictly taught the proper etiquette and deference to monks
from a very young age. Yet, while the more overt ritualistic

forms are learned fairly quickly, the inculcation of Buddhist ideology is a more gradual process, and total adherence to its precepts
is only expected of the maturing individual. The most illuminating
example of this latter point occurred whenever a chicken needed to
be killed: no adult wished to commit this sin, so the fowl would
usually be given to children to be killed, on the villagers' assumption that the children could kill the fowl and yet remain innocent,
being too young to be fully responsible for sins. Neither is the pre-
school child especially admonished to adhere to the Buddhist norms,
for parents are generally quite permissive. However, from the
age of about eight or nine when the child does become more subject
to discipline at home, is more able to comprehend sermons at the
temple, and nowadays attends school where there is a course in
"morals, " gradual awareness and internalization of the Buddhist
precepts begin. At adolescence, some boys enter the monastery,
and girls aid in the contribution of food and services to the temple.
They have by now become religious "adults" in the sense that they
are fully cognizant of earning merit and have begun in earnest to
accumulate their own supply.

Religious piety reaches its peak in old age when individuals
come to possess more physical and psychological leisure than is
ordinary. The somewhat younger adult generations in full activity
and vigor are usually observant enough, but the cares of the world
frequently impinge upon them too heavily for complete devoutness.
A field must be transplanted whether it is holy day or not; a little
surplus cash must be used for children's clothing rather than as a
gift to the temple; a man is too exhausted from a day's plowing to
attend a ceremony. Although the desire for earning merit is present in these individuals, practical realities and exigencies override good intentions; although one's fate is determined by religious
devotion, one must survive within the present life of poverty and
effort. However, when one's children are married and the labor
and worries of subsistence are given over to them, their filial piety
can then support the old people's religious piety, much as the layman supports the monk. Thus released from the usual arduous
strains of life and coming increasingly closer to the final tallying
of merit, the old people have both the heightened motivation and
increased time for religious activity. The woman past menopause
cuts off her hair or shaves her head to signify renunciation of
worldly vanities; some old people stay for extended periods of time
in small shelters on temple grounds to pray and meditate; both men
and women become much more observant of holy days and are seen
at all religious ceremonies, large and small, staying through all
the prayers and sermons which the younger adults often do not
bother or cannot afford to attend because of other concerns. Merit
is accumulated in large quantities during these latter years of life
and also earns a great deal of respect for the old people while they

are still in this world.

Religious observance also varies to some extent with sex.
Within Buddhism, women occupy a lower religious status than men;
their sex presumably reflects a limited amount of merit in the previous incarnation. Moreover, women are not only barred from becoming monks but various injunctions prevent them from close contact with monks. Thus the woman begins with several liabilities
and must work harder to compensate for them. This situation,
plus the fact that food is perhaps the main form of contributions by
villagers to the temple, seems to account for the preponderance of
women at various religious ceremonies. Some of the lesser events
are attended almost exclusively by females and a few old men (e.g.
at one Visak Bochià women outnumbered men almost four to one
and all the males were middle-aged or old).

Men generally know more about Buddhism because a greater
number of them have had education and experience in the monastery. But perhaps because they could obtain or had accumulated
so much merit as monks, and because secular and material concerns of subsistence weigh more heavily upon men than upon women, most adult men and adolescent boys tend to participate in
only the most important annual festivals. They rationalize non-
attendance at other events with comments such as: "I'm too tired,"
"My wife is going for the family," "I don't like crowds," etc. Men
are also more likely to break certain injunctions, e.g. against al-
cohol, than are women, who are characterized by more constant
devotion and obedience to religion from a young age. Generally,
men seem to "coast" until old age both releases and prods them
into more active observance.

Economic Organization and Buddhism

It is sometimes said or implied in the literature that Buddhism is a drain upon or hindrance to economic development because
large numbers of men are living unproductive lives in the monasteries, because a high proportion of food and money are given to
religion, because the doctrine of accepting one's fate is contrary
to our Protestant Ethic drive for economic success, etc. (Gourou
1945: 382; Delvert 1961: 140-42; Kleinpeter 1937: 76-78, 82-85).
Our discussion of some interconnections between religious and
economic systems might begin, then, with a reexamination of
these generalizations, because the reality at the Cambodian village
level is more complex than might be initially thought.

First, when one looks at a Buddhist nation as a whole, the
large number of males in monasteries does appear to cut off a
considerable supply of labor. Yet, within Village Kong, it is in-

teresting to note who had not been a monk and why. Of the nine
males over eighteen years of age in West Hamlet who have never
been monks, the following kinds of situations had been present.
Apart from two who were quite simply more interested in secular
pursuits (e.g. one is a professional musician) these men all came
from families which could not spare them because the father had
died, because a brother or brothers were already monks, or because the family needed all available manpower in the rice fields
or in alternative economic activity. In all of these cases, the
men came from poor families to begin with, and most even now reside uxorically. Though it remains true that the monastery can be
a haven for the poor, it is also true that a monk cannot work the
family's fields or remit regular income from a job. From the perspective of the family, a male will not become a monk unless he
can be spared. [9]

Second, it is sometimes thought that the contributions for
making merit are a drain on family budgets and food resources.
The partial validity of this picture will be discussed later, but for
now it should be noted that families seem to give only what they
can afford. (It is interesting that the families who attend very few
temple ceremonies during the year are precisely the poorest households in the hamlet, and one suspects not lack of piety but rather
embarrassment at inability to contribute.) Cash contributions are
generally limited, from the equivalent of a few cents at lesser
events to about a dollar at the larger festivals. More generally,
since cash is precious and scarce, contributions are made in the
form of services and especially food. The latter raises a significant point: the food given consists of special dishes (chicken curry,
beef, sweet delicacies, etc.) which the villager can afford to prepare only on very special occasions such as life-cycle or temple
ceremonies. After the monks finish their meal, there is always
considerable food remaining which the villagers themselves then
reclaim and eat, gathering in small groups to pool various dishes
brought by different families. The temple festivals are, therefore,
one of the few occasions when the usual diet of rice and fish is
supplemented by meat and other foods out of the ordinary, through
a small-scale redistributive system. Thus, while cash and service contributions bring important spiritual returns, the food donations generally bring returns to the stomach as well--or, to para-
phrase an old Western proverb, in this instance the villagers can
have their merit and eat it too.

There is, furthermore, one other way in which contributions for
merit-making bring other than purely spiritual rewards. The temple has traditionally performed a variety of social services for the
community: as a social center, an educational institution, a hostel
for travelers, and occasional means of employment on construction

jobs, etc. Its function in education is particularly significant: in
the past, the temple schools were the virtually exclusive means of
education in the rural areas, and they still retain significance as
part of the present-day public school system (e.g. Wat Kong main-
tains a primary school which now draws both boys and girls from
several villages). [10] Contributions for merit may thus substitute
for money that might otherwise have had to be spent in taxes to support public services performed by government agencies.

Finally, it is often said that the Buddhist idea of acceptance
of fate keeps the peasant from moving onward and upward to better
socioeconomic positions. Actually, for the peasant living twenty
or more years ago, I doubt very much whether mobility was likely
even with the greatest ambition, and resignation was perhaps the
only practical attitude. At the present time, however, an interesting development highlights one of the major spheres in which
the secular has considerable impact upon the sacred. I was struck
by the frequent comments made by villagers with the general tone:
"We are so poor," "We must work so hard to earn so little," "Life
is so difficult in the rice country." In part, these statements may
be simply a realistic perception of the peasant's fate. But this demanding and arduous fate is with one daily, and the statements contained a hint of sadness, sometimes even bitterness or envy. The
important fact is that mobility has become possible in contemporary
Cambodian society. A loosening of the traditional hierarchy has
made high status obtainable now through achievement as well as
ascription; and the expansion of public schooling makes education,
the major means of mobility for the peasant, more accessible
to all. It becomes increasingly clear that the doctrine of resignation does not in fact repress hopes of change, whether of geographical mobility to urban areas or of social mobility into the higher
stratum of the school teacher, the minor bureaucrat, the mechanic,
etc. An interesting question is how this desire for secular careers
and the requisite training will affect the number of males entering
monasteries in future years. Although my sample is too small to
be more than merely suggestive, one might note the following figures for West Hamlet Kong:

Age	Number of males who have been temporary monks	Number of males who have not been monks
50 and older	13	0
40-49	5	2
30-39	8	2
20-29	7	4
10-19	0	12

Indeed, of the youngest group, none have any immediate plans for
entering the monastery, their reasons ranging from poverty and

disinterest to concern with obtaining a secular education. Moreover, consumer goods have become increasingly available and necessary, and their possession is now a symbol of success and
prestige. Cash income, then, has assumed a much more significant role in contemporary life and may in future years seriously
override the nonmaterialistic emphasis of traditional Buddhism. [11]

    While I have just suggested that religious norms may not be
as important in certain spheres of economic organization as is often
thought, there are other areas of subsistence activity which do indeed evidence the influence of Buddhism. First, the injunction
against killing is not applied to certain creatures such as fish,
frogs, crabs, snakes, and insects, some of which are food resources but some of which may be injurious. Chickens are considered a borderline case, as we have seen. But the rule is strongly enforced in regard to pigs and oxen, which must be taken to
Chinese or Cham-Malay butchers respectively if slaughter is necessary. There are two further interesting points regarding the
raising of pigs and chickens for sale rather than consumption.
While some families do not undertake this enterprise because the
time and effort are not considered worthwhile, those households
headed by old couples refuse to do so specifically because they do
not wish to raise animals that are nurtured only to be killed. In
families which do raise pigs and/or chickens to provide supplemen-
tary income, the care and feeding devolve upon the woman. While
this may be a matter of pure expediency in the sexual division of
labor, one wonders whether there may not also be a religious factor operative in assigning this somewhat religiously suspect task
to the female.

    Second, it was noted previously that villagers seemed to give
only what they could afford as religious contributions. But it is
also true that any available margin of food or money, especially
fortuitous surplus, is frequently (though not always) used for
merit-making and that religious effort does seem to absorb many
resources that might ordinarily be utilized for secular purposes
(cf. Pfanner and Ingersoll 1962: 348). [12] For example, in the
Ceremony to Make a Mountain of Rice, (twùr bon phnom srau)
after the harvest, the villagers give whatever paddy can be spared
to the temple so that the rice may be sold to obtain money for the
wat's building fund. [13] Moreover, although the secular advantages
of money are appreciated and valued, it is definitely considered
praiseworthy to use wealth for religious concerns.

Social Organization and Buddhism

    Turning now to the interrelations between religion and social
systems, our discussion will focus primarily upon the influence

of Theravada on leadership and the formation of groups. The formal political structure of the village is dictated by the national
government's administrative hierarchy and is secular in nature.
The village and subdistrict chiefs are elected on the basis of criteria not overtly connectèd with religion.[14] Yet the distribution of
prestige and informal authority within the village does show the influence of Buddhism. Within the relatively egalitarian structure of
the village, an individual can gain some note because of official
position, wealth, age, special personal qualities and skills, or,
finally, exceptional piety and adherence to Buddhist norms. A
number of village men meet several or most of these criteria except the last one; yet none is accorded great prestige. Unusual
religious devotion, which suffices to bring tremendous prestige to
the monk, must also be a component of a layman's behavior if that
layman is to gain very high status within the village. When a number of distinguishing qualities plus unusual piety are possessed by
one individual, the result is almost inevitably a person of notably
high standing and informal power. The exemplar of this is Grandfather Iing, acknowledged by all to be "the most important person"
in West Hamlet Kong. Age sixty-six, he had once been a monk for
seven years and is now an achaa much in demand for healing and
for conducting private life-cycle and other ceremonies. All eulo-
gies of Iing stress his character, formed on the Buddhist ideals of
selflessness and adherence to the precepts. To quote the villagers
themselves:

> Since the time Iing was young, he would always help others.
> He would go to catch fish in the rice fields, and only if he
> got two fish would he keep one and give the other away; if he
> got only one fish, he would give it away. He knows only how
> to help others: if you are busy with work or your children
> are ill, he will come immediately to help, lend, give, with-
> out thought of making money. He never drank alcohol, even
> at weddings where wine was served. He never went with
> other women, just his wife. He does not like fighting and
> will not go near other people, even his own siblings, if they
> are quarrelsome. The people in the hamlet are "afraid" of
> him [in the sense that they would not disobey any orders he
> gives]. All the people in the village love him.

There are men in the village as old or older than Iing, as wealthy
or wealthier, who have been monks as long or longer, and who are
also achaas or hold positions of official authority. Yet only in Iing
do the villagers see a man who exemplifies the saintly life outside
of the robe. Only he combines adherence to the major precepts
with practice of the additional ten virtues advocated by the Buddha:
wholehearted generosity, moral integrity, contentment with one's
life, wisdom, intention to be good and just, patience to keep from

anger and injustice, sincerity, determined discipline to rules,
good will, and calmness in heart, senses, and passion (Leclère
1899: 524-26). Accordingly, Iing is the real leader of West Hamlet, without whose advice and consent no important community
matter can proceed, and whose influence reaches into the lives of
numerous families.[15] The second highest ranking informal leader
in the hamlet, Grandfather Pum, owes a great deal of his prestige
to his wealth, age, and the fact that he was once a subdistrict chief
but, again, all of these attributes are combined with notable religious devotion. It is only his general aloofness and detachment
from other villagers that keep Pum from earning the great affection
with which Iing is regarded.

Thus, in interaction with the social milieu outside the community, the villager will accord deference and respect to those who
are born into higher strata or come to occupy positions of acknowledged prestige or power, e.g. the aristocrat, the government
official, the priest. But within his own community or socioeconomic level, age combined with behavior that fulfills Buddhist ideals of
conduct constitute perhaps the most significant criteria for winning
respect, love, and informal authority. Moreover, the importance
of "good character" (chEt l'òò), such as Iing's, is also evident in
such evaluative acts as the selection of a marriage partner (village
endogamy is favored by many as a means of ensuring that one's
spouse has the proper qualities), the election of officials (who
would be disqualified if they were of disreputable character), and
legal decisions in which certain statutes specifically deny some
rights to individuals known to be drunkards, thieves, adulterers,
etc. The influence of Buddhist ideals is also cogently evident in
the basic provincialism and insularity of the villagers' outlook, in
which the residents of unknown or distant areas are invariably
stereotyped as thieves, rapists, and murderers.

The second aspect of social structure I wish to discuss is
the relation of Buddhism to group formation or integration. It has
sometimes been said that individualistic behavior is characteristic
of a number of Southeast Asian societies and is encouraged, at
least in part, by the Buddhist doctrine that each individual is responsible to and for himself. An individualistic and independent
streak has been noted for the Cambodians (Steinberg 1957: 319-20),
and their behavior patterns are similar in many respects to what
Embree (1950) characterized as a "loosely structured social system." But, again, there is danger in too broad a generalization,
for the Cambodian data suggest that Buddhism can encourage as
much group action and integration as individualism, if not more.

It is, of course, true that the accumulation of merit involves
individual responsibility and tally. Yet merit-making is frequently

performed by some group, usually a family, that has pooled its
efforts and resources to provide a contribution from the unit as a
whole, such contributions being taken to the temple by one or two
persons who are representatives for the entire group. The merit
thus earned is, in effect, "divided" among the members, but nonetheless there is action as a unit. Similar group effort occurs, as
mentioned previously, in the sponsorship of a Katûn festival.

The temple serves obviously as a moral-religious focal
point, integrating the village(s) within its congregation into a religious community through shared norms and common participation
in rituals. The temple also reinforces or creates bonds between
individuals in the course of performing other functions for its
people. For example, while attendance at Buddhist festivals is a
way to earn merit, these events and the temple are also the primary center for social gatherings and entertainment in the country-
side. The major annual ceremonies are eagerly anticipated months
in advance for their welcome punctuation of the drab cycle of rice
cultivation, and they bring together people from many different villages, even beyond the immediate vicinity. (Apart from visiting
kinsmen, these festivals are one of the few reasons for travel to
other regions.) Adults thus have an opportunity to visit and gossip
with acquaintances who are not usually encountered in the ordinary
course of daily life. Of special interest is the chance for adolescent boys and girls to see and be seen by one another, and the
overtly casual and disdainful glances exchanged at temple festivals
often lead to marriage offers and village exogamy. The temple
schools are another means whereby individuals from different villages may be drawn together into friendship. The temple, then,
not only serves as a major focus of loyalty but also offers opportunities for actual assemblages of and interactions among the individuals within its orbit.

In addition, both the temple itself and the larger religious
order sometimes serve to crystallize relationships. It was noted
before that Wat Kong is Thommayut, while Wat Somnang is Mohanikay. The general feeling is that differences between the two are
only superficial behavioral ones, and fifteen households within West
Hamlet either have varying loyalties within the same family or
attend both temples equally often, explaining: "Wherever there is
a festival, we go."[16] But another common statement asserted that
the hamlet was divided, the houses in the eastern section being
Thommayut and those in the west being Mohanikay. In fact, eleven
households (most indeed in the western part of the hamlet) do feel
their primary allegiance is to Mohanikay Wat Somnang, while five
households (all in the east) are devoted to Thommayut Wat Kong.
Overtly, the choice between the two is dictated by the fact that the
parents had attended, or men in the family had been monks in, one

or the other order, or simply by the feeling that one temple is
"prettier," "happier," or "more comfortable" than the other. On
a less obvious level, almost all the Thommayut are the wealthier
families in the hamlet, and their criticisms of the Mohanikay on
religious grounds seem to convey a sense of superiority they may
feel in other contexts but ordinarily can hardly express in the fund-
amentally egalitarian interaction of daily village life. (This egalitarianism, indeed, is reinforced by the Buddhist notion that merit,
accessible to everyone, is ultimately more important than wealth
or birth status.) The Mohanikay do appear to be more populistic,
and Wat Somnang is definitely the more popular temple with its
spacious grounds, its larger festivals, and especially its head
monk, an exceptionally lively, intelligent, and warm man who is
particularly beloved for being more sympathetic and affectionate
than the aloof head monk at Wat Kong.

The villagers ordinarily recognize this divided allegiance,
but it is relatively insignificant and does not usually disrupt their
daily relationships. On occasion, however, it can flare into factionalism, and during my stay the only evidence of divisiveness
was along religious lines. In 1959 the customary postharvest village festival (daà phum) to entertain the monks and visitors from
other communities was not held because of a dispute between the
Mohanikay and Thommayut adherents. The harvest had been poor
that year and there seemed to be enough money for only one feast
for only one group of monks (instead of separate feasts for the
monks from the two temples on two successive nights as in the
past). The Mohanikay villagers were unwilling to contribute if
only Thommayut monks were invited, and the Thommayut followers
felt similarly negative about the Mohanikay monks. No solution
was reached.

There is some truth in the assertion that independence and
individualism are important to the Cambodian: neolocal residence
is the preferred pattern; property is owned individually; there are
no clubs, political parties, or organized kindreds in village life;
and, even within the circle of kinship, personal likes and dislikes
determine one's closest bonds. However, the social reality is that
each individual, no matter how much independence may be treasured, is inextricably bound with others in his life. Buddhism
realizes this elemental sociological fact in its precepts which urge
harmonious, courteous, and generous relationships with others.
And although presumably only individual conscience and sensitivity
to critical gossip dictate adherence to the religious norms, certain
fundamental obligations and conformity are actually inescapable
unless one becomes a criminal, an outcast, or a ne'er-do-well.
For the individuals who do accept and wholeheartedly practice the
Buddhist virtues and precepts, particularly those of generosity and

kindness, there are the rewards of prestige, affection, and respect
in this life, as well as excellent prospects for the next. My own
assessment of Buddhism in Cambodian village life is expressed
aptly in the following:

> The [Buddhist] ideal is a society in which each individual
> respects the other's personality, an intricate network of
> warm and happy human relations: mutual respect and affec-
> tion between parent and child, teacher and student, husband
> and wife, master and servant, friend and friend, each helping
> the other upward in the scale of being . . . (DeBary et al.
> 1958: 116).

Buddhism thus can and does encourage integration in a society
where the family, village, and nation are the only other institutions
that can command much loyalty or influence behavior to any significant degree.

Other Religious Systems

Before concluding this paper, I should perhaps indicate that
Buddhism is not the only religious system in Cambodian culture.
Hinduism, once predominant in some of the ancient empires, no
longer survives as an organized religious system though elements
of it persist to the present time. Brahmanistic features are still
to be found in royal court ritual, art, literature, drama, some details of certain life-cycle and other ceremonies, and the recognition of various deities (tivoda) that are ultimately Indian in origin.

Of much greater significance is what might be called a folk
religion: beliefs and practices centering around a variety of supernatural beings which include animistic spirits of trees, stones, for-
ests, villages, etc. (neak thaa); ghosts (kmauit long); demon-like
spirits (praet); house guardian spirits (chmniàng pteah); ancestral
spirits (meba); guardian spirits for animals (mring kònvil); and
various others. Only the house spirits are wholly benevolent beings
who never create trouble. The neak thaa, ancestral spirits, and
animal guardians are harmless if proper conduct is followed and,
in the case of some neak thaa, may even be beneficial if begged for
aid; but an individual who displeases them will be struck down by
illness. The rest of the beings are all malevolent creatures whose
ill nature characteristically manifests itself by causing persons to
become sick. Respect and/or fear for these entities is virtually
universal among the villagers (even the few skeptics are more ag-
nostic than atheistic in their doubts) and is evidenced in a variety
of forms. Shrines, offerings, rituals, charms, potions, etc. keep
the spirits in good temper, atone for misdeeds, banish misfortunes,
or obtain special powers. Certain specialists acquire distinct com-
petence in mediating with the spirits: (1) the achaa, a term encoun-

tered earlier which may also be applied to an individual who has
extensive knowledge as to the proper conduct of ceremonials (particularly life-cycle and other private observances) and who may
also have some other skill such as curing; (2) the kru, a practition
er of magic who may possess any of a variety of talents or techniques such as curing, finding lost objects, making love potions or
charms for invulnerability, etc.; (3) the tmòp, a special kind of kru
who is noted for ability to practice a unique type of long-distance
murder; and (4) the rup arak, a medium who can be possessed by
spirits and speak for them.[17]

    The interconnections between this particular religious system
and social systems are not the specific concern of this paper and
cannot be discussed at length, but a few points might be mentioned.
First, there is little or no conflict or competition between this folk
religion and Buddhism.[18] Shrines for neak thaa are found on Buddh
ist temple grounds; life-cycle ceremonies combine offerings to
spirits as well as invitation of monks; and even the most devout
Buddhists such as Grandfather Iing make obeisance to both the
Buddha and the spirits. Rather, there appears to be a division of
labor between Buddhism and the folk religion. For while Buddhism
can explain more transcendental questions such as one's general
existence in this life and the next, the folk religion can give reasons
for and means of coping with or warding off the more immediate and
incidental, yet nonetheless pressing, problems and fortunes of
one's present existence. The accumulation of Buddhist merit may
enable a better rebirth, but in the meantime there may be drought
or illness which needs attention, and worry may be relieved by re-
course to the folk beliefs.

    Second, it is important to note that the folk religion also pro-
vides certain norms for behavior with sanctions that are more in-
stantaneous in their punishment for misconduct than in Buddhism.
Of particular interest in this regard are the ancestral family spirits
(meba) who watch over their descendents and frown especially upon
quarrels or sinful deeds within a family or among kinsmen, expressing their disapproval by visiting sickness upon an innocent
member of the offending group. Certainly Buddhism also urges
harmonious relationships among relatives (e.g. the Sigalovada
Sutta in Burtt 1955: 109-10), but the consequences of antagonistic
behavior toward kinsmen are remote at best in its doctrine. Cambodian kinship is, in fact, characterized by a very loose bilateral
structure in which there are no larger organized kin groups beyond
the family, and personal likes and dislikes greatly determine the
extent and content of kin bonds (Ebihara 1960). But fear of the
meba's wrath offers a strong injunction to maintain friendly com-
patibility with kinsmen and has conciliated more than one family
quarrel, although it does not succeed in completely suppressing

all discord. In much the same manner, the belief concerning the
guardian spirit of animals specifies that these creatures, which
the Buddha says should not be killed, must also be cared for and
treated properly or the owner will be punished with illness. Cur-
iously, pigs and chickens do not come under the mring kònvil's
guardianship. But oxen and water buffalo, the animals most crucial for agricultural labor, thus receive a double-barreled supernatural protection. A further interesting point is that illness is
the characteristic retribution for offense to the spirits. Surely
various forms of physical ailments are endemic in a peasant population, and the folk religion thus offers a variety of explanations
and cures for ill health.

From even this brief exploration of some of the interconnections between religious and social systems in Cambodian village
life, it is evident that both Theravada and the folk religion are potent forces in the society. They penetrate numerous institutions
and provide basic values, explanations, and patterns of behavior
for their adherents. With increasing Westernization, the future of
the religious systems as these are known today is unclear; some
elements are even now subjected to secular influences and modifi-
cations. But their basic simplicity seems to imply also a flexibility and adaptability that will probably allow their persistence as
critical elements of Cambodian culture.

NOTES

1. For further details, see Briggs 1951: 217, 242-43,
    251-56; Leclère 1899: 506-07; 1914: ch. IX.

2. Research was conducted during 1959 and early 1960 under a
    Ford Foundation Fellowship. The village, located about thirty
    kilometers from Phenom Penh in a region considered one of
    the most typical ecologically and culturally in Cambodia, had
    a total population of about 780 persons divided into three ham-
    lets. West Hamlet, the main focus of research, was com-
    posed of some 160 individuals.

3. All transcriptions are of spoken rather than written Khmer.
    ò = ɔ ; u̇ = ʌ ; à = shwa. Double vowels (e.g. oo) represent
    length. An h after t indicates an aspirated t.

4. The exact reasons for this change are unclear. Evidently the
    head monk decided to leave (suk) the Mohanikay order and
    enter (buàh) the Thommayut. Any monks who did not wish to
    follow him went to other Mohanikay temples.

5. The monks are differentiated into: head monk (<u>chau atikaa</u>),
    two assistant monks (<u>kru sot</u> of the right and of the left) who
    aided in the management of the temple and in the conduct of
    services, monks (<u>pikuk</u>), and novices (<u>samne</u> or <u>nin</u>).

6. The term <u>chbap</u> is generally applied to secular rather than re-
    ligious laws, but villagers may use it to refer also to moral
    (religious) as well as civil codes of conduct. The exact term
    for "merit" is somewhat unclear. The word <u>bon</u> usually desig-
    nates "ceremony" or "festival, " as does the phrase <u>twùr bon</u>
    (twùr = to make, to do). But <u>bon</u> is also sometimes used by
    the villagers in a phrase, e. g. <u>yok bon</u> (yok = to take, to pick
    up, to carry), to speak of performing virtuous or meritorious
    deeds. The word <u>kosal</u> may also be used for merit or the
    achievement thereof, according to Gordon Elliot, who taught
    for several years at the Buddhist Institute in Phnom Penh. My
    thanks to him for his commentary on these terms in general.

7. The major yearly Buddhist ceremonies are: New Year (<u>chol
    chnam</u>) in mid-April, Visak Bochià in May, the entry of monks
    into retreat (<u>chol vosaa</u>) in July, Prachum festival for the
    dead in September, the monks' coming out of retreat (<u>chEng
    vosaa</u>) in October, Katùn in October or November, and Miàk
    Bochià in February. For details of these ceremonies, see
    Porée-Maspero et al. 1950 and Leclère 1899.

8. Some notion of the importance of a Katùn may be gained from
    the information that the 1959 festival at Wat Somnang received
    cash contributions alone of 69,210 riels (about $1,000 at the
    unofficial exchange rate) as well as a great variety of gifts of
    clothing, utensils, furniture, etc.

9. In all fairness it must also be stated that many men who <u>were</u>
    monks also came from poor families, often with identical cir-
    cumstances. But in these instances some arrangements were
    worked out whereby the man could be spared for a temporary
    period in the monastery (e. g. a brother-in-law supplied the
    necessary labor for the family in one case). Also, uxorilocal-
    ity is a common residence pattern in Cambodia for several
    reasons (Ebihara 1960). In the cases under review here, how-
    ever, it was due specifically to the male's lack of resources.

    It should be noted, too, that sending a male into the monk-
hood may not be a hardship for a family if the individual is still
a child or a very young adolescent who would contribute little
or no labor power or income anyway, or if the period in the
monastery is very brief (a few weeks or months). For West
Hamlet, however, neither of these patterns was common. Of

the men who had been monks, mid- or late adolescence was the usual time for taking the vows, and the time spent as a monk ranged from one to eight years.

10. The importance of the temple schools is evidenced by the fact that all literate males over eighteen years of age in West Hamlet, with only two exceptions, had been educated while monks. By contrast, all females over eighteen are illiterate.

11. Rather similar situations may be seen in Pfanner and Ingersoll 1962, which also contains a host of other excellent comparative data.

12. Although I have no figures for Village Kong itself, a recent study by Delvert (1961: 524-32) estimated budgets for five representative peasant families in Cambodia. Contributions to religious ceremonies comprised 2.6, 3, 3.6, and 12 per cent respectively of expenditures in four households where expenditures were less than the total income. However, in the fifth family, whose expenditures exceeded income, there were no contributions listed for religious purposes. Note that the figures did not specify the type of religious ceremonies supported nor account for food alms, etc.

13. There are surprisingly few religious ceremonies or beliefs connected with agriculture in Village Kong. At one time there was an animistic fertility ritual for rice that has since been discarded because it necessitated killing chickens. At present there are only a few folk superstitions, occasional incantations to folk spirits to obtain rain, and the Ceremony to Make a Mountain of Rice. Nationally, there is the Plowing of the First Furrow Ceremony (a mélange of Buddhist, Hindu, and folk elements) that is ritually observed only by the king, or his surrogate, in Phnom Penh (see Porée-Maspero et al. 1950). Perhaps, however, other villages have retained more agricultural rituals. For a general study of this topic, see Porée-Maspero 1962.

14. It might be mentioned that the monks associated with Wat Kong and Wat Somnang played no role in political matters, other than the wats acting as one channel for dispersal of news of national events because they had radios. The village as a whole, in fact, was basically unconcerned with political issues. However, in Phnom Penh where political parties and conflicts do occur among the intelligentsia and elite group, monks have participated in political movements and debates. This tendency, however, has been discouraged and criticized by the king (Steinberg 1957: 301-02).

15. Even within the national structure, the influence of religious norms on the popularity of leaders can be observed. Sihanouk, the former king who resigned to become prime minister in order to have greater contact with the people, is revered and adored. He has entered the monastery several times and is faithful to Buddhism; he has made considerable efforts to associate with the masses in a friendly manner; his ideas of egalitarianism have enabled the possibility of increased mobility for peasants; etc. In short, he appears to have fulfilled many of the criteria which a good Buddhist king should have. For a discussion of these qualities, see Leclère 1899: 504, 509.

16. Each family was asked: "Which temple do you usually attend?" If the response specified one particular temple, they were asked if they ever attended the other. In addition, records of villagers' presence at five representative festivals or events at both temples were kept in order to determine actual attendance patterns.

17. The term kru is applied actually to any specialist in a certain kind of knowledge, e.g. school teacher (kru bòng riàn), medical doctor (kru pEt), etc.

18. The only example I encountered of any conflict between Buddhism and the folk religion concerned the fertility ritual mentioned above (see note13) that was discontinued because the killing of chickens was contrary to the Buddhist doctrine of not taking any life.

REFERENCES CITED

Briggs, Lawrence P.

    1951   "The Ancient Khmer Empire," Transactions of the
                American Philosophical Society (Philadelphia), 41,
                pt. 1.

Burtt, E. A.

    1955   Teachings of the Compassionate Buddha, New York,
                Mentor.

DeBary, Theodore et al.

    1958   Sources of Indian Tradition, New York, Columbia.

Delvert, Jean

 1961   Le paysan cambodgien, Le Monde d'Outre-Mer
             Passé et Présent, Première série, Etudes no. X,
             Paris and The Hague, Mouton.

Ebihara, May

 1960   "Cambodian Kinship Organization," paper presented
             at the 59th annual meeting of the American Anthro-
             pological Association, Minneapolis, Minnesota.

Embree, John F.

 1950   "Thailand: A Loosely Structured Social System,"
             American Anthropologist, 52, 181-93.

Gourou, Pierre

 1945   Land Utilization in French Indochina, Washington,
             Institute of Pacific Relations.

Ingersoll, Jasper

 1961   "Religious Roles and Economic Behavior in Village
             Thailand," paper presented at the 60th annual meet-
             ing of the American Anthropological Association,
             Philadelphia, Pennsylvania.

Kleinpeter, Roger

 1937   Le problème foncier au Cambodge, Paris, Les
             Editions Domat-Montchrestien.

Leclère, Adhémard

 1899   The Buddhism of Cambodia, New Haven, Human
             Relations Area Files translation.

 1914   Histoire du Cambodge, Paris, Librairie Paul
             Geuthner.

Martini, François

 1955a   "Le bonze cambodgien," France-Asie, 12, 409-15.

 1955b   "Organisation du clergé bouddhique," France-Asie,
             12, 415-24.

Pfanner, David E. and Jasper Ingersoll

 1962   "Theravada Buddhism and Village Economic
             Behavior," Journal of Asian Studies, 21, 341-61.

Porée-Maspero, Eveline et al.

[1950]   Cérémonies des douze mois: Fêtes annuelles
          cambodgiennes, Phnom Penh, Commission des
          Moeurs et Coutumes du Cambodge, Albert Portail.

Porée-Maspero, Eveline

1962   Etude sur les rites agraires des cambodgiens, Le
         Monde d'Outre-Mer Passé et Présent, Première
         série, Etudes no. XIV, Paris and The Hague,
         Mouton.

Steinberg, David et al.

1959   Cambodia, Survey of World Cultures, 5, New
         Haven, Human Relations Area Files Press.

DUAL ORGANIZATION IN CENTRAL CEYLON

Nur Yalman

University of Chicago

Un modèle quelconque peut être conscient ou inconscient, cette condition n'affecte pas sa nature. Il est seulement possible de dire qu'une structure superficiellement enfouie dans l'inconscient rend plus probable l'existence d'un modèle qui la masque, comme un écran, à la conscience collective. En effet, les modèles conscients -- qu'on appelle communément des 'normes' -- comptent parmi les plus pauvres qui soient, en raison de leur fonction qui est de perpétuer les croyances et les usages, plutôt que d'en exposer les ressorts.

Claude Lévi-Strauss
Anthropologie Structurale

My concern here will be an examination of symbolic and social dual organization, a subject still surrounded by some confusion. Does "dual organization" refer to those rare social systems in which the total community is in one way or another bisected into two definable "groups" which have certain formal relations with each other? Or, alternatively, can we speak of "dual organization" when the society is not so divided, or when the social divisions are obscure but there is a symbolic system in which binary categories are prominent? And, furthermore, just what is the relationship between dualism as a symbolic order, which appears quite widespread, and dualism as bisected social structure, which has rarely been satisfactorily analyzed?

Dualism has moved in and out of the central arena of anthropology in a bewildering fashion. Lévi-Strauss traces the interest in dualism directly back to Rivers and asserts that some of the best ideas of Radcliffe-Brown and Malinowsky may be seen in their genesis in his work.[1] After Rivers, the study of dualism was pursued particularly by Hocart in some erudite and highly interesting articles.[2] Recently Lévi-Strauss, in a tradition which stretches from Durkheim and Mauss[3] to Hertz[4] (not to carry the fascination of the subject back to the Pythagoreans or the Chinese) has brought

---

This article, with minor revisions by the author, is reprinted from the Journal of Asian Studies (XXIV, No. 3) with the kind permission of the editors.

the problems of dualism back into the focus of anthropological interest. Needham, too, in his more recent articles has given binary categories greater prominence.[5]

Lévi-Strauss' main article on this subject "Les organisations
dualistes existent elles?"[6] has recently been bitterly criticized by
Maybury-Lewis for being misleading, ambiguous, and based on
flimsy and dubious evidence.[7] Maybury-Lewis acknowledges the
originality of the author, but underlines the distinction between
social systems and symbolic systems. We should observe, however, that it is precisely this distinction which Lévi-Strauss, in
all his works, has attempted to dissolve.

The relation between social systems and symbolic systems
leads directly to a theoretical issue of fundamental importance. It
concerns the interpretation of religious phenomena. Just how does
religion relate to "social structure?" To what extent are we justified in tracing various features of religion and ritual to the mere
presence of social groups. There has been a tendency at times to
see a one-to-one connection between groups and their rituals. Yet
it is obvious that the simple parallel statement of groups and their
rituals leaves a vast mass of religious phenomena unaccounted for.
Here the approach deriving from Durkheim and Robertson Smith
leads to an oversimplified conception of the "congregation" or the
"group."

As I will indicate, a more fruitful line of investigation lies
in the direction not of the morphology of social groups but of the
principles on which they are formed. In other words, we should
seek to relate religious and ritual phenomena to "structural principles," for when adequately analyzed such principles may be seen
in operation, as it were, behind both social groupings and moral
and religious concepts. We must therefore shed our empirical
bias and be prepared to consider not the caste congregation in a
temple but the caste principle, or not the members of the lineage
meeting under a particular tree but the lineage principle. For it
seems as if culture is its own best analyst and these structural
principles which anthropologists attempt to distill from their mountains of field material are quite often to be seen beautifully analyzed
and perfectly framed in religious concepts, myths, symbolism, and
ritual. The unexpected directions to which such premises lead will
be revealed below.

I will attempt to elucidate this problem in the context of
material from Ceylon. I am concerned with an intriguing ritual
during which a goddess and her consort are first joined and then
pulled apart with great pomp. In one village, Terutenne, the ritual is closely associated with extensive evidence for "dual organ-

ization." Indeed, there appears to be a one-to-one connection between the ritual and the structure. Yet when we move to another
village, Panama, we find the ritual but not the bisection. How
then are we to proceed?

II

I have drawn attention to some structured features of Sinhalese healing rituals elsewhere. [8] It was noted that while most healing rituals were directed to demons (yakās) and were intended to
appease and chase these creatures away, others were directed to
deities (dēva) and were intended as requests for their assistance in
fighting the demons and as pleas for their intercession in everyday
existence.

I will now pursue further the analysis of certain major rituals, directed again to the male and female deities of the Sinhalese
pantheon and undertaken on behalf of an entire community after the
harvest.

These communal rituals are identical in intention and similar
in structure to the private healing rituals directed to the deities,
but they are more elaborate and ostentatious. The rituals for the
deities may be referred to with a generic term as deviyangē sellama (literally, "the play of the gods"). The tone of levity in the
term sellama (play or game) does not detract from the precision
of the term for the Sinhalese male and female gods are quite play-
ful creatures and, in their anthropomorphic aspects, not unlike the
gods of the Greeks. Their playfulness contrasts strongly with the
high moral tone associated with the Buddha. "The play of the gods"
would include all rituals undertaken by a kapurāla priest for the
deities. The village rituals may be more obliquely referred to as
mangalaya (festivals) or mangala davasa (festival day, also
wedding). It is notable that ordinary villagers may in their casual
moods refer to these "games" as "female-male intercourse" (ganu
purussaya sambandham), thus bringing out the central concern of
these harvest rites. Indeed, the term keliya often associated with
these sacred "games" has lewd sexual implications (e.g. rata
keliya, night play, copulation).

Most harvest rituals in central Ceylon are developed around
the theme of a food offering (first fruits, alut sāl, also adukku or
multeng) to the deities. This offering may be a separate ritual by
itself but is often part of a larger sequence in which gods and goddesses are brought to the ritual location with separate processions
and then united in a hut. The Gam maduva ritual of Terutenne is
of this kind. [9] The same occurs in Udumulla (Wellassa division),

and in the ritual at Kataragama, as we shall see, the god is taken
in a magnificent nocturnal procession to visit his mistress. The
ritual of Kotabowe Vidiya (Wellassa division) is identical in structure to the one at Kataragama and also consists of nocturnal visi-
tations and the offering of food to the deity. There are elements of
this kind in the main annual festivals (perah̃ara) at Hanguranketa
and Kandy, but they include the Buddhist vihāra and their sexual
content is less evident. [10]

The An keliya ritual described below stands in direct contrast to these rites of "unification" for in this case, after the male
and female deity are laboriously locked together, the "game" consists of their being pulled apart by two opposing teams in the village. It is appropriate therefore to speak of An keliya as a "rite
of separation." Let me now briefly indicate the place of these harvest rites in the annual ritual cycle of the Kandyan Sinhalese dry
zone villages.

III

The most prominent cyclical rituals in a Sinhalese village
are in fact concerned with the Buddha. So there are daily rituals
such as food or flower offerings (dāna) to the Buddha in every temple. Just as the Buddhist priest (bhikkhu) according to tradition
is offered food by the householders every day before noon, the
bhikkhu in his turn offers food to the image of the Buddha in his
vihāra (image chamber) before noon every day. In the evening,
when the priest is permitted to partake of liquid refreshments, the
Buddha image is also not neglected.

On the four quarters of the moon, the poya days, the ritual
is basically the same, though there may be more lay visitors to
the temple, and other sacred objects in the temple grounds, such
as the dāgoba and the bo tree, may receive ritual attention and
offerings (mainly flowers). [11]

Leaving aside the daily and poya activities, the following
occasions of the year were ritualized in the dry zone villages in
which I worked:

Sinhalese lunar month	Date of full moon	Occasion	Rite
Bak	April	"Sinhalese New Year"	Family feasts, new fires in houses, new oil on hair, etc.

Sinhalese lunar month	Date of full moon	Occasion	Rite
Vesak	May	"Real New Year," the Buddha born, reached Buddhahood, and died, Buddhism brought to Ceylon	Dāna service at temple, bo tree decorated and fed with milk
Poson	June	Mahinda came to Ceylon	
Äsala	July	Mahinda's sister came to Ceylon, brought bo tree, started Bhikkuni order, Vas commences	Vas offering to priest
Nikini	August	Kandy perahära	Elaborate village rituals, pilgrimages to other ritual centers
Binara	September	Mahiyangana perahära	
Vap	October	Vas ends on poya day	Offering of katina robe to priest within a week of ending of Vas
Il	November		
Unduvap	December		
Durutu	January	Buddha came to Mahiyangana on poya day	
Navam	February		
Madin	March		

It is clear from the above account that the main efflorescence of ritual activities in the dry zone falls precisely into the dry season from about May to October. Again in this region the full moon day in May (Vesak) which commemorates the birth and Buddhahood of the Buddha coincides precisely with the main (maha) harvest on the paddy fields. After Vesak, each full moon day has some kind of ritual associated with it, and it is precisely at this time that the great ritual processions (perahära) at such sacred centers as Kandy, Anuradhapura, Mahiyangana, and Kataragama take place.

Vas (sometimes described as Buddhist Lent) is the traditional rainy season in the Buddhist calendar and coincides with the proper season in northern India. This is traditionally the time when the bhikkhu were unable to make their expected "begging" rounds in the villages because of the rain and stayed in one place to be looked after by the laity (Vas vahinava). Contrary to tradition, Vas in Ceylon also falls squarely in the height of the dry season.

The special rituals in the Buddhist temples during the dry season are confined to the full-moon days of Vesak and Äsala, i. e. the birth of the Buddha and the commencement of Vas. It is noteworthy that the most significant "play of the gods" associated with the centers of Kandy, Mahiyangana, and Kataragama take place in those months within the Vas season. Apart from the main rituals, the celebrations at secondary centers such as Panama, Kotabowe Vidiya, and Hanguranketa, which draw large regional crowds, also fall into this period. [12] It so happens that the Buddhist priests are confined to their temples exactly at the time when the main after-harvest fertility rituals are undertaken.

We should further observe that the priests are said to be explicitly forbidden to see the "play of the gods," or indeed any rites that include "dancing and singing." Parallel to this prohibition, they also may not attend births, weddings, or puberty rituals. This latter prohibition, at least, is explained by the association of the priests with funerals and death. [13]

IV

Having noted this concentration of ritual activities in the dry season, and in particular the Buddhist Vas period, I turn to the rituals in the villages, taking up first those of Terutenne (Walapane division). In 1954-56 the main dry season activity of the inhabitants was to visit the sacred shrine at Mahiyangana. Formerly, in addition to the Mahiyangana pilgrimage, the village held two "plays of the gods" -- Gam maduva and An keliya. But a communal Gam maduva had not been performed for three years and, even though the paraphernalia were still treasured in the homes, An keliya had apparently not been performed for twenty.

The Gam maduva ritual, described before, [14] consists brief- ly of the following activities. First, a hut (madura) is erected and various symbols of the deities, arrows and tridents for the gods, and anklets and necklaces for the goddess brought in processions and placed on an altar there. Then certain objects made by the washermen from starched cloth (haluva, ritually clean clothes?) are taken to the hut. In the second important phase of the rite, food is cooked and offered to the assembled gods and goddesses. Each object representing a deity is handled separately by the kapurālas, who go into trances and relate the myth of the birth and other events associated with the deity. Some of the events related in the myth may be theatrically enacted, e.g. "shooting the mango" (amba vidamana), the arrival of Devol Dēva in Ceylon (see below), both associated with Pattini, or "the tying of elephants" (at bandana) are special sequences which may be included in the ritual. [15] The total impression is one of divine nuptials, and the twofold purpose to purify the village of "mistakes" (varada) and to enhance the fertility of its fields, cattle, and women.

The An keliya ritual has similar purposes but a different and more intriguing structure based on an event in Pattini's life. First, the myth:

The Goddess Pattini and her consort Pālanga were out in the jungle looking for some sapu (temple tree) flowers. [16] They dis- covered a beautiful one, but it was too high up on the branches of a tree to reach so they found some long poles with hooks at the end and attempted to pick the flower with these. They still could not reach the flower. Climbing the tree, Pattini always on a "lower" branch (yata) than her consort, the two went from branch to branch until suddenly their hooks became entangled. They climbed back down and tried unsuccessfully to pull the hooks apart, finally re- pairing to the legendary city of Madura in southern India, where all the maidens on the side of Pattini and all the men on the side of Pālanga had a tug of war. When Pālanga's hook broke, Pattini was delighted and in her pleasure demanded that henceforth she be pro- pitiated annually in this fashion. Thus Pattini's side became Yata pila (below side) and Pālanga's became Uda pila (top side). Pāl- anga, however, was not a very good husband, and although Pattini allows him to win now and again she is not pleased when it happens.

The An keliya rite consists of an enactment of the central theme of this myth. The village has a traditional division into two, spoken of as Yata pila and Uda pila and thought of as a topographi- cal and hereditary bisection of Terutenne by the mountain stream

called pin arawa (merit stream). Each side possesses enormous
hooks (an) which are handed down as prized possessions in the
family.

During An keliya two enormous wooden hooks, one for Yata
pila and one for Uda pila, are locked and tied together with great
ceremony. Then the opposing groups, using the leverage provided
by an enormous tree trunk placed upside down in a ditch, pull on
the hooks until one breaks. The winners shower the losers with
obscene language and, because the losers have not always been
able to take such abuse in good spirit, serious fights and killings
are said to have occurred.

The sides are not in fact equal in status, the Goddess' side
being considered superior. In Terutenne the Yata pila by customary right usually arranged their hook in such a fashion that the Uda
pila had no chance of winning, which led to fights even before the
rite had commenced. This significant bias in favor of Yata pila is
noted by all the observers of An keliya. It was said in Terutenne
that Yata pila is the side of the Goddess, whereas Uda pila is only
the side of her consort who is not important in his own right. Besides, if Pālanga won, the village would be ravaged by disease
brought on by the angry Pattini, whereas her victory would be
auspicious. [17]

The central features of the rite do not appear to have changed
since the seventeenth century when it used to be held on a grand
scale, perhaps even between sections of the Kandyan kingdom. The
sexual content is tersely underlined by Robert Knox writing at the
time:

> Upon the breaking of the stick, the party that hath won
> doth not a little rejoyce. Which rejoycing is exprest by
> dancing and singing and uttering such sordid beastly ex-
> pressions, together with postures of their bodies,as I
> omit to write them . . . This filthy solemnity was for-
> merly much in use among them; and even the King him-
> self hath spent time in it, but now lately he hath abso-
> lutely forbidden it under penalty of a forfeiture of money. [18]

V

Just what is the relation of this rite to the social organization
of Terutenne? To what extent was the village bisected? And what
was the significance of the dualism? A general topographical division into two was definitely recognized in the village. The people
spoke of the community in terms of sides: "that side, this side"

(egoda, megoda). And thus the old (parana) fields of the village
were divided into "that-side" fields and "this-side" fields (egoda
wela, megoda wela); the same was true of the lands for slash-and-
burn cultivation (egoda hen, megoda hen); and, finally, the village
itself was spoken of as egoda gama and megoda gama.

That this bisection was not simply a matter of the special
topography of Terutenne alone was clear since a similar bisection
of the community could be observed in neighboring villages as
well. The division was partly related to the agricultural cycle in
this area. There are essentially two forms of cultivation in dry
zone villages; paddy and slash-and-burn (chena) agriculture. The
paddy fields, which are dependent on elaborate irrigation systems,
are always permanent and form the focus for agricultural communities. Slash-and-burn agriculture, however, entails a cultivation
cycle of at least four years: the jungle is cut, allowed to dry, fired,
sown, and cultivated, after which the community moves on to another plot the next year. Thus while the paddy fields are in valley
floors, or around streams, chena is movable. In Terutenne the
chenas move from year to year and, in certain years, the chenas
worked on one side of the hills are many miles apart from those
cultivated on the other side. Owing to the very extensive areas
required for low-yield chena cultivation, it is impossible for the
entire village to move as a group on the highlands. Thus in Terutenne the chenas were in principle divided between the two halves
of the village, with one side always going to the east and the other
side to the west.

The egoda-megoda bisection coincided exactly with the Yata
pila-Uda pila division. It was furthermore claimed, first, that all
those in Uda pila (west) were low-status persons and that all the
families with "clean" caste-pedigrees were Yata pila. Second, it
was claimed that there could be no intermarriage across Uda and
Yata pila even though there were members of the same castes in
both sections. And it is true that during many months in Terutenne
I came across very few such unions. There was, however, no un-
animous agreement on the "marriage barrier."

Let me now summarize the bisection of the community. If
the two sides on either side of the pin arawa (merit stream) are
listed, the following picture emerges. I will take the west to be
"this side."

West - megoda	East - egoda
a. all Uda pila	a. all Yata pila
b. megoda gama (village)	b. egoda gama

c. megoda hen (chena)   c. egoda hen

d. megoda wela (paddy fields) d. egoda wela

e. megoda pansala (temple)   e. egoda pansala

f. megoda Maluvegoda   f. egoda Boddhisukkaramaya
    dayakaya samitiya   dayakaya samitiya

[two temple benefactors' societies]

g. aristocratic high caste   g. same
    (goigama) families

h. ordinary high caste   h. same
    families

i. low caste goigama   i. same
    families

j. low caste washermen   j. low caste tom-tom beaters,
    and some tom-tom   blacksmiths, and potters
    beaters

Some points call for comment. Under (e) it should be noted
that there are two temples in Terutenne, one of the Amarapura
order (east) and one of the Siam Nikaya (west). The priests of
the two orders never mix in Buddhist rites, even though the laity
is not so divided and the rites are identical. The annual ritual
which concludes the Vas season is the <u>katina pinkama</u> in which the
Buddhist priest is offered a specially prepared and stitched cloth.
During the period of Vas in Terutenne in 1955 the two temple societies separately organized the food offerings to the priests so that
each household took turns in preparing the food and offering it at
the temple. Anyone could join in on this act of merit, but it is
significant that no household from the west provided food for the
eastern temple and only three wealthy households from the east
entered their names, among a list of eighty, for the food offerings
to the western temple.

The paddy fields are also divided. The parts called egoda
and megoda wela have separate water supplies. However, labor
in these fields does go across the division. Of the 71 holdings in
megoda wela (west) 27 are owned by people in the east; again, of
the 71 holdings, 15 are cultivated on a sharecropping basis by
people of the east and 56 by those of the west. In the fields below
the place where the separate streams of egoda-megoda fields meet,
18 lots out of 39 are owned by people of the east, but only 4 culti-
vate the fields themselves, the rest being given on a sharecropping
basis to the west.

A fuller account of land tenure in Terutenne would indicate
more clearly that there is definite imbalance in wealth in the village. The west consists of poorer people; all the large landlords
and rich schoolteachers are concentrated in the east. So, in Terutenne at least, the ideal pattern of Yata pila being superior to Uda
pila did coincide with actual figures of land ownership.

The bisection of Terutenne into "that side" or "this side"
village, and the association of these sections with the Yata and
Uda pila divisions, was also repeated in the organization of other
villages in the Walapane region. Thus the immediately neighboring village of Udamadura is similarly bisected by a stream: Uda
pila live on one side and Yata pila on the other. I have a statement
from an informant who claims that the Yata pila of one village always marry Yata pila from another and that marriage between Uda
and Yata pilas is forbidden. "Why should one marry Uda pila?
They are 'low!'" The same is true of Tibbotugoda village, and in
Abangelle I was told that a great fight had developed at the last An
keliya and allegedly some people were killed. My informant stated
that those who did have wives from the "other" side sent them back.

Having described the "ideal" blueprint of the village, it should
be observed that after a residence of ten months in the community I
became convinced that, whatever the situation in the past, in 1955
neither the dual organization nor the alleged marriage barrier between Uda and Yata pila was of any immediate importance in the
social life of the village. It is true that the divisions were concep-
tualized and that informants spoke, when asked, in Uda pila-Yata
pila terms, but marriage was obviously a matter of negotiation
with wealth, caste, and status as the factors of prevailing importance. If it was still true that there were extremely few marriages
across the egoda-megoda division in Terutenne, this was not because of An keliya or the division but simply a reflection of the fact
that, in the first place, those who lived in the Uda pila area were
-- for reasons other than An keliya -- considered to be "polluted"
and, secondly, they were in general poorer than the persons in the
Yata pila part of the community. [19] Hence, even though the ritual
division was perpetuated by de facto conditions in the village, the
division itself was not the central concern of the villagers and we
can not attribute much importance to it.

However, a similar pattern of Uda pila-Yata pila division
could be observed not only in this region but also in other parts of
central Ceylon. I noted it for the village of Udumulla in the Uva
province, where An keliya had also not been performed for some
years. The Yata pila side was again stated to be superior to the
Uda pila; and the marriage barrier was mentioned. My informants
added a detail to the An keliya procedure by explaining that Pattini

and Devaya (consort not named) were first placed together in a
gedara (house) or madura (hut), and the splitting came only after
this "joining together" (sambandam) had been accomplished.

VI

So far our evidence on the relations between the bisected
community and the rite is inconclusive. Let me now turn to another community which will render further precision to the problem. The best material on An keliya comes from the intriguing
village of Panama on the east coast of Ceylon. This village with
its curious mixture of Hindu Tamils and Buddhist Sinhalese, has
been described elsewhere. 20 An keliya is one of the annual rituals
performed by the entire village just before the Kataragama ceremonies. The fact that Panama lies on the main pilgrimage route
from Batticaloa to Kataragama, and that the rite is observed not
only by the inhabitants of the village but also by pilgrims on their
way to this jungle shrine, should be recalled in assessing the persistence of the rite in this region.

The Panama An keliya is more elaborately organized than
any I have come across in the literature. In 1955 there were six
persons formally associated with the proceedings, the following
three officials being named by each of the two hereditary divisions,
Yata pila and Uda pila:

Basnayaka	Lay lord of temple
Wattandiya	Priest who handles hook (an) and food
Kattandiya (kapurāla)	Priest who gets possessed

These positions, like the pila affiliation, are hereditary in the
male line, but accession to the Wattandiya and Kattandiya posts is
ratified by the Basnayakas, who are the lay heads of the sides. In
1955 the Basnayakas in Panama were rich and influential members
of the village.

Until about 1943 Panama did not have any permanent constructions at the an pitiya (the An keliya place), which was simply
a large flat rock to the west of the extensive paddy fields. On
either side of the rock stood two large trees which served as
images (gas deka rupaya) of Pattini and Alut Swami (new holy
man), as her consort was known in this region. In 1943 the location was "improved" by the addition of two temples (kovil or
devāle) facing each other, one for Pattini and one for her consort.

The temples, like the location, are deserted most of the year but are activated at the proper time (in the month of Bínara).

Before the An keliya is to be held, the officials go around the village shouting "Hoo! Must purify the place!" At the same time new rice (first fruits, alut sāl) is collected by the Wattandiya of each party. During the fifteen days preceding the An keliya, villagers must be clean and refrain from fishing and from sexual intercourse. Each Basnayaka, in the past, had to construct a hut (madura or geyak) for his deity at the an pitiya. Now with the permanent constructions, his duty is to provide a clean mat and clean cooking pots for the food offerings to be prepared.

From the first to the sixth day the rituals are said to be "small." In the second week the interest mounts and many more visitors from the village as well as the region go to see the proceedings. The climax comes on the fourteenth night when the final An keliya takes place. On the fifteenth day the unbroken hook (always the hook of the Goddess Pattini) is taken in procession to the sea and bathed. The rite of "water cutting" (die kapanava) follows and the ritual is ended.

During the period leading up to the final An keliya, the kapurālas (Kattandiya) remain in their respective temples day and night, keeping very clean and bathing fully after all bodily functions. The Wattandiya cooks the food offerings for the God and the food (adukku) is offered by the kapurāla, who falls into trances during this procedure. In particular, the alut dēva kapurāla is much in evidence. He dances (alut dēva natanava); he "becomes" the God (alut dēva venava); he loses consciousness (sihi neti venava); and he describes his visions of the future (pena kiyanava).

In the actual ritual the Yata pila Wattandiya brings his hook to the stone in the middle, all the while reciting various verses (kannalav). His mouth, however, is covered like a doctor's in an operating room so that no "polluting" saliva will fall on the sacred object. Then the Uda pila Wattandiya ties up the Yata pila hook, and the Yata pila Wattandiya does the same for the hook of Alut Swami. In the smaller An keliya leading up to the grand finale, the broken hooks are replaced by others and the rite goes on.

The contest apparently provokes great excitement. The victors may tie the vanquished to the central rocking post with a rope and dance around them, at first uttering obscene language but finally singing certain charmed songs referred to significantly as "reversing the fault" (varada horavanava).

In the day ritual after the final night (the fourteenth), when

the winning hook is taken in procession to the sea, three Yata pila
and three Uda pila pots are filled with saffron water (kaha pen) and
offerings of coins (panduru) dropped in. The kapurālas, again with
their mouths covered, bathe the Goddess with the saffron water.
The Goddess "plays in the water" (die kelinava) and is then taken
back to her temple.

Such is the course of the Panama rite. Let me observe immediately that if some association with a topographical and hereditary dual organization could be detected in the Terutenne region,
the evidence was to the contrary in Panama. First, the village
was not topographically bisected. Second, even though the people
mentioned Yata pila and Uda pila, and even though in theory pila
affiliation was hereditary in the male line, in fact these matters
were hardly taken seriously. Some said that Yata pila was the side
of grown-ups and Uda pila the side of the children. (Note the asym-
metry between the sides.) Others said that separate household
lists were prepared for the rice offering to the two devāles, and
although these lists were traditional, one could change one's affiliations by making vows to the Goddess. It seemed extremely unlikely, at any rate, that the Yata pila-Uda pila division in Panama
was related to a fundamental cleavage between specific social
groups in the community. It should be understood then that no
analysis of the An keliya rite in Panama is possible by way of an
itinerary through "social groups." We must look elsewhere.

                                    VII

I have suggested that An keliya is a rite of separation. Although the Goddess and her consort are made to cohabit, they are
in the end forcibly split. The significance of this act is more
clearly indicated in contrast to the other main annual rituals in the
Panama region where the divine personages are joined. The most
intriguing and esoteric ritual in Ceylon takes place at the jungle
shrine of Kataragama, near Panama. Thousands of pilgrims from
Ceylon and South India, Buddhists as well as Hindus (and even
Muslims and Christians), flock to this deserted locality and bring
it alive for a few weeks every year. The myth is as follows:

The god Kataragama (Supramanyar), who has a wife (Tey-
vannai Amma) and children in South India, comes to Ceylon on a
hunting trip with his brother Ganesha. Near Kataragama the two
brothers see a young girl (Valli Amma), who has been brought up
by the Veddas. Kataragama falls in love with her and together
with Ganesha devises a trick to win her. Putting on an elephant
head, Ganesha frightens the girl. Kataragama, present and available, saves her, and because she is grateful to him the two start

cohabiting. Teyvánnai Amma in South India is understandably
annoyed with the god and his new mistress and sends all sorts of
messengers to induce the god to return to her -- but to no avail.

It should be observed that while Valli Amma's birth is also
supernatural, she is not of equal birth to Kataragama. Her birth
story is told as follows: a hermit living in the jungle masturbated
one day and his semen fell on grass which was eaten by a hind; the
hind became pregnant and gave birth to a daughter, Valli Amma,
who was brought up by the Veddas around Kataragama. It is worth
adding here that <u>valli</u> is the usual feminine suffix indicating caste
status for those in the lowest Sinhalese caste, the <u>rodiya</u>.[21]

The ritual of Kataragama consists essentially of the great
mysterious god going to his mistress twice a night for fourteen
nights. The magnificent nocturnal ceremony takes place in the
light of flares, sacred fires, and torches held by thousands of
pilgrims thronging the route of the god. Drum-dominated music
comes from the temple of Kataragama, and at the right time two
priests emerge to the great shouts of "Saddhu" from the Buddhists
and "Haro Hara" from Hindus. One of the priests, wearing a full
crimson cloak, walks in front with the crouched figure of the second priest close behind and completely shrouded under the cloak of
the first. The symbols of the god are said to be carried under the
red cloak. Mounting a caparisoned elephant, the two priests go
slowly in a colorful procession, tom-toms beating, dancers and
singers leading the way through the great sea of crowds, toward
the temple of Valli Amma. The second temple is about half a
mile down the road and faces the Kataragama temple. The procession halts in front of the Valli Amma temple; the god and priests
go in and disappear behind a curtain which has a picture of Valli
and her hind and which covers the sacred chamber where the symbols of the mistress are to be found. After the visitation (about
45 minutes) the priests come out, again the devoted shouts of
"Haro Hara" fill the air, and the procession returns to the Kataragama temple.

When I asked people in the crowd what actually takes place
in the Valli Amma temple, some claimed they did not know, some
said it was a secret. Others, however, answered with an amused
glance that the god was having intercourse with his mistress. Being
already married, the god had to visit Valli secretly, which explained why he hides behind the cloak of his priest. The people
appeared to be uncertain about exactly what takes place inside the
chamber of Valli Amma, but some thought that an arrow and some
oil is taken from the Kataragama temple to Valli Amma. Valli
Amma's symbol is a necklace; the arrow is put through the necklace and the oil poured on top of the sacred objects. In the meantime the priest, in a trance, dances in front of the symbols, after

which they are taken back.

This ritual is repeated, on a smaller scale but in almost exactly the same form, in the shrine of Kotabowe Vidiya in the Bilile
region. The details of that ritual, which bring out this theme of
male-female union, will be described elsewhere. I should also
note that the building of two shrines facing each other -- one male,
one female -- is a prominent part of the ritual healing ceremonies
(madai) I observed in Panama.

For our purposes, the most striking aspect of the Kataragama
ritual is that it is a union between a god of high status and a woman
of relatively low status, in this respect presenting no violation of
the rules of hypergamy. The low status of Valli Amma is emphasized, first, by the distinction made between her and the "legitimate" wife and, second, by the fact that valli is a usual name for
the women of the lowest caste, the rodiya.

The contrast with An keliya is forceful. An keliya consists
of a union between a goddess and a man of low status, and appears
to run counter to the rules of hypergamy.

                              VIII

I think that the Pattini-Pālanga union is in fact a "wrong
marriage" (varada) and that the two are forcibly split in order to
"correct" the mistake (varada horavanava). The Kataragama-
Valli Amma union, though secret, is according to the rules -- and
indeed particularly fertile. Therefore not the split but the union
is emphasized. In order to elucidate the symbolic implications of
this splitting act, I propose to examine the other contexts in which
this male-female splitting theme is repeated. For example, the
most frequent ritual act in Ceylon is the splitting of a coconut with
a knife. Most rituals contain this act in some fashion. There is
no specific explanation for the act except that it forecasts (like the
Yata pila-Uda pila contest) whether the future will be auspicious
or not. More specifically, the coconut is described as having a
male and a female end. One side of the nut has three holes in it,
and this is the female, inauspicious end; the opposite end has an
erect tuft and is male and auspicious. It is these two sides which
are split. The Tamils, who have greater finesse in their interpretation of ritual, say that the coconut for Valli Amma can be split
with a knife but the coconut dedicated to Kataragama must be
smashed and broken on the ground. At the end of the Kataragama
ritual hundreds of coconuts are broken by the devotees in front of
the temples in this fashion.

Other fruits are also supposed to have male and female sides, and splitting fruits apart is one of the major healing rituals in Sinhalese villages. All kinds of fruits may be split but one in particular is singled out for special potency: the limes. Lime-cutting specialists (dehi vedarala) have a special place among ritual healers. Lime-cutting (dehi kapang) is a complex ritual in which hundreds of limes are cut with scissors over the person of a patient. The specialist cuts limes over the head first and then proceeds to do the same over every joint down to the feet. One explanation of this act is that it splits the person into two sides: the right side, which is pure and male, and the left, which is impure and female. The ritual is intended to drive away sin (dos), mistakes (varada), poison (vas), etc. Wirz, who describes lime-cutting in detail, also provides the myths associated with it.[22] It must be observed that these myths, indeed like almost all the myths recorded by that indefatigable ethnographer, appear to center around themes of patricide, incest, and "wrong" sexual intercourse. It is pertinent here to consider some of these myths, through which runs the basic theme of the demon (yakā) "birth stories."

One myth begins with an "origin story."[23] The population of the earth comes from an original couple. At first there are no sun and stars, no animals and plants, nothing to eat but mud. Desire arises in the couple; one becomes man, the other woman. Stars start shining; they procreate and people the earth.[24]

The second part of this myth repeats a typical "wrong" intercourse theme. There are a king and a queen in this population, and many desire the queen. Among these is Maraya (Death), who tries to commit sexual intercourse with her in the guise of her husband. The queen wants to open the door of her bedchamber but her maid stops her. Maraya, fooled in this attempt to get through the door, sends an eighteen-foot "polanga" snake into the room. This makes the queen ill and the lime-cutting ritual is prescribed. The limes must be cut over the queen's body.[25]

A different version of the story repeats the structure but changes some of the items. There is again a creation episode and this time Sakra creates a couple who populate the earth. Sakra again makes a king and a queen. Maraya wants to copulate with the queen but, being unable to do so himself, instead sends a lizard (geta-polanga), which gets into the queen's room and hides in her genitals. The lime-cutting ritual is prescribed.[26]

The "message" appears to be that at first there is no life but also no death. Then life and procreation appear but the "wrong" intercourse (of the couple?) is followed by death (Maraya). Hence to avoid death the male-female splitting act must be performed.

There is a long series of birth stories with precisely this
structure but with the addition of the patricide theme after the
"wrong" intercourse. In many of these the queen bears a "demon-
son" who attempts to kill his father. In one of these stories, the
theme of incest is brought out. There are a king and a queen. The
queen is pregnant and astrologers tell the king that she will bear a
son and a daughter. The son will have supernatural powers and
the daughter (Giri Devi) will be irresistibly beautiful -- so beautiful in fact that her brother will want to copulate with her. He must
be banished. The son is sent away and many years pass. The girl
is about to be married when her brother finds out who he is and becomes furious at not being invited to the wedding. He arrives at
the wedding, eats everything up, and carries off his sister, who
then commits suicide. The brother is dismayed and very angry,
goes berserk, and begins to torment both gods and men.[27]

So far we may be allowed to draw one simple conclusion: the
male-female splitting act as exemplified by the rituals of lime-
cutting is considered a palliative of "wrong intercourse. " But it
is really the case that Pattini and Pālanga are involved in a "sexual
mistake" that must be "corrected" by a public ceremony. Let us
consider some other myths to elucidate this particular point. It
may be noted that the relations between Pattini and Polanga repeat
this theme of the king and queen and "wrong" intercourse on the
part of the queen. Pattini marries Polanga Therunaanse, a man
"with neither profession nor income. " Polanga takes Pattini's gold-
en anklets (halang), which are the symbol of Pattini and the female
organ (symbolism explicitly made by informants). The golden anklets are sold to a goldsmith (low caste). There are a king and a
queen, and the queen also has anklets. She takes them off while
bathing and loses them. They are "eaten" by a peacock (the "vehi-
cle" of the god Kataragama). The angry king, over the protesta-
tions of the queen, catches Polanga, accuses him of "stealing" the
golden anklets of the queen, and kills him. (Adultery in Sinhalese
is also referred to as "stealing" or thievery!) Pattini comes back
to the scene, now angry with the king. The king tries to kill Pattini.
Pattini wreaks havoc and must be appeased.[28]

I would suggest that the idea of "wrong intercourse" (i.e.
against the rules of hypergamy) is fairly explicit in the relations
between Pattini and Polanga. In the above myth, for instance,
there is a clear juxtaposition between the "anklets" of the queen
"eaten" by a "peacock" and the accusation that the "anklets" were
"stolen" by Polanga. The first indicates a connection between the
god Kataragama and the queen (hypergamy) to which the king could
have no objection, whereas the second describes the suspicion of
intercourse between the queen and Polanga (hypogamy) to which
the king would have serious objections. In fact, certain other Pattini myths appear to center around this preoccupation.

In one such myth intruders from Malabar (among them Devol
Dēva) sail over to Ceylon. Pattini wants to keep them off Ceylon
and sends up seven layers of fire. This proves unsuccessful and
three men land. One is experienced in charms and ritual healing
(often associated with tom-tom beaters), another is experienced in
transforming "potsherds into money" (potter caste), and the third
is experienced in changing sand into sugar (jaggery makers caste).
The caste occupation comes to the surface in the second part of the
story when one of the men settles and marries a local girl. He
secretly continues his occupation of transforming sand into sugar.
His children discover his "secret" (low caste?) and tell their mother. The mother is angry and the man kills his children.[29]

There is little doubt that the landing of the intruders against
Pattini's will is seen by the informants in its sexual undertones.
Gunasekera writes:

> The priest impersonates Devol, asks to be let into the
> shed which is obstructed by two men holding the cloth
> across, which is said to represent the obstruction
> created by Pattini when the former wanted to land in
> Ceylon. In the dialogue that follows there is much
> humorous dialogue (sic), at times bordering on ob-
> scenity. The priest is ultimately allowed to come in
> and worship at the main booth re-enacting the prostra-
> tion of Devol at Pattini's shrine.[30]

These Pattini myths are clearly imbued with the anxiety of
"wrong intercourse" but they are not unequivocally concerned with
the particular myth of An keliya. They may strengthen our argument, but they do not clinch the case since the same myths may be
given different interpretations. It is for this reason noteworthy
that another route through a different set of myths leads directly
back to our issue. It will be recalled that in the original myth of
An keliya Pattini and her consort are in the jungle trying to pluck
flowers and that they start climbing a tree. Now we may ask why
a tree is inserted at this point in the myth? And why are they both
climbing to reach the flowers? The answer to this seemingly innocent question takes us back again to the theme of incest.

In this connection let us first consider the myth of origin of
the lowest caste in Sinhalese Ceylon, the rodiya. Once upon a time
there was a king, Parākrama Bāhu, whose daughter, Ratnā Valli
(Gem Valli), became addicted to flesh and began demanding that
some kind of flesh be given to her every day.[31] One day the people who were charged with finding provisions for the palace could
not find any animal flesh and so substituted human flesh. The
daughter liked this so well that she became quite addicted to it.

Soon afterward a barber (or in some accounts a weaver) discovered
what was going on and broke the news to the anxious population
whose youths had been disappearing that human flesh was being eat-
en in the palace. Thereupon the king expelled his daughter and gave
her to a roddā, a "sweeper" who was a poor relative of the royal
household in the palace. The progeny of these two formed the rodiya caste.

We should draw attention to the following points. To begin
with, eating in the context of caste is often associated with sex.
Hence the daughter was not only a cannibal but also guilty of "eating" human beings, i. e. having improper intercourse. She was
therefore guilty of a double crime, both eating polluted food, i. e.
disregarding caste rules concerning commensality, and having sexual relations with persons below her station, i. e. flouting the rules
of hypergamy. The punishment meted out in this myth is entirely
according to the rules laid down in the Laws of Manu: she is given
to low caste. The Laws of Manu explicitly state this kind of wrong
intercourse to be the origin of the castes in general. I should observe that the "wrong intercourse" is not always in clear focus in
the rodiya myths: some versions make it clear that there has been
"an illicit love affair between princess Ratnā Valli and the roddā,
the sweeper at the palace" which led to their excommunication, but
others disguise the crime behind metaphors.

What has this story of "wrong intercourse" to do with our
tree ? Here we should return to the songs which the rodiya sing
about the mythical ancestress, Ratnā Valli (Gem Valli). The famous Ratnā Valli is always said to be atop a telambu tree, and all
the incantations are intended to bring her down -- not simply off
the tree but down to the caste level of the rodiya.

> Leaning against the tree of thick green foliage,
> Oh! woman with your heavy bluish braided tresses,
> Oh, Ratnā Valli, like a peacock resplendent,
> Descend from the telambu tree. [32]

We may further note that the association between Ratnā Valli and
the Goddess Pattini is explicitly made both by Raghavan and by
Nevill. [33] Even leaving aside the many other intriguing problems
raised by the story of Ratnā Valli and the incantatory songs addressed to her, not to speak of the curious treatment of the telambu
tree which must be cut down before the Ruvan Vali saya dāgoba can
be built, it is clear that there is more to this goddess who likes to
remain on top of trees. [34] But if this myth, too, is not sufficient
to allow us an insight into the splitting act dramatized by the An
keliya we have the myth about "trees" in nirvāna and "hell." (This
is one of the very first stories I recorded in the village of Terutenne.)

Hell is apāya: people who are guilty of wrong behavior de-
scend to apāya. Those who are involved in wrong sexual acts,
people who copulate with others' wives, in fact people who copulate
with anyone besides a proper mate are condemned to climb the
"Katuimbula" (thorn? sour?) tree. This tree has big thorns like
crowbars, which point down when you climb up and point up when
you climb down. There are always two climbing the tree, the woman and the man, and when one goes up the other comes down; they
will never meet. If you sleep with your sister the same thing may
happen. The tree in nirvāna has a special name (?). Only good
people have a chance of seeing that tree. The tree will provide one
with everything or anything that is desired. But the people who go
to nirvāna never want bad things! That tree has no thorns on it!

There is, no doubt, much more to be said on the subject of
the ritual as well as the above myths. One feature of both the
myths and the ritual seems quite definite: each rite and myth refers to the basic principles of caste hypergamy and copulation in
one way or another and all lead to and amplify the same conclusion
-- that the health and prosperity of the community depends upon
correct caste behavior. Perhaps it is not entirely accidental that
the rodiya, illegitimate offspring of Ratnā Valli, are still associated with disease through their name, which Raghavan says derives
from the words roga (disease) and dadi (deformity).

An keliya may now be seen in its total context of Sinhalese
rituals concerned with splitting males from females. Furthermore, the examination of the particular rituals and the myths
associated with them clearly suggest that, even though the rituals
may be described by informants as being generally beneficial, they
are in fact specifically concerned with "mistakes" (varada) in
sexual relations. In the Sinhalese context there are two kinds of
such mistakes. The basic rule is that a man may only have intercourse with a woman in the category of cross-cousin, all other
women being considered to be in the incestuous relationship of
"sisters" or "mothers." So any union outside the prescribed category would be described as a "mistake" or "wrong." The other
"mistakes" would concern cross-caste unions, i.e. hypergamous
unions would be accepted but hypogamous sexual intercourse would
be considered a severe offense. In practice the two rules are associated; the kinship rule is only an aspect of the caste rule. If
the kinship rule were rigidly followed, caste mistakes would not
take place. I would suggest that while the "birth stories" of the
demons appear to center around the theme of "incest" rather than
"caste," and while the rodiya are living examples of the dreadful
consequences of hypogamy, the rituals are in fact meant to reverse (or split) all mistaken unions. [35]

Still, the specific "mistake" that An keliya deals with is
hypogamy. This is exemplified by the agreed status differences
between Yata pila (the side of the Goddess, superior, but female
and hence "under") and Uda pila (the side of Pālanga, inferior,
but male and hence "on top"). An keliya, therefore, counteracts
unions "against the grain" (pratiloma), thereby protecting the
purity of the castes and the community. The purity of the community enhances its luck, fertility, health, wealth, and the general well-being of the inhabitants. For this reason An keliya is
especially appropriate as an after-harvest rite.

Kataragama deals with the opposite theme. It represents a
correct, "with the grain" (anuloma) union. As an approved union
it is more directly concerned with fertility. And this concern is
shown by the widespread belief that the rains never fail to come
either immediately following upon the last ritual at Kataragama
or very soon thereafter.

The concern with sexual relations, the male-female dichotomy, is obvious in the rites we have described. It is hardly necessary to draw the contrast between the realm of gods and goddesses, demons and demonesses, on the one hand, and the all that lies
within the purview of Buddhism, on the other. In the devāle and in
connection with those beings concerned with everyday existence,
the sex distinctions are markedly elaborated. In the Buddhist temple (vihāra) and in connection with the Buddhist priesthood, precisely these divisions are negated, denied, obliterated. The
priests must be asexual.

Buddhism is more concerned with eternity than life, with the
other world than this world, with the moral being than the physical
being. The denial of the world, life, and sex is of course more
forcefully underlined in the birth stories of the Buddha and we may
recall, for instance, the occasion when as Prince Siddharta the
Buddha tires of all the beautiful women in the palace and goes out
for a walk in the garden. There he sees an old man, a priest, and
a corpse and decides to turn away from the sensual life.

It is interesting also that in nirvāna there is no life but also
no death. In the world of sense, of pleasures, there is life, but
there is also death. And it would appear from the myths that the
distinctions of sex also belong to the region of existence rather
than eternity. In a sense, the distinctions of sex, which imply life,
also bring with them death. And in order to escape from this pain-
ful cycle of life and death, sex and sexual distinctions, in particular, have to be negated. These questions appear to be the central
concerns of Buddhism in the villages. [36]

IX

I began with dual organization. It appeared at first from the analysis in Terutenne as if the An keliya ritual could directly and immediately be related to the social divisions in the community. Yet further attention to the contexts of the rite showed that the Yata pila-Uda pila division itself was part of the ritual, and that to explain the ritual in terms of divisions created in order to play the "game" would beg the question of why the rite was performed. At the conclusion of our itinerary through healing rituals and demon myths, we did end up at the concept of structure. But it was clear that the rite was concerned with the deeper principles of the structure (i.e. incest, hypergamy, etc.) rather than directly with specific social groups. It looks as if specific social structures generate anxieties around the preservation of certain core principles on which they are based. Caste structures raise problems concerned with the regulation of sexual intercourse within and across the castes, and in particular the preservation of the purity of high caste females. I have already indicated the potency of this concept in connection with female puberty rites in Malabar and Ceylon. [37] It is noteworthy that another one of the major rituals of Sinhalese villages has brought us back to the same anxiety. [38] My argument that the ritual is not related to the topographical divisions in Sinhalese villages but concerns the institution of caste and hypergamy is best shown by the fact that Hindu Tamils of the east coast also perform An keliya. In Tirukkovil and Tambilivil the population divides into east and west (sen seri and wada seri) and the rite is repeated. The concern is clearly not embedded in the particularities of Sinhalese social structure but in those deeper principles of caste which they share with Tamils.

To conclude, although the distinction between dual organization at the "group" level and dualism at the cognitive level is useful for heuristic and empirical purposes, we must agree with Lévi-Strauss that both can be treated as surface phenomena and as expressions of fundamental structural principles which indeed do lie at a greater depth and may not be consciously recognized by the informants. [39]

NOTES

1. C. Lévi-Strauss, Anthropologie Structurale (Paris, 1958), p. 179n.

2. A. M. Hocart, "Buddha and Devadatta, " Indian Antiquary (Bombay and London), 52 (1923), 267; and "Duplication of Office in the Indian State, " Ceylon Journal of Science (Colombo and London), vol. 1 (1928), section G, part 4, pp. 205-10.

3. Durkheim and Mauss, "De quelques formes primitives de
    classification, " Année Sociologique, 6 (1901-1902).

4. Hertz, "La pré-éminence de la main droite, " in Death and the
    Right Hand, R. Needham, tr. (Chicago, 1960).

5. See for example "The Left Hand of the Mugwe, " Africa, 30
    (1960); and "Genealogy and Category in Wikmunkan Society, "
    Ethnology (Pittsburgh), 1 (1962), 254 f.

6. Reprinted in Anthropologie Structurale (Paris, 1958), pp.
    147-80.

7. Maybury-Lewis, "The Analysis of Dual Organizations: A
    Methodological Critique, " Bijdragen Taal-, en Volkenkunde,
    No. 115 (1960), pp. 18-44; see also reply by Lévi-Strauss,
    "On Manipulated Sociological Models, " ibid. No. 116 (1960),
    pp. 45-54.

8. Yalman, "The Structure of Sinhalese Healing Rituals, " in Re-
    ligion in South Asia, ed. E. Harper (Seattle, 1964), pp. 115-50.

9. Ibid.

10. Hocart, "Buddha and Devadatta, " observes that the ritual in
    the Temple of the Tooth imitated the daily ceremonial of the
    Sinhalese king in the palace and mentions the continued pre-
    sence of two women in the temple known as alatti amma though
    only hinting at their functions. J. Cartman, Hinduism in
    Ceylon (Colombo, 1957), p. 155, reports that alatti amma
    play a central part in Tamil marriage rituals and are present
    before the couple partake of their common ritual meal of
    bananas mashed in milk prior to retiring to their chamber.
    It is noteworthy that the celebrations at Kandy, where the
    Temple of the Tooth is located, did not include the Buddha
    until the final days of the kingdom. E. R. Sarathchandra, The
    Sinhalese Folk Play (Colombo, 1953), p. 5, states that the
    "sacred tooth" became part of the ritual by order of King Sri
    Rajasinha in 1775. There is a possibility that folk rituals such
    as Gam maduva are also related to palace ceremonial.

11. The poya days are named: māsa poya (lit. "month poya, " no
    moon), attavaka poya (half moon), pasalos vaka poya (full
    moon), etc. The period when the moon is getting larger is
    auspicious, the period after full moon inauspicious. Annual
    rites are normally timed to begin soon after māsa poya, grow
    with the moon, and come to climax on the night of the full moon

12. There is some suggestion that these secondary rituals are
     timed to form a cycle, but the evidence on this point is not
     extensive. It is said that at least in the Uva (Eastern Pro-
     vinces) Kataragama area the rites of Panama, Kotabowe
     Vidiya, and Mahiyangana take place in a set order and even
     that the god visits these centers in a fixed order. In the
     same way, it is said that the Kandy and Hanguranketa rituals,
     and others in the same district, are also part of a special
     cycle.

13. A. M. Hocart, "The Mortuary Use of the Bo Tree, " Ceylon
     Journal of Science, vol. 2 (1928), section G, part 1, ob-
     serves that the Bo tree had an important association with
     funerals. See also Yalman, "The Ascetic Buddhist Monks
     of Ceylon, " Ethnology, 1 (1962), 315-28.

14. U. A. Gunasekera, "Puna Maduva, " Spolia Zeylanica (Colom-
     bo), vol. 27 (1953), part 1, pp. 63-75; M. D. Raghavan, "The
     Pattini Cult as a Socio-religious Institution, " Spolia Zeylan-
     ica, vol. 26 (1951), part 2, pp. 251-61; and Yalman, "Sin-
     halese Healing Rituals. "

15. Sarathchandra, Sinhalese Folk Play, pp. 44-47.

16. Pattini's consort is often referred to as Polanga (Russell's
     viper?) in myths; see below.

17. For further material on An keliya see P. Wirz, Exorcism
     and the Art of Healing in Ceylon (Leiden, 1954), pp. 168-78;
     C. J. R. LeMesurier, "An Keliya, " Journal of the Royal
     Asiatic Society (Ceylon), 8 (1884-1886), 369; M. D. Raghavan,
     "The Pattini Cult. "

18. Robert Knox, An Historical Relation of the Island of Ceylon
     (London, 1681), p. 97.

19. For a fuller analysis of status divisions in Terutenne see
     Yalman, "The Flexibility of Caste Principles in a Kandyan
     Community, " in Aspects of Caste in S. India, Ceylon and
     N. W. Pakistan, ed. E. R. Leach, Cambridge Papers in
     Social Anthropology, No. 2 (1960), 78-112.

20. Yalman, "Sinhalese-Tamil Intermarriage on the East Coast
     of Ceylon, " Sociologus, 12 (1962), 36-54.

21. Most castes appear to have special suffixes to indicate status
     in personal names. The rodiya use valli and villi for female
     and male respectively.

22. Wirz, Exorcism and the Art of Healing.

23. Penetrating and highly suggestive analyses of the "origin
     stories" will be found in C. Lévi-Strauss, "La structure des
     mythes, " Anthropologie Structurale, and in E. R. Leach,
     "Lévi-Strauss in the Garden of Eden, " Transactions of the
     New York Academy of Science, series 2, vol. 23 (1961),
     no. 4.

24. Here is the latent incest problem indicated by Lévi-Strauss
     and Leach (see note 23).

25. Wirz, Exorcism and the Art of Healing, p. 70.

26. Wirz, pp. 72-74.

27. Wirz, pp. 129 f.

28. Wirz, p. 175.

29. Wirz, p. 141.

30. Gunasekera, "Puna Maduva, " p. 69.

31. I am aware that in yet other myths Ratnā Valli is described
     as the mother of Parākrama Bāhu I and that Vijaya Bāhu pre-
     dicted her body "shall be the place for the birth of a son who
     will surpass all former and future monarchs in glorious
     qualities (Mahavamsa 59. 34 sq.). But that evidently was a
     "correct marriage"; see Wilhelm Geiger, Culture of Ceylon
     in Medieval Times (Wiesbaden, 1960), p. 114.

32. M. D. Raghavan, Handsome Beggars: The Story of the Ceylon
     Rhodiya (Ceylon, Colombo Book Center, 1957), p. 62. Rag-
     havan also gives some information about the telambu tree:
     "Sterculia Foetida. A tree common in the dry region of
     Ceylon, with dull orange flowers. The great pendulous red
     follicles gaping open and showing the black seeds within are
     very striking objects. The seeds are eaten roasted. "

33. Nevill, The Taprobanian (1887), vol. 2, part 3, p. 87.

34. Raghavan, Handsome Beggars.

35. There is undoubtedly also a theme of the "original incest
     sin" running through the demon birth stories. This is why
     they are often associated with myths of the creation of the
     world and the first couple, e. g. by Lévi-Strauss and by

Leach. The concept of "original sin" is not particularly strong among Sinhalese Buddhists and, even though a latent preoccupation with this subject may be present in the rituals, they appear to me to be directed more specifically against sexual mistakes which have occurred in the community during the past year.

36. For further discussion see Yalman, "On Some Binary Categories in Sinhalese Religious Thought," Transactions of the New York Academy of Science, series 2, vol. 24 (1962), no. 4, pp. 408-20.

37. Yalman, "On the Purity of Women in the Castes of Ceylon and Malabar," Journal of the Royal Anthropological Institute, 93, (1963), 25-58.

38. For a vivid description of this fear of low caste pollution among high caste women, see Raghavan, Handsome Beggars, p. 35.

39. See his discussion of conscious and unconscious models in Anthropologie Structurale, p. 308.

A NOTE ON THE GLOSSARY

We are grateful to Mr. John K. Musgrave, Jr., Librarian of Yale University's Southeast Asia Collection, for the preparation of the Glossary of Religious Terms derived from Indian sources. It should facilitate the identification of such terms rendered in the individual, local variants in the various papers. Pali and Sanskrit words, as well as their English meanings, are largely based on Dines Andersen's A Pali Reader (Copenhagen, 1907), supplemented by references to The Pali Text Society's Pali-English Dictionary, edited by T. W. Rhys Davids (Chipstead, Surrey, 1925). Pali and Sinhalese words and their English meanings were carefully checked with the Rev. Bhikkhu Anuruddha, whose friendly cooperation we should like to acknowledge gratefully. We are similarly indebted to Professor William S. Cornyn of Yale University for his assistance with the tracing of Burmese expressions to their Pali origins, and to Daw Tin Tin, of Yale's Institute of Far Eastern Languages, for additional help with Burmese terms. Transliterations of Burmese by and large follows the official usage of British Burma, those of Thai being a modified form of the Romanization by Professor Mary R. Haas of the University of California at Berkeley. Words from the Thai-Lue dialect and from Cambodian are rendered in the transliterations created by the authors of the relevant papers, Professor Michael Moerman and May Ebihara respectively.

H. J. B.

GLOSSARY OF RELIGIOUS TERMS

Pali	Sanskrit	Definition	Burmese	Cambodian	Sinhalese	Thai
ācariya	ācārya	teacher		achaa		acan
Abhidhamma	Abhidharma	higher dhamma, transcendant doctrine				
ahimsā	ahimsā	harmlessness			ahimsā	
akusalaṁ		evil deed, demerit	akutho			
anicca		impermanence	aneiksa			
anatta	anatta	destitute of soul, no-self	anatta			
apāya	apāya	hell			apāya hell	
arahaṁ		fully ordained monk	yahan			
arahat	arhat	one who has attained highest stage of sanctification			arhat	
bhikkhu	bhikshu	monk		pikuk		

bodhi	bodhi	sacred tree under which Buddhahood attained, Bo tree			Bo tree / Bōdhi tree
Buddhasāsana		Buddhism		Pot sasnaa	
dāna	dāna	giving, especially of alms			dāna
deva	deva	deity	dewa		deva
devaloka	devaloka	heaven			devlova
devatā	devatā	deity		tivoda	
dhamma	dharma	law, doctrine, scriptures			tham
Dhammayutta		reformed monastic order		Thommayut	Tamayud
dhātu	dhātu	sacred relic			dhātu
dukkha	duḥkha	suffering	dokhka		dukkha

Pali	Sanskrit	Definition	Burmese	Cambodian	Sinhalese	Thai
gāthā	gāthā	verse, (Pali) incantation or prayer			gāthās	kaataa
guru	guru	teacher, practitioner of magic		kru		
iddhi	rddhi	supernatural power, e.g. to float in air			irdhi	
kathina.	kathina.	ceremonial presentation of gifts to monks	kahtein	katŭn	katina	gatin
kamma	karman	(past) deed, influence of past deeds on future destiny			karma	
karunā	karunā.	pity, mercy, compassion			karunā	
kusalaṁ	kucalaṁ,	good deed, merit	kutho	kosal		
Mahānikāya				Mohanikay		Mahaanigaai
metta	maitra	loving-kindness			maitreya	
maṅgala	maṅgala	auspicious	mingala			

Maṅgalasutta		(name of sutra)	Mingala thok			Pbaatimoog
nibbāna	nirvāna	Nirvana	neikban	nipean	nirvāna	
okāsa	avakāca	permission	awgatha			
pārami	pārami	perfection, virtue	parami			
paritta	paritrāna	protection	payeit, Payeitkyi			
Pāṭimokkha	Prātimoksha	collection of moral precepts	Patimauk			
peta	preta	spirit of dead		praet	preta	
pūjā	pūjā	worship, ceremony				buuchaa
puñña	punya	merit		bon	pin	bun
sadda	cabda	sound, voice, word, grammar	Thada			
sādhu	sādhu	well done!	thadu			satho

GLOSSARY OF RELIGIOUS TERMS (continued)

Pali	Sanskrit	Definition	Burmese	Cambodian	Sinhalese	Thai
Sakka	Cakra	Indra, king of the nats (Burma)	Thagya Min			
sālā	cālā	house, mansion, meeting hall		salaa		saalaa
sāmaṇera	crāmaṇera	Buddhist novice		samne		nen
saṅgha	saṃgha	congregation or order of monks	thanga			song
saṃsāra	saṃsāra	life in this world, round of existence			saṃsāra	
sāsana	cāsana	teaching, religion			sāsana	
sīla	cīla	morality, virtue, precept		sūl	sīla	sin
sīmā	sīmā	boundary, limit, ordination hall	thein		sīma	
saṅgaha	saṃgraha	collection, text	Thingyo			
saṃkama	saṃkrama	passage, New Year Water Festival	Thingyan			

sutta	sūtra	passage or chapter in Buddhist scriptures	thok			
upekkha	upeksa	equanimity				ubekha
vihāra	vihāra	Buddhist monastery, temple		vihiå	vihāra	vihāra
Vinaya	vinaya	rules of the order, section of the Tipitaka	Wini			Winai
vassa	varsha	rain, rainy season, rainy season retreat		Vosaa		Phansaa
Visākha pūjā	Vaisākha pūjā	celebration of Buddha's birth, enlightenment and parinirvāna		Visak Bochiå	Wesak	Wisaak Buuchaa

LIST OF PUBLICATIONS

Southeast Asia Studies   Yale University

BIBLIOGRAPHY SERIES

2.   Embree, John F. and Lillian Ota Dotson, Bibliography of the Peoples and Cultures of Mainland Southeast Asia (1950), xxxiii, 821, xii pages, with maps; out of print [available as photographic reprint: OP 6654, $31.15].

4.   Hart, Donn V., An Annotated Guide to Current Philippine Periodicals (1957), xxi, 116 pages; out of print [available as photographic reprint: OP 16716, $8.30].

5.   Irikura, James K., Southeast Asia: Selected Annotated Bibliography of Japanese Publications (1956), published by arrangement with the Human Relations Area Files, Inc., xii, 544 pages. $8.50

6.   Kennedy, Raymond, Bibliography of Indonesian Peoples and Cultures (1955, 2nd rev. ed. 1962), ed. Thomas W. Maretzki and H. Th. Fischer, published by arrangement with the Human Relations Area Files, Inc., xxii, 207 pages, with maps. $8.50

TO ORDER

Southeast Asia Studies publications are distributed by:

· The Cellar Book Shop, 18090 Wyoming, Detroit, Michigan 48221

Publications with the Human Relations Area Files or HRAF Press are also available from:

· Taplinger Publishing Co., 119 West 57th St., New York, N.Y. 10019

Photographic reprints may be ordered from:

· University Microfilms, Inc., 313 N. First St., Ann Arbor, Mich. 48107

---

7. Pelzer, Karl J., Selected Bibliography on the Geography of Southeast Asia, 3 vols., published by arrangement with the Human Relations Area Files, Inc.
    Part I. Southeast Asia: General (1949), 43 pages.
    Part II. Philippines (1950), 76 pages.
    [Parts I and II available only as combined photographic reprint: OP 11000, $7.00 soft cover, $9.25 hard cover.]
    Part III. Malaya (1955), 162 pages. $1.75

8. Trager, Frank N., Furnivall of Burma: An Annotated Bibliography of the Works of John S. Furnivall (1963), ii, 55 pages. $1.75

CULTURAL REPORT SERIES

1. Coughlin, Richard J., The Position of Women in Vietnam (1950), 43 pages; out of print [available as photographic reprint: OP 17125, $3.10].

3. Hart, Donn V., The Philippine Plaza Complex: A Focal Point in Culture Change (1955, second printing 1961), 55 pages, with charts. $1.50

4. Koentjaraningrat, R. M., A Preliminary Description of the Javanese Kinship System (1957), 111 pages; out of print [available as photographic reprint: OP 17124, $4.20].

5. Cunningham, Clark E., The Postwar Migration of the Toba-Bataks to East Sumatra (1958, second printing 1962), xii, 187 pages. $4.50

6. Koop, John C., The Eurasian Population in Burma (1961), 66 pages. $2.00

7. Hart, Donn V., The Cebuan Filipino Dwelling in Caticugan: Its Construction and Cultural Aspects (1959), 148 pages, with charts, drawings, photographs; out of print [available as photographic reprint: OP 17126, $5.55].

9. Textor, Robert B., From Peasant to Pedicab Driver: A Social Study of Northeastern Thai Farmers Who Periodically Migrated to Bangkok and Became Pedicab Drivers, 2nd ed. (1961), 83 pages, with photographs; out of print [available as photographic reprint: OP 25039, $4.05].

10. Cooley, Frank L., Ambonese Adat: A General Description (1962), 99 pages, with map, photographs. $4.00

11. Alisjahbana, S. Takdir, Indonesian Language and Literature: Two Essays (1962), 40 pages. $1.75

12. Jay, Robert R., Religion and Politics in Rural Central Java (1963), viii, 117 pages, with charts, maps. $3.75

13. Nash, Manning et al., Anthropological Studies in Theravada Buddhism (1966), xiv, 236 pages, with maps, charts, glossary.

TRANSLATION SERIES

1. Langrand, Gustave, Social and Religious Organization of a Vietnamese Village (1950), summary translation, 33 pages; out of print [available as photographic reprint: OP 14590, $2.50 soft cover, $4.50 hard cover].

2. Maspero, Georges, The Kingdom of Champa [Chapter 1. Le Royaume du Champa] (1949), 56 pages; out of print [available as photographic reprint: OP 14603, $3.60 soft cover, $6.35 hard cover].

3. Nguyen Van Vinh, Savings and Mutual Lending Societies [Ho] (1949); out of print [available as photographic reprint: OP 14158, $2.50 soft cover, $4.50 hard cover].

4. Odaka, Junio, Economic Organization of the Li Tribes of Hainan Island (1950), 92 pages; out of print [available as photographic reprint: OP 17127, $6.05].

5. Rajadhon, Phya Anuman, The Life of the Farmer in Thailand (1956); out of print [reprinted as Part I in William J. Gedney, trans. and ed., Life and Ritual in Old Siam (1961), HRAF Press, 191 pages, $4.50].

6. Benda, Harry J., James K. Irikura, and Kōichi Kishi, Japanese Military Administration in Indonesia: Selected Documents (1965), xxvi, 300 pages, with charts, glossary. $7.00

MONOGRAPH SERIES

2. McHale, Thomas R. and Mary C. McHale, Early Ameri-
    can-Philippine Trade: The Journal of Nathaniel Bowditch
    in Manila, 1796 (1962), 65 pages. $3.25

3. Paauw, Douglas S., ed. Prospects for East Sumatran
    Plantation Industries: A Symposium (1962), xiii, 68
    pages, with maps. $2.75

4. Halpern, Joel M., Government, Politics, and Social
    Structure in Laos: A Study of Tradition and Innovation
    (1964), xii, 202 pages, with map, tables. $4.50

5. Halpern, Joel M., Economy and Society of Laos: A
    Brief Survey (1964), xii, 234 pages, with drawings,
    maps, photographs, tables, bibliography. $5.25

6. Landé, Carl H., Leaders, Factions, and Parties: The
    Structure of Philippine Politics (1965), xvi, 148 pages,
    with maps, charts, bibliography. $4.25

7. Silverstein, Josef et al., Southeast Asia in World War
    II: Four Essays (in press).

SPECIAL PUBLICATIONS

Maung Maung, Aung San of Burma (1962), published for Yale
University Southeast Asia Studies by Martinus Nijhoff,
The Hague, 162 pages. $5.75

United States Economic Survey Team to Indonesia, Indonesia:
Perspective and Proposals for United States Economic
Aid: A Report to the President of the United States
(1963), xi, 205 pages, with tables. $4.50

McVey, Ruth T., ed. Indonesia (1963), published by arrangement with HRAF Press, xx, 600 pages, with maps,
charts, tables. $12.00